Community College Library Job Descriptions and Organizational Charts

CJCLS Guide #4

compiled and edited by

Judy Born
Sue Clayton
Aggie Balash

Manatee Community College
Bradenton, Florida

Community and Junior College Library Section
Association of College and Research Libraries
A division of the American Library Association
Chicago 2000

The paper used in this publication meets the minimum requirements of
American National Standard for Information Sciences–Permanence of
Paper for Printed Library Materials, ANSI Z39.48-1992. ∞

Library of Congress Cataloging-in-Publication Data
Community college library job descriptions and organizational charts / compiled and
edited by Judy Born, Sue Clayton, Aggie Balash.
     p. cm. -- (CJCLS guide ; #4)
  Includes index.
  ISBN 0-8389-8119-4 (alk. paper)
    1. Community college libraries--United States--Administration. 2. Library
administration--United States. 3. College librarians--United States--Job descriptions. 4.
Organizational change. I. Born, Judy. II. Clayton, Sue (Sue N.) III. Balash, Aggie. IV.
Series

Z675.J8 C665 2000
025.1'977--dc21

                                                    00-059443

Printed on recycled paper.

Printed in the United States of America.

04 03 02 01 00   5 4 3 2 1

Contents

iii

iv   **Contents**

Introduction

Organizational change and technological developments have impacted community college library staffing. Today every job description at every level requires some degree of computer expertise. Many libraries have developed new computer-related positions, while other libraries have incorporated these responsibilities into existing staff positions. Technology has also impacted the library's relationship to the rest of the college organization, and in many cases library directors have assumed collegewide responsibility for computer systems. This guide provides examples of 93 job descriptions, 32 college organizational charts, and 29 library organizational charts.

The Association of College and Research Libraries has established Standards for Community, Junior and Technical College Learning Resources Programs. *Standard Two* includes recommendations for Organization and Administration and *Standard Three* covers Library Staff. These standards recognize that "the structure and function of a learning resources program within an institution are determined by the role assigned to learning resources in the institutional organization." This guide is intended to supplement the ACRL Standards, providing details about how community college libraries are staffed, what services are provided, and the role the library plays within each institution.

We received over 600 pages of job descriptions and organizational charts from 86 libraries for this guide. The majority of community colleges follow the traditional academic reporting structure, and we included organizational charts from both multi-campus and single-campus libraries of this type, as well as a representative sampling from colleges of various sizes nationwide. We also included examples from as many different types of college organizational structures as space allowed.

A list of job titles appears at the beginning of each section, followed by a sampling of job descriptions. Most libraries have added responsibilities for automation and computer systems to the employee most willing and able to assume new technical duties. We included every position description we received for specific computer-related positions. The most difficult descriptions to select were in the paraprofessional area, since the educational requirements and responsibilities for these positions vary greatly. The college's human resources department often determines the style and format for job descriptions, whether there are position levels (I, II, III), and how much detail is included in the position description.

Librarians and college administrators are continuously reviewing position descriptions and organizational structures both within the library and collegewide. We hope that the selected readings and sample documents in this guide will provide a starting point for this process.

Library Organizational Survey Results

The Library Organizational Survey was sent to 268 libraries, which included members of the Community and Junior College Library Section of ACRL and 28 Florida Community Colleges. Eighty seven surveys were completed and returned; however, one was a duplicate, which gave us a total of 86 surveys. This is a return rate of 32%. Below are the totals for each question, and, at the end of the survey is an evaluation of each question.

1. Number of full-time equivalent (FTE) students, as listed in the latest HEGIS report:
   - <u>15</u> fewer than 1000
   - <u>34</u> 1000 – 3000
   - <u>8</u> 3000 – 5000
   - <u>14</u> 5000 – 7000
   - <u>5</u> 7000 – 10,000
   - <u>10</u> more than 10,000

2. Number of full-time equivalent staff in your library/learning resources center (include professional, paraprofessional, and clerical, but do not include student assistants):
   - <u>21</u> fewer than 5
   - <u>31</u> 5 – 10
   - <u>14</u> 11 – 15
   - <u>11</u> 16 – 25
   - <u>6</u> 26 – 40
   - <u>3</u> more than 40

3. How does the library/LRC fit into your institutional organizational structure? Please send a copy of your institution's organizational structure.
   a. Is your institution <u>41</u> single campus <u>45</u> multi-campus? Multi-campus, how many? <u>12 – 2 campus, 16 – 3 campus, 4 – 4 campus, 1 – 5 campus, 2 – 6 campus, 1 – 7 campus, 1 – 8 campus, 1 – 9 campus, 1 – 17 campus, 4 – no answer</u>
   If multi-campus, does each campus report to
      - <u>17</u> Institution library/LRC administrator
      - <u>15</u> Campus administrator (Provost, Vice President, President)
   b. The library/LRC administrator reports to
      - <u>2</u> College President

      <u>49</u> Vice President of ....
      - <u>18</u> Academic Affairs
      - <u>13</u> Instruction or Instructional Services
      - <u>8</u> Education or Educational Services
      - <u>2</u> the College
      - <u>2</u> Education and Student Services
      - <u>1</u> Information Technology
      - <u>1</u> Educational Technology Services
      - <u>1</u> Planning & Institutional Effectiveness
      - <u>1</u> Continuing Education & Evening Programs
      - <u>1</u> Learning Systems & Technology
      - <u>1</u> Health and Transfer Programs

      <u>15</u> Academic Dean of....
      - <u>4</u> Instruction or Instructional Affairs
      - <u>4</u> the College
      - <u>2</u> Learning Resources
      - <u>1</u> General Education
      - <u>1</u> Humanities
      - <u>1</u> Student Services
      - <u>1</u> Learning and Instruction
      - <u>1</u> Facilities and Operations

      <u>18</u> Other
      - <u>1</u> Academic Vice President
      - <u>1</u> Assistant Director of IT/Operations
      - <u>1</u> Assoc. Dean of Learning Resources
      - <u>1</u> Dean of Instructional Support
      - <u>1</u> Dean of Learning & Student Dev.
      - <u>1</u> Exec. VP for Academic Affairs

<u>1</u> Assoc. Dean of Instructional Affairs   <u>1</u> Executive VP of Instruction
<u>1</u> Executive Campus Dean   <u>1</u> Exec. Dir. of Information Tech.
<u>1</u> Dean of Info. Resources & Tech.   <u>1</u> Head of Educational Resources
<u>1</u> Dean of Info. Tech. & Resources   <u>1</u> Provost
<u>1</u> Dean of Information Services   <u>1</u> Vice Chancellor for Instruction
<u>1</u> Dean of Instruction   <u>1</u> Vice Chancellor of Acad. Affairs

4. What services does your library/LRC offer? Please check all that apply.
    <u>83</u> Automated circulation system   <u>35</u> Distance learning
    <u>69</u> AV/Media services   <u>83</u> Online Public Access Catalog
    <u>84</u> Bibliographic Instruction Classes   <u>81</u> Public access computers
    <u>48</u> Computer services   <u>26</u> Web Page Development
    <u>18</u> Credit courses   ___ Other <u>included: ITV, Test Monitoring,
    Instructional Technology, ILL Adaptive equipment,
    Multi-media Lab, Staff Development, and
    Teleconferences via Satellite</u>

5. Are any library/LRC services outsourced? No – 71, Yes – 15
    Please list <u>Cataloging – 8, Circulation – 1, OPAC – 2, Equipment Maintenance – 1, Access to
    OCLC – 1, Equipment repair – 1, Video Tape Duplication – 1</u>

6. How is your library/LRC organized? Please give a brief description of staffing in each
    department (i.e. Administration, circulation, technical services, etc.).
    <u>Answers to this question varied greatly and are best represented in the organizational charts
    found on pages 241-274.</u>

7. How many hours is the main library open to the public in a typical week? <u>Ranged from 37.5 to
    82</u>

8. Is a librarian available to serve the public during all hours the library is open? <u>Yes - 48</u>
    If not please describe your staffing arrangement.
    <u>Answers to this question are addressed in the survey summary found on page 5.</u>

9. How many librarians teach bibliographic instruction (BI) classes? <u>Ranged from 1 to 12</u>

10. How many BI classes were taught during the 98-99 fiscal year?
    <u>9</u> no classes   <u>7</u> 101 – 150
    <u>29</u> less than 50   <u>3</u> 151 – 200
    <u>18</u> 51 – 100   <u>18</u> more than 200

11. Do professional librarians at your institution belong to a union? <u>Yes - 33</u>

12. What is the length of contracts for librarians in your library?
    <u>60</u> 12 month   <u>14</u> 10 month   <u>11</u> hours per week
    <u>4</u> 11 month   <u>20</u> 9 month

13. Do all librarians at your institution have faculty status? Yes – 43
    If not, do any librarians have faculty status? 10
    Are the librarians at your institution considered
    _3_ non-classroom faculty   _20_ support faculty
    _19_ non-teaching faculty   _11_ academic support faculty
    _22_ other Administrative staff – 7, Administrative/Professional Support – 1, Support staff – 5,
        academic support staff – 4,   non-faculty professionals – 2, professional staff - 3

14. Do the librarians have levels and/or Faculty Ranks (ie. Librarian I, II, III, or Instructor, Asst.
    Professor, Professor, etc.)? yes – 24

15. Do librarians have tenure and/or continuing contract? Yes – 61

16. Do paraprofessional/clerical staff at your institution belong to a union? Yes – 28

17. What is the length of contracts for paraprofessional/clerical staff in your library? Please indicate
    the number of paraprofessional/clerics in each category.
    _67_ 12 month   _8_ 10 month   _20_ hours per week
    _4_ 11 month   _4_ 9 month   _1_ no contracts

18. Has the organization structure of your library changed in the last five years? Yes – 52

Narrative Review

In the survey narrative we will use the terms students and enrollment to indicate full-time
equivalent (FTE) students and the terms staff or employees to indicate FTE staff. We will also be
using the following terms and abbreviations:

> ALA – American Library Association
> ACRL – Association of College and Research Libraries a division of ALA
> ACRL guidelines – refers to the *Standards for Community, Junior, and Technical College
> Learning Resource Programs* found at http://www.ala.org/acrl/guides/jrcoll.html

Questions 1 and 2
According to ACRL guidelines the minimum number of staff for an institution with fewer than
1,000 students are seven. At the other end of the spectrum colleges of 7,000 – 10,000 minimum
staffing is 25 – 31. The answers to questions one and two indicate that 15 colleges are fewer than
1,000 in enrollment yet 21 colleges have fewer than five employees. By the same token there are
15 colleges with enrollment of 7,000 – more than 10,000, yet only nine colleges have 26 or more
employees. Using the ACRL guidelines we can conclude the majority of colleges responding to the
survey are under staffed.

Question 3
The respondents were almost equally split between single campus institutions (41) and multi-
campus institutions (45). The reporting structure varied widely, this is best seen in the

organizational charts on pages 205 – 239. We were particularly struck by the variety of titles of the administrators the library reports to.

Question 4
We are surprised to find that three institutions do not have an automated circulation system, all three are in the 1,000 – 3,000 size. There are also three institutions that do not provide an online public catalog, one at the fewer than 1,000 size, one at the 1,000 – 3,000 size and the third at the more than 10,000 size. One college reports that the only service provided is bibliographic instruction, this college is in the 1000 – 3000 size. There are two institutions reporting that they do not offer bibliographic instruction, both are multi-campus in the 1,000 – 3,000 size.

Question 5
Of the services offered by the institutions 15 (17%) of the 86 do some outsourcing. Of the services reported as outsourced three seem to be non-library functions, i.e. equipment maintenance, repair, and videotape duplication. Of the other outsourced services cataloging is outsourced by eight (9%) institutions. Four (5%) are 1,000 – 3,000 size, two (2%) are 5,000 – 7,000 size, and two (2%) are more than 10,000.

Question 7
There are a wide range of hours each library/lrc is open, 37.5 to 82. Also within each FTE group there are a wide range of hours. The fewer than 1,000 size range from 37.5 to 81.5 and just over half (nine of 15) do not have a librarian covering all open hours (question 8). In the 1,000 – 3,000 group the hours range from 55.5 to 79.5 and 19 (56%) of the 34 do not have a librarian covering all open hours, again over half. The 3,000 – 5,000 size cover hours of 61 to 69.5, the smallest range of hours of any group. There are two of eight libraries in this category that do not have a librarian covering all hours, a much smaller percentage (25%). Institutions with 5,000 – 7,000 students range in hours from 56 to 80. Of the fourteen institutes in this category two do not have librarians covering all hours (14%). The range of hours for the 7,000 – 10,000 group starts at 70 and goes to 81.5 and one of the five in this category do not cover all hours with a librarian (20%). The last category, more than 10,000, cover hours from 65 to 82 and one of the ten in this category does not cover all hours (10 %).

Question 8
This question shows that 48 (56%) of institutions have librarians available all hours the library is open. Six of the institutions report that librarians work a typical 8 – 5 day or slight variations of 8 – 5. Others have consistent times such as, ½ - 1 hour every morning, every Friday afternoon, Saturday, and Sunday. Fifteen (17%) of the institutions that do not have a librarian available all hours have a staff of fewer than 5. The next highest group is the 5 – 10 staff of which there are fourteen (16%). Four (5%) of the institutions have staffs of 11 – 15. Two (2%) institutions have staffs of 16 – 25, one (1%) in the 26 – 40 staffing range, and two (2%) in the greater than 40 staffing range.

Question 9
Answers indicate a range of one to eleven librarians at the institutions offering bibliographic instruction (BI) classes. In examining the answers we found that five institutions do not offer classes, of these three offer individual BI. Nineteen institutions have one librarian that conducts BI

classes. Nine of these institutions are in the fewer than 1,000 size, seven in the 1,000 – 3,000 size, two in the 3,000 – 5,000 size, and one in the 5,000 – 7,000 size. Twenty-one institutions have two librarians teaching BI. Five institutions are in the fewer than 1,000 size, thirteen in the 1,000 – 3,000 size, one in the 3,000 – 5,000 size, and two in the more than 10,000 size. Of the institutions that have three librarians teaching BI classes seven are in the 1,000 – 3,000 size and one is in the 5,000 – 7,000 size. There are thirteen institutions that reported four librarians teach BI classes. Three of those are in the 1,000 – 3,000 size, three in the 3,000 – 5,000 size, five in the 5,000 – 7,000 size, one in the 7,000 – 10,000 size, and one in the more than 10,000 size. Five institutions report that five librarians teach BI classes; one in the 3,000 – 5,000 size, two in the 5,000 – 7,000 size, one in the 7,000 – 10,000 size, and one more than 10,000 size. Five institutions use six BI class instructors; two in the 5,000 – 7,000 size three in the 7,000 – 10,000 size, and one in the more than 10,000 size. Two institutions in the 5,000 – 7,000 size and one greater than 10,000 size has eight librarians that teach BI classes. One institution in greater than 10,000 size has nine BI instructors. Two institutions have eleven librarians that conduct BI classes, one in the 5,000 – 7,000 size and one in the more than 10,000 size. Nine institutions indicate that all the librarians teach BI classes. One institution of greater than 10,000 size has twelve librarians that teach BI classes. Two institutions indicated all librarians teach BI but no number was given.

Question 10

In looking at question ten an interesting aspect is the wide range of the number of BI classes over the different size institutions. Of the twenty nine institutions that taught less than 50 classes two are in the 5,000 – 7,000 size and two in the greater than 10,000 size. Of the remainder nine are in the fewer than 1,000 size and fourteen are in the 1,000 – 3,000 size. On the other end, of the eighteen institutions that taught more than 200 classes during 98-99 one is in the 3,000 – 5,000 size. The majority of more than 200 classes were in the larger institutions, five each in 5,000 – 7,000 and 7,000 – 10,000 and seven in the more than 10,000 size. Of the institutions that taught 51 – 100 classes the majority (10) are in the 1,000 – 3,000 size. The remainder in that group are pretty evenly distributed between fewer than 1,000, 3,000 – 5,000, and 5,000 – 7,000.

Question 11

We find that of the 86 institutions 33 (38%) have faculty unions that include librarians. In looking at the geographic distribution of those with unions, only eight (24%) of the 33 are in Southern or Southwest states (4 in Florida, 1 in Louisiana, 3 in California). The area with the most is the Northeast with ten, next is the Northern middle states with eight and the Northwest with seven.

Question 12

Many institutions have librarians on more than one contract term. Sixty of the 86 have at least some librarians on 12 month contracts. Four institutions have 11 month contracts and eleven are hourly employees, so this leaves at least 11 libraries that do not have librarians available more than ten months of the year.

Question 13

Librarians have faculty status at 43 institutions; also, at ten institutions some of the librarians have faculty status. At seven institutions librarians are classified as administrative staff and one institution classifies librarians as administrative/professional support staff. Other classifications include support staff (five), academic support staff (four), and non-faculty professional (two). Fifteen gave no indication of a classification for librarians.

Question 14
Of the 86 institutions 24 (27%) have a ranking system which librarians can use to advance and climb the proverbial ladder of success.

Question 15
We find it interesting that 61 of the 86 institutions have tenure and/or continuing contracts when only 52 have at least some staff with faculty status (question13).

Question 16
We find that 28 (32%) institutions have unions for paraprofessional/clerical staff. This is four less than the number that have unions for librarians.

Question 17
Sixty-seven (77%) of the 86 institutions do have 12 month contracts for staff. The next largest group is the hourly contracts, which make up 20 (23%) of the total. Ten month contracts constitute 10 (9%) of the total. Both 11month and 9 month contracts make up 4 (5%) of the total. There was only one institution that reported no contracts for paraprofessional/clerical staff.

Question 18
Of 86 institutions 52 (60%) have had a change in the organizational structure in the last five years. This is only surprising in that it is not a greater percentage. With the changes in technology change in organizational structure is inevitable.

Question 19 – additional comments:
➢ Added Assistant Director and "team leaders", previously a flat organization.
➢ Administration took away professional status of Public Services Librarian and eliminated Media position.
➢ Functions of positions change as people retire. Shifting to teaching learning environment.
➢ 1997 changed governance from K-12 School Board to Board of Regents.
➢ In the last year moved from administrative Director to team management to library department chair.
➢ Library merged with IT in 1996, reorganization is ongoing.
➢ New responsibilities added, i.e. Instructional Technology
➢ Added Public Services Librarian position in 1995.
➢ Managed by a team of 5: 3 librarians, 1 professional staff and 1 paraprofessional.
➢ Planning to implement BI this next year.
➢ Recently switched reporting from Academic Dean to Dean of IT.
➢ Now have a computer lab run by a lab specialist.

List of Contributing Institutions
Ancilla College, PO Box 1, Donaldson, IN 46513
Andrew College, 413 College St., Cuthbert, GA 31740
Anne Arundel Community College, 101 College Pkwy, Arnold, MD, 21012
Bakersfield College, 1801 Panorama Dr, Bakersfield, CA 93305
Barton County Community College, 245 N.E. 30 Rd, Great Bend, KS, 67530
Black Hawk College, 6600 34th Ave, Moline, IL 61265
Blue Mountain Community College, 2411 N.W. Carden Ave., Pendleton, OR 97801
Bossier Parish Community College, 2719 Airline Dr., Bossier City, LA, 71111
Carl Sandburg College, 2232 S Lake Storey Rd., Galesburg, IL 61401
Central FL Community College, P.O.Box, 1388, Ocala, FL 34478
College of DuPage, 425 22nd St., Glen Ellyn, IL 60137
Columbia Basin College, 2600 North 20th Ave, Pasco, WA 99301-3379
Columbus State Community College, 550 East Spring St., Columbus, OH 43215
Cottey College, 1000 W. Austin, Nevada, MO 64772
Dallas County Community College District, www.dcccd.edu
Dawson Community College, P.O.Box 421, Glendive MT 59330
DeVry Inst. Tech., 1350 Alum Creek Dr., Columbus, OH 43209
Dyersburg State Community College, 1510 Lake Rd, Dyersburg, TN 38024
Eastern Idaho Tech College, 1600 S. 25th E., Idaho Falls, ID 83404
Eastfield College, 3737 Motley Dr, Mesquito, TX 75150
Edison Community College, P.O. Box 60210, Ft. Myers, FL 33906
Edmonds Community College, 20000 68th Ave. W., Lynnwood, WA 98036
Estrella Mountain Community College, 3000 North Dysart Road, Avondale, AZ 85323
Everett Community College, 801 Wetmore, Everett, WA, 98201
FL Keys Community College, 5901 College Rd, Key West, FL 33040
Great Basin College, 1500 College Pkwy, Elko NV 89801
Gulf Coast Community College, 5230 West U.S. Highway 98, Panama City, FL 32401
Harrisburg Area Community College, One Hacc Dr., Harrisburg, PA 17110
Hillsborough Community College, P.O. Box 30030, Tampa, Fl, 33614
Holmes Community College, P.O. Box 439, Goodman, MS 39079
Horry Georgetown Technical College, P.O. Box 261966, Conway, S.C. 29528
Hudson County Community College, 25 Journal Sq., Jersey City, N.J., 07306
Hutchinson Community College, 1300 N. Plum, Hutchinson, KS 67501
Iowa Lakes Community College, 3200 College Dr, Emmetsburg, IA 50536
Ivy Tech State College, 590 Ivy Tech Dr, Madison, IN 47250
Jefferson Community College, 4000 Sunset Blvd., Steubenville, OH, 43952
Kellogg Community College, 450 North Ave, Battle Creek, MI 49017
Kirtland Community College, 10775 N. Saint Helen, Rescommon, MI, 48653
Manatee Community College, 5840 26th St. W., Bradenton, FL 34207
Miami-Dade Community College, 11011 S.W. 104th St., Miami, FL 33176

Monroe Community College, 1000 East Henrietta Rd, Rochester, NY 14623

Montgomery College, 7600 Takoma Avenue, Takoma Park, MD 20912

Nicolet Area Technical College, P.O.Box 518, Rhinelander, WI, 54501

North Idaho College, 1000W Harden Ave, Coeur d'Alene, ID 83814

Northeast Community College, P.O. Box 469, Norfolk, NE 68702

Northeast Iowa Community College, P.O.Box 400, Calmar, IA 52132

Northland Pioneer College, P.O. Box 610, Holbrook, Arizona, 86025

Norwalk Community-Technical College, 188 Richards Avenue, Norwalk, CT 06854-1655

Nortwestern CT Community Technical College, 100 South Main St, Winsted, CT 06098

Nunez Community College, 3710 Paris Rd, Chalmette, LA 70043

Ocean County College, P.O. Box 2001, Toms Rivers, NJ 08754

Okaloosa-Walton Community College, 100 College Blvd, Niceville, FL 32578

Panola College, 1109 West Panola, Carthage, TX 75633

Pasadena City College, 1570 E. Colorado Blvd., Pasadena, CA 91106

Pasco-Hernando Community College, 36727 Blanton Rd, Dale City, FL 33523

Paul Smith's College, Library, Paul Smiths, N.Y. 12970

Pensacola Junior College, 1000 College Blvd., Pensacola, FL 32504

Phillips Community College, P.O. Box 785, Helena, AR 72342

Phillips Community College, P.O. Box 921, Stuttgart, AR 72160

Pierce College, 9401 Farwest Dr SW, Lakewood, WA 98498

Portland Community College, P.O. Box 19000, Portland, OR 97280

Prairie State College, 202 South Halsted St, Chicago Heights, IL 60411

Prince George's Community College, 301 Largo Rd, Largo, MD 20774

Pueblo Community College, 900 West Orman, Pueblo, CO 81004

Quinebaug Valley Community-Technical College, 742 Upper Maple St, Danielson, CT 06239

Richland College, 12800 Abrams Rd., Dallas, TX 72543

Riverland Community College, 2200 Riverland Dr., Albert Lea, MN, 56007

St. Petersburg Junior College, 7200 66th Street West, Pinellas Park, FL 33781

Salt Lake Community College, 4600 South Redwood Rd, Salt Lake City, UT, 84130

San Diego Mesa College, 7250 Mesa College Dr, San Diego, CA 92111

Seminole Community College, 100 Weldon Blvd., Sanford, FL 32773

South Florida Community College, 600 W. College Dr., Avon Park, FL 33825

Southern Maine Technical College, 2 Fort Rd., South Portland, ME 04106

Springfield Tech Community College, 1 Armory Square, Springfield, MA 01105

Tallahassee Community College, 444 Appleyard Dr., Tallahassee, Fl, 32304

Technical College of the Lowcountry, P.O. Box 1288, Beaufort, SC 29901

Temple College, 2600 South First St., Temple, TX, 76504

Trident Technical College, P.O. Box 118067, Charleston SC, 29423

Umpqua Community College, 1140 College Rd/ P.O.Box 967, Roseburg, OR 97470

Villa Maria College, 240 Pine Ridge Rd, Buffalo, NY 14225

Western Nebraska Community College, 1601 East 27th St., Scottsbluff, NE 69361

Western Oklahoma State College, 2801 North Main, Altus, OK 73521

10 Contributing Libraries

Western Piedmont Community College, 1001 Burkemont Ave, Morganton, NC 28655-4511
Western Wisconsin Technical College, 304 North 6th St, La Crosse, WI 54602
Wharton County Junior College, 911 Boling Highway, Wharton, TX 77488
York Technical College, 452, S Anderson Rd, Rock Hill, SC, 29732

Library Directors

Community College Library Directors duties vary from responsibility for the operation of one library, several campus libraries, or supervision of other campus activities. The following job titles were submitted from all the responding libraries.

Associate Director of Library Media Services
Associate Director of Libraries
Associate Vice President of Academic Affairs/Dean of Learning Resources and
    Distance Learning
Dean, Learning Resources
Dean of the Learning Resource Center
Dean of Learning Resource Services/Evening Administrator
Dean of the Learning Resource Center
Director, Educational Resources
Director—Learning Resources
Director of Learning Resources
Director of Libraries
Director of Library Services
Director of the Library
Director of the Library and Instructional Technology
District Director of Learning Resources
Head Librarian
Information Services Director
Learning Resources Coordinator
Library Department Chair

<u>Carl Sandburg College</u>

Job Description

<u>Position Title:</u>	Dean of Learning Resource Services/Evening Administrator (Galesburg Campus)
<u>Classification:</u>	Administration
<u>Level:</u>	II
<u>Supervises:</u>	LRC Staff
<u>Reports To:</u>	Vice President of Instructional Services
<u>Principal Working Relationships:</u>	Vice President of Instructional Services, LRC Staff, and Faculty
<u>Purpose:</u>	To facilitate the daily operations of the Learning Resource Center

<u>Essential Functions</u>

<u>Major Responsibilities</u>

1. Assume primary responsibility for the planning, organization, coordination, administration, and evaluation of all learning resource services and personnel at all college sites.

2. Supervisory responsibility for all formats of distance learning (video conferencing, telecourses and teleconferencing).

3. Advise the Vice President of Instructional Services on integration of new technologies into the instructional programs.

4. Maintain a viable service program which will engender maximum utilization of learning resources.

5. Serve as college Affirmative Action Officer.

6. Responsible for preparation and administration of LRC budget.

7. Ensure LRC services support college curriculum.

8. Have final authority for selection and de-selection of LRC materials.

9. Maintain LRC Archives Room.

10. Serve as college Copyright Officer.

11. Serve as the evening administrator at the Galesburg campus.

<u>Coordinates</u>

1. Faculty development programs for full and part-time faculty.

2. Sandburg Scholars Program.

3. International Studies Program.

4. LRC exhibits and informational programs.

Assists With
----

1.   Other duties as assigned by Vice President of Instructional Services.

Risk Management and Loss Prevention Activities
----

1.   Participate in and support the college Risk Management Program in a capacity appropriate to this position.

2.   Monitor hazardous conditions, events, and circumstances present in the college operation and communicating observations to the appropriate supervisor and/or Risk Management Committee.

3.   Perform administrative night duty.

Minimum Necessary Skills, Experience, and Educational Background
----

1.   Master's degree in information science, library science or instructional media with some administrative experience preferred.

2.   Basic computer knowledge desirable.

3.   Organizational and communications skills essential.

Physical Requirements to Perform Job Functions
----

1.   The specific motor skills and sensory perception to effectively perform daily tasks.

10/June 1999

CENTRAL FLORIDA COMMUNITY COLLEGE

JOB DESCRIPTION

JOB TITLE: DIRECTOR - LEARNING RESOURCES

PAY GRADE: H

OVERTIME STATUS: EXEMPT

MAJOR RESPONSIBILITY:

Plan for, administer, advance and evaluate the policies, procedures and operations of the Library (Learning Resource Center), Media Center and Distance Learning. Provide Leadership, direction and support for Learning Resource personnel. Collaborate with faculty and staff in providing services, in a learning centered environment, to the students and communities of Marion , Citrus and Levy Counties.

PREREQUISITES FOR POSITION (Qualification Standards):

1. Education or training: Requires a Master's degree in Library Science or a related field from an accredited college or university.

2. Years of experience in field: Five (5) to nine (9) years of experience in education, distance learning, supervision, computers, and library science, or an equivalent combination of education, training and experience that provides the required knowledge, skills and abilities. Community college experience preferred.

3. Special skills or abilities related to position: Working knowledge of automated learning resource systems. Experience in leading and implementing distance learning courses/programs. Ability to direct the operation of a center and to establish good working relationships with the faculty, staff and public. High level of communication and human relations skills that support a collaborative learning environment. Experience in evaluating the effectiveness of programs, policies, procedures, resources and equipment that are included in this position.

ESSENTIAL JOB FUNCTIONS:

1   Develop and implement policies and procedures relating to the Library/Learning Resources Center and its various functions. Oversee the acquisition of suitable materials and equipment to operate the center.
2. Supervise activities of Learning Resources personnel; evaluate assigned personnel, sign payroll, time cards and other various forms; initiate hiring process for Learning Resources staff; resolve personnel issues; analyze staffing needs.

09/17/98

Central Florida Community College

DIRECTOR - LEARNING RESOURCES   Page 2

ESSENTIAL JOB FUNCTIONS (Continued):

3. Analyze budgets and plans expenditures; approve requisitions and purchase orders and resolve any problems associated with them.
3. Communicate to various individuals and groups the programs, services, activities and needs of Learning Resources.
4. Assist in the implementation of the statewide automated library system.
6. Recommend the purchase of books, equipment, films, videos, and supplies needed for the operation of the center. Help develop grant applications and monitor progress of approved grants.
7. Plan for the security and maintenance of books and other materials located in the Learning Resource Center.
7. Coordinate information relating to new technology and developments in telecommunications. Assist in coordinating the CCTV system, including program design, operation and maintenance.
8. Participate in professional development to maintain professional competence.
9. Conduct management meetings to provide direction for Learning Resources, develop plans for future activities and collaborate with the Provost and Learning Resource Center staff at the Citrus and Levy Campuses.
10. Participate on College and Statewide committees and task forces.
11. Report to the Vice President for Instruction.
12. Analyze programs, services and evaluate for existing and future needs; initiate and conduct user surveys to identify needs, analyze a variety of data as it pertains to the Learning Resource Center.
13. Identify training needs, initiate plans for developing staff training as related to the Learning Resource Center.

(These essential job functions are not to be construed as a complete statement of all duties performed. Employees will be required to perform other job related marginal duties as required.)

ESSENTIAL PHYSICAL SKILLS:

- Acceptable eyesight (with or without correction).
- Acceptable hearing (with or without hearing aid).
- Ability to communicate both orally and in writing.

ENVIRONMENTAL CONDITIONS:

- Work inside in an office environment.

(Reasonable accommodations will be made for otherwise qualified individuals with a disability.)

PRIMARY LOCATION OF JOB: Building 3, Ocala Campus

SUPERVISOR OF POSITION: Vice President, Instruction

09/17/98

Central Florida Community College

EDISON COMMUNITY COLLEGE
<u>District Director of Learning Resources</u>

<u>Position Function:</u>

This is advanced responsible work in providing innovative and effective leadership to Learning Resources services within the College district. Work includes determining, implementing and evaluating policies and procedures and overseeing all operations to provide student-centered Learning Resources programs. The employee in this position directly supervises Learning Resources on the Lee County Campus, oversees the district-wide activities at the Charlotte and Collier campuses, and coordinates the state-wide library automation systems employed by the College.

<u>Supervision:</u>

Work is performed under the leadership and direction of the Provost of the Lee Campus who provides direction and establishes overall goals for Learning Resources.

The District Director of Learning Resources works collaboratively with and provides innovative leadership and direction to a staff of faculty members and support personnel in providing student-centered learning resources programs.

<u>Responsibilities:</u>

Oversees the overall operation of Learning Resources services for the Lee County Campus and provides general direction and supervision to the Collier and Charlotte Campuses and the district as a whole.

Coordinates with and through the Collier and Charlotte Provosts to ensure appropriate learning resources services to these campuses.

Serves as liaison for the College with the College Center for Library Automation, the Learning Resources Standing Committee for the Council of Instructional Affairs and other appropriate state-wide groups relating to the overall Learning Resources responsibility.

Provides long-range planning for the development of Learning Resources and implements appropriate movement of the library into the 21st century and toward mutually cooperative efforts with Florida Gulf Coast University and the Lee County library system.

Maintains adequate resources to serve the demands of the teaching/learning environment within allowable economic constraints.

Supports Distance Learning projects through access to electronic information.

Prepares and submits the budget for all areas supervised.

Supervises and controls all expenditures from the budgets supervised.

Plans and coordinates the orientation of all students, faculty and staff to services provided by Learning Resources.

Maintains accountability and/or delegation of accountability for all furniture and equipment in the areas supervised.

Provides for centralized processing in the acquisition and cataloging of all library materials.

Coordinates the implementation and operation of the state-wide library automation systems used within the district.

Provides for the selection, training, evaluation and maintenance of adequate staff to perform overall responsibilities.

Performs related duties as assigned.

<u>Minimum Requirements:</u>

A Master's degree from a regionally-accredited institution of higher education. A degree in library or information science is preferred.

Demonstrated knowledge of library automation, advanced information technologies and management of non-print collections.

Experience with decision-making in a highly collaborative environment.
Skill in supervision, verbal and written communications, interpersonal relations, budget analysis and development, organization, program development, team work and knowledge of learning resources issues and practices.

Commitment to the philosophy of a student-entered comprehensive community college preparing to meet the needs of the 21st century.

The ability to act as an advocate and possess a sound understanding of issues affecting academic libraries, computing, telecommunications, media services, and their relationship to a student-centered learning environment are preferred.

Approved: 2/20/97; revised 9/16/97.

Edison Community College

Gulf Coast
Community College

TITLE	Job Description Director of the Library and Instructional Technology	NUMBER	2.3
DATE	April 1998	PAGE	1 of 1

JOB TITLE: Director of the Library and Instructional Technology

REPORTS TO: Vice President of Instructional Services

BASIC FUNCTION: Supervision of the Library and Administration of College
                                                      Information and Instructional Technology Services

CLASSIFICATION: Administrative (Managerial)

DUTIES AND RESPONSIBILITIES:

Administer and provide leadership to all services, activities and programs of the library (i.e. circulation, periodicals, books, technical services, audio-visuals and informational technologies).

Develop and articulate a campus-wide vision for the use of existing and developing technologies in support of the college's instructional programs and activities. Provide direction, support and supervision to the college's instructional technology services.

Supervise and manage a team-oriented library staff who strive to anticipate and respond to the teaching, research and service needs of the faculty, staff, students and community.

Coordinate and supervise all aspects of the fiscal management of library departments, to include budget preparation, inventory, purchases and expenditures.

Schedule and coordinate the preparation and completion of reports and statistical collections required by the college or state and federal agencies.

Provide leadership and support to develop and extend current services, technologies and collections of the library.

Maintain, with adequate review and revision, appropriate policies and procedures to insure the efficient and effective operations of the library. Articulate and implement goals for library services as well as informational and instructional technologies.

Serve as an advocate and spokesperson for the library. Represent or delegate representation of the library in college or related groups in order to maintain communication and support the mission of the college.

Serve as an active member of the college's administrative/leadership team, sitting on the Instructional Affairs Council, the Executive Council, and other appropriate councils or committees as appointed.

Perform other duties as may be assigned.

MINIMUM QUALIFICATIONS:

A Master of Library Science from an ALA-accredited program or a master's degree or higher in a relevant field is required. Prior experience with automated integrated library systems, a computer-intensive environment, and new information/instructional technologies is critical. Strong organizational skills, excellent communication skills, the ability to act as an advocate or spokesperson, grant writing experience, and prior related work experience with increasing levels of responsibility is highly desirable.

Gulf Coast Community College

HILLSBOROUGH COMMUNITY COLLEGE

JOB DESCRIPTION

Class Title: Dean, Learning Resources	*Date:*	Feb 25, 1998
Level: D	*FLSA Status:* Exempt	*Class Code:* A0476

GENERAL DESCRIPTION

Plans, directs, and evaluates all aspects of the daily operation of the campus library and district library services.

	KEY RESPONSIBILITIES	% OF TIME
1.*	Plans, directs, and evaluates all aspects of the daily operation of the campus library.	20%
2.*	Provides and coordinates centralized control of district library services, including acquisition, cataloging, and processing of material, and audiovisual and automation services.	15%
3.*	Hires, trains, supervises, and evaluates all assigned campus and district library services faculty and staff. Prepares and administers budgets for the campus library and district library services.	15%
4.*	Coordinates college-wide learning resources mission, goals, objectives, administrative policies and procedures.	10%
5.*	Coordinates and monitors collection assessment and development, reference services, and bibliographic instruction at the campus library.	10%
6.*	Handles student concerns and complaints about library services at the campus.	10%
7.	Prepares and disseminates library information. Accumulates statistics and maintains records.	5%
8.	Acts as building supervisor for the campus library facility. Interacts with other campus departments.	5%
9.	Performs other similar and related duties as required.	

* Indicates an "essential" job function.

Class Title: Dean, Learning Resources	Class Code: A0476	Level: D

KEY JOB REQUIREMENTS

Education:	Master's Degree in library or information science from an ALA accredited program required.
Experience:	Five to seven years prior related work experience required, preferably in an academic library.
Planning:	Makes formal plans that exceed one year, but not three years beyond normal operational planning.
Impact of Actions:	*Operating Budget Responsibilities:* Has controlling influence on decisions affecting expenses/revenues. *Grant Fund Responsibilities:* Has recommending influence on decisions affecting expenses/revenues. *Revenue Generating Impact:* Has supportive budget role which may impact on methods used to generate revenues.
Impact of Decisions:	Major responsibility for making decisions and final recommendations which routinely affect the activities of a campus. Position duties may include responsibility for developing strategic plans for one or more campuses.
Complexity:	Work is non-standardized and widely varied requiring the interpretation and application of a substantial variety of procedures, policies, and/or precedents used in combination. Frequently, the application of multiple, technical activities is employed: therefore, analytical ability and inductive thinking are required.
Decision Making:	Supervision is present to review established departmental and/or campus objectives. Independent judgement is required to recommend departmental or campus objectives, evaluate new approaches to problem solving, and assess changing facts or conditions.
Problem Solving:	Problems are complex, varied and only mildly related to those seen before. Simply determining what the problem is requires major individual effort and/or consultation with others within the department or College. A high degree of analytical ability and inductive thinking may be required to solve highly intricate, technically complex problems. Must be able to develop new and nonstandard approaches.
Communications with Others:	*Internal Contacts:* Requires regular contacts to carry out programs and to explain specialized matters. Also requires continuing contacts with officials at higher levels on matters requiring cooperation, explanation, and persuasion. *External Contacts:* Requires regular external contacts to carry out organization programs and to explain specialized matters. Occasionally requires personal contact with the public involving the enforcement of regulations, policies and procedures
Supervision of Others:	Plans, assigns, and evaluates the work of subordinates for effective operation and results of the unit. Nature of work supervised requires training and experience, a thorough knowledge of departmental or divisional activities, and an understanding of and appreciation for work conducted in other departments or campuses.
Job-Related Knowledge:	Requires extensive knowledge of their professional discipline and a working knowledge of related fields. Understands information in several unrelated professional disciplines.
Innovation/ Creativity:	Work requires the development of innovative methods, procedures, products or systems. This is a significant part of the job and results generally affect several campuses.
Work Conditions/ Physical Effort:	Work requires only minor physical exertion and/or physical strain. Work environment involves only infrequent exposure to disagreeable elements.

MANATEE COMMUNITY COLLEGE
Job Description
JOB TITLE: Library Department Chair

GENERAL DESCRIPTION/PRIMARY PURPOSE: This individual coordinates the planning, administration, and evaluation of library policies, procedures and operations. The Library Department Chair is a twelve-month faculty position reporting to the Vice President of Institutional Effectiveness, Planning and Information Service.

> *NOTE: Position descriptions and essential functions are subject to change due to advances in technology, utilization of work force, and facts which may impact the College's need to modify position requirements.*

ESSENTIAL JOB FUNCTIONS: The following essential job functions identify various types of work performed in this position. The omission of specific statements of duties does not exclude them from the position if the work is similar, related, or a logical assignment to the position. To perform this job successfully, an individual must be able to perform each essential duty satisfactorily. Reasonable accommodations may be made to enable individuals with disabilities to perform the essential functions of the position. Applicant may be asked to demonstrate any or all of the following essential duties:

Is responsible for the overall organization and administration of the library.

Coordinates short-term and long-range planning and development of library services with other library staff.

Communicates with the college administration on library issues.

Administers library policies and rules.

Collects and reports library statistical data on services provided, i.e. IPEDS.

Represents the library at standing, advisory, and administrative committee meetings.

Coordinates library services on both MCC campuses.

Communicates with the College Center for Library Automation (CCLA) as the Administrative Contact.

Supervises library staff, approves work schedules, and assigns duties and responsibilities.

Works with other members of the library to meet the goals and mission of the library.

Keeps current on changing professional practices; participates in local, state, regional, and national library organizations.

QUALIFICATION STANDARDS: The requirements listed below are representative of the knowledge, skill and/or ability required for the position.

Education and/or experience:
Master's degree in Library Science or equivalent, with at least five years experience working in an academic library with supervisory experience.

Language skills:
A high level of communication and human relations skills.

Mathematical skills:
Ability to create and analyze statistical data.

Reasoning ability:
Excellent problem solving skills.

Other skills and abilities:
Extensive knowledge of library systems. Ability to work well with all other college employees and patrons.

PHYSICAL DEMANDS: The physical demands described here are representative of those that must be met by an employee to successfully perform the essential functions of this job.

> While performing the duties of this job, the employee is regularly required to touch, handle, feel or reach objects, tools and controls; and verbally communicate with co-workers. The employee is frequently required to sit for extended periods of time. The employee is occasionally required to stand.

> The employee is occasionally required to independently transport oneself over uneven surfaces to various locations on two 100-acre campuses.

> The employee must occasionally lift and/or move up to 20 pounds.

> Specific vision abilities required include close vision, distance vision, identification and discernment of colors, peripheral vision, depth perception and the ability to focus.

WORK ENVIRONMENT: The work environment characteristics described here are representative of those an employee encounters while performing the essential functions of this job.

> The noise level in the work environment varies from very quiet to moderate as is typical of an office or classroom environment.

> The environment is usually indoors in a centrally heated/air-conditioned climate.

> Lighting conditions meet recommended standards and are provided by direct and/or indirect electric light fixtures of various kinds.

PERFORMANCE STANDARDS AND EXPECTATIONS:

1.   Knowledge of the College's mission, purpose, and goals.

2.   Grooming and Appearance: Manatee Community College seeks to maintain a neat and professional image at all times. When issued, College personnel must wear uniforms and maintain a neat, clean, and well-groomed appearance.

3.   Safety Awareness: Manatee Community College employees are expected to work diligently to maintain safe and healthful working conditions and to adhere to proper operating practices and procedures designed to prevent injuries and illness. Employees are required to wear personal protective devices as provided.

4.   Attendance Standards: Manatee Community College employees are expected to attend their work assignments and schedules at all times in accordance with College Rules and Procedures.

5.   Manatee Community College employees are expected to attend College-provided training sessions and meetings when deemed necessary.

JOB DESCRIPTION

JOB TITLE: **Director of Libraries**

REPORTS TO: **Provost (East Campus)**

BASIC FUNCTION: **Districtwide leader and manager of library services. Supports the Vice President of Instructional Services with needed information, reports schedules and budget requests. Directs the activity of the East Campus Library, supervises and evaluates the full-time, part-time, and volunteer staff under the guidance of the East Campus Provost.**

CLASSIFICATION: **Managerial and Other Academic Personnel**

DUTIES AND RESPONSIBILITIES:

DISTRICTWIDE RESPONSIBILITIES:

1. Provides leadership to and management of all Library services to include print and non-print materials.

2. Coordinates the districtwide satellite and certain cable and other media services.

3. Provides information, reports, and schedules to the Vice President of Instructional Services as needed.

4. Prepares and recommends to the Vice President of Instructional Services the budgets for all Libraries.

5. Recommends programs and delivery system changes and improvements for instructional support services to the Vice President of Instructional Services.

6. Establishes and monitors appropriate instructional support standards and recommends action to the Vice President of Instructional Services.

7. Assists other college personnel in resolving problems associated with Library services.

8. Provides input to the Provosts of the West and North campuses concerning the evaluation of the Associate Director of Libraries on their campuses.

1

Job Description
Director of Libraries

9.   Develops and provides for training of Library staff.

10.   Coordinates the communications between District Library functions and campus functions.

11.   Serves as a member of such committees as the Council on Instructional Services and the Technology Committee.

CAMPUS RESPONSIBILITIES:

12.   Initiates selection of print and non-print materials.

13.   Supervises the scheduling, circulation, and reference services for campus learning resource materials.

14.   Provides for student and faculty orientation to the Library and media services.

15.   Arranges for maintenance and small repair of the Library equipment and materials.

16.   Responsible for inter-campus and inter-library loan services involving the assigned campus.

17.   Provides operational and usage reports.

18.   Provides Library services to faculty and students.

19.   Responsible for supervision of the campus museum, arranges for the display of various exhibits, and meets with the Museum Advisory Committee.

20.   Performs such other duties as may be assigned.

MINIMUM QUALIFICATIONS:

A Master's Degree in Library Science or a related field from an American Library Association accredited institution required. An earned Doctoral Degree preferred. A minimum of three years of administrative experience in a postsecondary institution required.

file: moap19
last revised: 7/1/98

Quinebaug Valley Community-Technical College
Job Description
Director of Library Services
Spring, 1996

I . <u>Narrative Description</u>: Under the supervision of the Academic Dean, the Director of Library Services plans, develops and manages the college library and, depending upon the size and philosophy of the individual college, such other instructional media as learning resources laboratory and audiovisual resources.

II. <u>Effectiveness Areas</u>: Among key managerial effectiveness areas, representing the output requirements of this position, are (but are not necessarily limited to the following and are subject to change depending upon the size and complexity of the institution):

      Collection development and management
      Library and media facilities planning
      Library and media center operations
      Library and media center services
      Information retrieval systems
      Instructional program enrichment

III. <u>Functional Responsibilities</u>:

    A. Plans and maintains the library and media collections in close cooperation with the professional staff;

    B. Supervises all library and media operations and services at the college and its off-site center in Willimantic;

    C. Oversees cataloging and other technical services;

    D. Provides learning support services for faculty, students, staff and the community;

    E. Designs and plays an active role in offering bibliographic instruction that meets specific objectives of instructors at various class and subject levels; offers in-service training to the professional staff;

F. Develops and manages efficient maintenance procedures for the library and media center and for the equipment and materials in them;

G. Develops and maintains inter-library loan programs and a shared, on-line automated circulation system; develops and maintains other cooperative inter-library and media services as needed;

H. Develops, manages, and reviews the policies and regulations of the library and media center; establishes effective procedures for informing the professional staff and students about resources, policies, and services;

I. Develops and manages an annual library and media budget; initiates all library and media requisitions; coordinates the purchase of books, equipment, supplies and services;

J. Prepares reports and evaluations of the services and operation of the library and media center;

K. Supervises all professional and non-professional library and media personnel; evaluates staff for purposes of retention, promotion, and tenure;

L. Provides creative and effective leadership in building and maintaining community relations, promoting the college, and presenting a positive image of the colleges learning support services;

M. Serves on college, local, state and other committees as related to the needs of the college;

N. Provides in-service training for staff members as needed;

O. Performs such other duties as may be determined by the Academic Dean and/or the President of the college.

SALT LAKE COMMUNITY COLLEGE

POSITION DESCRIPTION
   Exempt
   (Do not use more than allotted space.)

Date: June, 1995   Job Code:
Position Title: Director of Learning Resources
Department: Learning Resources
Incumbent Name:

POSITION PURPOSE: Responsible for organizational leadership and management of Learning Resources, which includes the SLCC Library System, Media Services, and the Television Studio.

REPORTING RELATIONSHIP:
   REPORTS TO: Academic Vice-President
   AS DO: 1 Dean, School of Business and Industr (E); 1 Dean, School of Continuing and Community   Education (E); 1 Dean,School of Humanities and Sciences (E) ; 1 Dean, School of Technolog (E) ;
   1 Coordinator, Sandy Center (E) ; 1 Administrative Assistant (N); 1 Technician (N)
POSITIONS REPORTING DIRECTLY TO THIS POSITION: 1 Librarian, Administrative Services (E); 1 Librarian Systems/Technical Services (E); 1 Librarian, Media Services (E); 1 Learning Resources Computer Analyst (E); 1 Director of TV Production (E); 1 Librarian, Branch Campus (E); 1 Administrative Assistant (N).
FTE Personnel directly supervised: Exempt - 6, Non-Exempt - 1; FTE Personnel indirectly supervised at Redwood, South City, and Sandy locations: Exempt - 7, Non-Exempt - 12, Hourly (headcount) - 36.

JOB DIMENSIONS:

Annual Op Budget:	Ann Payroll:	Ann Revenue, Accounts:
$371,236 plus supplemental	$582,863 salaries	Total operating, acquisitions, and
and grant funds $203,300 hourly		payroll: $1,268,356
$110,957 acquisitions funds	$786,163 total payroll	

Library collection of 53,699 books, 9,927 media items, 465 periodical subscriptions. Library operates two computer networks: Dynix library management system and Novell-based reference databases system with approximately 25 CD-ROM products and more than 65 computer and terminal workstations. Library collection valued as of 1994 at $2,008,440. Library system includes 62,000 sq ft Markosian Library (Redwood Campus), South City Campus Library, and Sandy Center Library. Services provided to other sites as needed. Cost of Markosian Library (construction and furnishings): $8,000,000. Television Studio valued at $1,273,000 (equipment replacement cost). Television Studio is designated Salt Lake Valley regional fiber hub for state Utah Education Network telecommunications system.
Services provided to approximately 19,440 students, 811 contract and adjunct faculty, and 1654 full-time and part-time staff, plus off-campus users through Utah Academic Library Consortium (UALC) and community user programs.

POSITION SUMMARY:
ESSENTIAL:
1. Plan, organize, and implement all aspects of Learning Resources program to support college mission and role assignment within Utah State System of Higher Education. Develop Learning Resources tactical and strategic plans and goals.
2. Provide leadership, direction, and training for reporting directors and managers in the provision of library services to both on and off campus users.
3. Provide leadership, direction, and training for reporting directors and managers in management of campus media distribution system, TV studio production, teleconference services, and operation of regional UEN fiber hub.
4. Interview and hire new Learning Resources staff. Provide new employee orientation and ongoing staff training for all Learning Resources personnel.
5. Represent College on a statewide basis by providing leadership and direction for management of Learning Resources role in electronic highway, library, and instructional television networks and systems.
6. Provide leadership and direction for management of Learning Resources role in campuswide information technology strategic planning and expansion of campus information access\networking systems.
7. Establish, implement, and interpret Learning Resources policies and operating procedures within the context of general College operating policies and procedures.
8. Manage allocation of resources to improve quality and productivity of Learning Resources services including organizational design, staff development and utilization, management of multiple site physical plants, equipment selection and allocation, and collection and resources development.
9. Plan and manage Learning Resources budget, including educational and general funds, grant, supplemental, and special purpose funding accounts.
10. Provide leadership and direction in establishing and maintaining community and professional contacts to facilitate delivery of services; work closely with both on and off-campus groups to achieve service goals.
11. Represent Learning Resources on the UALC Directors' Council, in the Utah Library Association, in the National Council for Learning Resources, and in other professional and community assignments.

MARGINAL:
12. Other projects as assigned which may include College or state projects.

Salt Lake Community College

DIFFICULT AND COMPLEX PROBLEMS OR CHALLENGES: May include one or more of the following: Directing library and media system development so as to meet the needs of a diverse population of both on-site and distance learners. Directing television services development so as to maintain up-to-date equipment platform and meet differing needs of a wide variety of users. Facilitating communication among a wide variety of people and groups in order to meet service expectations and achieve the mission of Learning Resources and of the College. Resolving personnel problems and conflicts arising from a variety of sources, including students, faculty, staff, and members of the community. Assuring personal and professional growth and development for all personnel in Learning Resources.

MAJOR PROBLEMS NORMALLY REFERRED TO SUPERVISOR OR OTHERS: May include one or more of the following: Problems between instructional support organizations and academic schools that cannot be resolved through available means. Budgeting deficiencies that cannot be resolved through allocated resources. All matters requiring approval by the Legislature, Board of Regents, President, Vice Presidents, and designated by law or policy.

PRINCIPAL ACCOUNTABILITIES:

1. Plan, organize, implement, and promote a unified vision of the Learning Resources role in statewide information highway, library, and instructional television networks and systems.
2. Plan, organize, implement, and promote a unified vision of the Learning Resources role in campuswide information technology strategic planning and information network expansion.
3. Improve quality of Learning Resources collections and services through collection evaluation and acquisitions programs, effective advisory committees, faculty/staff and student involvement, technology upgrades and enhancements, and staff development.
4. Provide an environment and a structure that assists Learning Resources personnel to be productive contributors and assures continued personal and professional growth and development.
5. Manage Learning Resources physical plant and fiscal resources so as to meet College goals and statewide network commitments.

SPECIFIC TYPES OF KNOWLEDGE, SKILL, AND EXPERIENCE REQUIRED FOR THIS POSITION:

Knowledge of: College operations, policies, and procedures
      Library management, operations, policies, and procedures
      Instructional television services management and operation
      Information technology planning, management, and utilization
      Federal and state funding and regulations
      Budget and financial planning, management, and development
      Personnel management and team building
      Strategic and tactical planning
      Physical plant management
      M.L.S. from ALA-accredited institution or M.Ed in media required. PhD or EdD. preferred

Ability to: Effectively represent Learning Resources to the College and the community
      Foster positive organizational development
      Organize and direct staff training and development
      Manage fiscal resources effectively
      Use integrated information systems
      Manage many projects and tasks concurrently
      Manage multiple physical sites and services to remote locations

Experience: Five years academic library or learning resources experience, including at least two years of progressively more responsible administrative experience
      Two years full-time teaching experience at an accredited college or university

Prepared by:
(Signature)

Edited by:
Date:

Supervisor Approval:
Date:

Evaluation
Date:

VP Signature: Date:

WESTERN NEBRASKA

COMMUNITY COLLEGE
INFORMATION SERVICES DIRECTOR

*Class specifications are intended to present a descriptive list of the range of duties performed by employees in the class. Specifications are **not** intended to reflect all duties performed within the job.*

DEFINITION
The Information Services Director is responsible for the organization and supervision of the Libraries and the Instructional Technology Centers of both campuses, directing the resources and services of these entities in supporting and strengthening the educational program of the institution. The Information Services Director has the responsibilities for determination of policy regarding services to students, faculty/administration and the public and in development organization, and maintenance of library resources in instructional technology. Preparation of annual budget and accountability for expenditures is required.

SUPERVISION RECEIVED AND EXERCISED
Receives direction from the Executive Director of Information Technologies.

Exercises direct supervision over Administrative/Professional, Support and Student staff of the Library.

Essential and marginal function statements – Essential and other important responsibilities and duties may include, but are not limited to the following:

Essential functions:
- • Prepares annual budgets ; arranges for internal financial records and supervises expenditures.
- • Directs and supervises staff, setting schedules and supervising training for new personnel; plans and implements in-service and staff development; evaluates personnel; makes recommendations to the Vice-President of Educational Services and Executive Director of Educational Technologies for selection of personnel.
-
- • Prepares Federal and State reports; annual institutional reports; applications and reports for grant programs; prepares accreditation studies; prepares statistics and inventory reports.
- • Communicates with college and community by providing for liaison with faculty, staff, students and public; plans and conducts staff meetings; participates in general councils and committees; promotes public relations, including publications, displays, etc. in accordance with Library standards.
- • Cooperates with outside organizations by representing the College in professional library organizations, and participates in planning with area and state libraries to improve and extend the resources and services for all; represents the College in cooperative ventures regarding educational technology.

- • Plans for optimal arrangement of the physical space and equipment of the libraries and their instructional technology requirements; notes maintenance and repair needs and notifies the appropriate staff.
- • Plans development of a balanced collection of materials to support the educational objectives of the institution with final responsibility for selection of materials.
- Coordinates and assists the Learning Resource Center Coordinator with reference to library activities and instructional technology.
- Works with Division Chair, Dean of Instruction, Learning Resource Center Coordinator and faculty in selection of materials.
- • Supervises the program of instruction in library use and materials used in such instruction.
- • Supervises reference services, including on-line computer reference services.
- • Prepares or supervises preparation of bibliographies to encourage and promote library use.
- • Supervise the technical services, encouraging use of available technology to achieve optimal efficiency.
- • Plan overall development of the collection of AV software, developing standards and setting goals.
- Plans overall development of equipment resources including setting long-term acquisition schedule of major equipment.
- Is cognizant of new developments in educational technology.
- • Performs any other duties assigned by the Vice-President of Educational Services and/or the Executive Director of Educational Technologies or President.

QUALIFICATIONS

Knowledge of:

Breadth and diversity of information services in higher education today.

Library administration, including the role of the library in the overall academic mission is necessary.

Current educational technology, its future possibilities, requirements, benefits and pitfalls is required.

Ability to:

Develop harmonious staff relationships and focus staff efforts to serve the informational needs of the institution .

Possess good communications skills, both oral and written.

Experience and training guidelines: Any combination of experience and training that would likely provide the required knowledge and abilities is qualifying. A typical way to obtain the knowledge and abilities would be:

Experience:

Course work and/or experience in all aspects of educational technology is required; or any equivalent combination of education and experience which provides the required knowledge, skills and abilities will be considered.

Training:

Master's degree in Library Science is strongly preferred with emphasis and experience in administration highly desirable.

WORKING CONDITIONS

Environmental Conditions:

Office environment; irregular work hours.

Physical Conditions:

Essential functions may require maintaining physical condition necessary for sitting for prolonged periods of time.

Revis'd: 8/98

disk - jobdescp.98

Campus Library Supervisor

The following job titles and descriptions are for multi-campus college libraries.

Campus Director of Learning Resources
Campus Supervisor
Coordinator of LRC Instructional Services
Learning Resources Coordinator

<u>Carl Sandburg College</u>

Job Description

<u>Position Title:</u>	Coordinator of LRC Instructional Services
<u>Classification:</u>	Faculty
<u>Level:</u>	N/A
<u>Supervises:</u>	LRC Circulation Clerk, Technical Services, LRC Assistant
<u>Reports to:</u>	Dean of Learning Resource Services
<u>Principal Working Relationship:</u>	TRIO Project Director/Dean of Learning Resource Services, Staff, Students, and AV Coordinator

<u>Essential Functions</u>

<u>Major Responsibilities</u>

1. Serve as a reference librarian, interpreting both on-site and externally available collections of resources to the user.

2. Collection development recommendations to Dean for purchase of materials, or contracting for on-line services that enhance the ability of the LRC to support instructional programs includes making determination on disposition of donated materials. Works with AV Coordinator to provide faculty and students with equipment and software needed for instruction.

3. Assume the position of liaison with faculty for the design and evaluation of an information skills program. Tailor LRC orientation programs covering research skills to meet the requirements of faculty and students in various college programs and teach these skills as required.

4. Proper functioning of automated systems to include both hardware and software components. Troubleshoots problems and solves them or makes referrals to technical personnel who can.

5. Proper cataloging of acquisitions. Does all original cataloging.

6. Perform database searches as requested.

7. Designs, constructs, and maintains LRC web pages.

8. Maintains LRC procedures manual. Makes recommendations for additions or deletions to Dean.

9. Supervision of archives and special collections.

10. Adhere to the guidelines of any negotiated labor contract involving faculty.

11. Enforce college regulations concerning student behavior and building regulations.

12. Other duties as assigned.

Carl Sandburg College

Coordinates

1. Repair and/or replacement of damaged or worn out materials and equipment.

2. Schedules and approves displays.

Preventive Risk Management Activities

1. Participate in and support the college Risk Management Program in a capacity appropriate to this position.

2. Monitoring conditions, events, and circumstances present in the college operations and communicating observations to the appropriate supervisor and/or Risk Management Committee

Minimum Necessary Skills, Experience, and Educational Background

1. Master's degree in Library Science.

2. Ability to work with computer systems and software.

Physical Requirements to Perform

1. Ability to bend, reach, and lift weights of at least 20 lbs.

2. Basic dexterity skills (computer work, telephoning).

May 7, 1999

EDISON COMMUNITY COLLEGE
Campus Director of Learning Resources

Position Function

This is professional work in planning, directing and coordinating the activities of the Campus library. Work includes providing library services and learning resources to students, faculty and staff through the maintenance of effective and efficient materials selection and provision for reference, informational and instructional services which support the educational programs of the College.

Supervision

Duties are performed under the leadership and direction of the provost, who reviews work through conferences and reports. Policies and procedures regarding learning resources activities which have district-wide implications are developed and interpreted in cooperation with the District Director of Learning Resources.

Responsibilities

Provides leadership for and direction to faculty and staff in the selection, distribution, use and maintenance of learning resources materials in all formats.

Supervised and monitors learning resources staff and operations; provides instruction, guidance and leadership for progressive enhancement of quality services. Supervises all aspects of circulation operations, comprehensive reference services and collection development.

Develops and maintains policies, procedures, work flows, schedules and systems to enable students, faculty and staff to effectively access information and select learning resources.

Provides effective communication systems within the Learning Resources area which foster the exchange of ideas and provide opportunities for staff participation in decision-making.

Provides an effective organization through the hiring, training, evaluation and motivation of staff. Maintain and organizational structure that ensures effective and efficient operations.

Coordinates the preparation of the Learning Resources budget with campus faculty and staff in consultation with the District Director of Learning Resources, and recommends the budget for approval by the Campus Provost. Monitors budget expenditures to maximize utilization of existing resources.

Maintains currency in the latest developments and technology relating to the Learning Resources area of responsibility.

Maintains appropriate liaison with individuals and organizations within the State of Florida that support and enhance the Learning Resources operation locally. Participates in the activities of the organizations.

Recommends programs to enhance staff development.

Performs related duties as assigned.

<u>Position Requirements</u>

Earned Master's degree in Library Science from an ALA-accredited institution.

Demonstrated competence as a librarian with appropriate administrative, budgetary and supervisory experience at the college level, community college preferred.

Effective oral and written communication skills.

Personal and educational philosophy compatible with the mission, goals and objectives of Edison Community College.

Approved 4/24/96

HILLSBOROUGH COMMUNITY COLLEGE

JOB DESCRIPTION

Class Title: Learning Resources Coordinator	*Date:*	June 22, 1998

Level: G	*FLSA Status:* Exempt	*Class Code:*	E0730

GENERAL DESCRIPTION

Manages and oversees the operation and administration of a Learning Resources Center (LRC).

KEY RESPONSIBILITES	% OF TIME
1.* Supervises, initiates, and disseminates work assignments and schedules for assigned staff. Monitors and evaluates staff performance, trains and provides staff development opportunities.	25%
2.* Manages and oversees daily operations of the campus LRC which may include circulation, audiovisual services and lab, slide collection, campus processing, periodicals, etc. Conducts meetings as needed.	15%
3.* Communicates LRC and College policies and procedures to staff and explains LRC policies and procedures to students. Handles routine student concerns and complaints, and recommends appropriate action.	15%
4.* Writes, reviews, and updates LRC and College procedures; reviews forms and recommends changes.	5%
5.* Coordinates campus LRC budget process for equipment and supplies; coordinates requisitions, and documents LRC materials and supplies.	5%
6. Ensures the security and maintenance of the physical assets of the campus LRC; assists students and troubleshoots LRC equipment problems.	15%
7. Prepares and maintains essential LRC records and files, and prepares correspondence, reports, etc.	10%
8. Coordinates the acquisition and distribution of LRC equipment and supplies. Establishes rapport with the library faculty and assists them in preparing materials and providing professional support.	5%
9. Serves on College, regional and statewide committees. Keeps abreast of new developments for learning resources and/or technical services.	5%
10. Performs other similar and related duties as required.	

* Indicates an "essential" job function.

Class Title: Learning Rsrcs Coord	Class Code: E0730	Level: G

KEY JOB REQUIREMENTS	
Formal Education:	Bachelor's Degree required.
Work Experience:	3 to 5 years.
Planning Scope:	Four to Twelve Months: Plan events that will occur during the year, and have some effect on the department's annual expenditures, and or revenues.
Planning Level:	The primary scope of planning activities in this position affects the department or equivalent.
Budgets Impact:	Recommending/Contributory: Have a strong, but not controlling voice in decisions on the budget; can authorize or recommend expenditures within an approved budget. Actions may have a direct contribution on the methods used to generate revenues.
Grants/Revenue Impact:	No impact on grant funds or revenue generation.
Impact of Decisions:	Makes recommendations or decisions which typically affect the assigned department, but may at times affect operations, services, individuals, or activities of my campus.
Complexity:	Varied: Work is complex and varied and requires the selection and application of technical and detailed guidelines. Moderate analytic ability is needed to gather and interpret data where results/answers can be found after analysis of several facts.
Decision Making:	Analytic: Independent judgment is required to study previously established, often partially relevant guidelines; plan for various interrelated activities; and coordinate such activities within a work unit or while completing a project.
Problem Solving:	Problem solving involves identification and analysis of diverse problems; answers are usually found by reviewing standard technical manuals and administrative procedures and modifying them for unusual situations.
Internal Communications:	Regular contacts to carry out programs and to explain specialized matters, or occasional contacts with officials at higher levels on matters requiring cooperation, explanation and persuasion.
External Communications:	Regular external contacts to carry out organization programs and to explain non-specialized matter, or work requiring continuing personal contact with the public involving the enforcement of laws, ordinances, polices and procedures.
Level of Supervisory Responsibility:	Provide limited supervision for one or more functions within a department. Formally plans, assigns, directs, and coordinates the work of these functions.
Nature of Work Supervised:	Nature of work supervised is primarily technically oriented or complex, includes additional administrative responsibilities, and requires a working knowledge of unit or departmental activities.
Job-Related Knowledge:	Entry Professional Skills: Requires entry-level knowledge of theories and practices of a professional field. This level is reserved for an individual with a four-year degree or with high-level vocational skills demonstrated by a number of years of on-the-position experience. Writes reports using technical data requiring considerable interpretation, developing new methods and procedures. Frequently applies knowledge to practical issues.
Innovation/Creativity:	Work requires using original and creative thinking to develop new, moderately complex results. The results generally impact several work groups, a large project or an extended customer base.
Working Conditions/ Physical Effort:	Work requires only minor physical exertion and/or physical strain. Work environment involves only infrequent exposure to disagreeable elements.

Job Description: Learning Resources Coordinator/Calmar Campus

Areas of Responsibility:

Library:

- Select materials to strengthen library collection.
- Collaborate with teachers on materials to support curriculum.
- Involve the advisory committee in supporting library activities.
- Lead the library staff to develop schedules, procedures, and solve problems.
- Cooperate with the Peosta librarian to develop policies, manage the automation system, and select shared resources to assure standard services across the College.
- Market library and its services among staff, faculty and students.
- Work with Learning Resources Supervisor to manage budget, acquire material and equipment, supervise workers, and generate reports.
- Coordinate library orientation and reference lessons for classes.
- Be available for backup in the reference area.

Learning Center:

- Increase faculty & student awareness of Learning Center through promotion & orientation activities.
- Provide leadership for emerging technologies & their use in developmental education.
- Supervise Learning Center faculty at Calmar to insure that services are provided when students need them and in the variety of needs students have.
- Coordinate curriculum, computer-assisted instruction, tutoring, tracking of students, staffing, reporting & budgeting for Calmar campus Developmental Ed Services.
- Work with Coordinator of Developmental Education at Peosta to develop staff training opportunities for Learning Center faculty at both campuses & for others involved in developmental education.
- Cooperate with Coordinator of Developmental Education at Peosta to generate various reports that are needed.

Testing Services:

- Supervise & coordinate testing services for ASSET & and other tests.
- Be the Chief GED examiner—arrange for GED testing and coordinate with Peosta GED staff people as well as the CIS staff to assure that GED is done in accordance with GEDTS rules & regulations.

Librarians

Job descriptions in this section all require a Master's Degree in Library Science. Some descriptions are for generic librarian I, II, III, others are for specific duties, such as reference or cataloging. These job titles represent every title that was submitted for this publication.

General Librarian Titles
Assistant Librarian
Associate Librarian
Learning Resource Faculty
Librarian I, II, III
Librarian, Branch Campus
Librarian (Faculty)
Library Services Specialist
Library Specialist

Public Services Librarians (Circulation, Reference, BI)
Assistant Librarian, Circulation
Assistant Librarian, Library Instruction
Assistant Librarian, Public Services
Audiovisual/Circulation Librarian
Evening/Center Librarian
Information Literacy Librarian
Information Services Librarian
Learning Resources Administrative Team Coach/Public Services Librarian
Librarian Electronic Resources/Reference
Librarian Instruction/Reference
Librarian—Reference and Instruction
Library Technician
Public Services Librarian
Reference Librarian
Reference and Instruction Librarian

Technical Services
Assistant Librarian, Technical Services
Catalog Librarian
Cataloger
Coordinator, LRC Technical Services
Dept. Coordinatior Technical Services
Librarian—Cataloger/Technical Services
Learning Resources Administrative Team Coach/Technical Services Librarian
Learning Resources Administrative Team Member/Assistnat Technical Services Librarian
Librarian Collection Development, Acquisition, Etc.
Supervisor Technical Serices
Technical Services Liberarian

BARTON COUNTY COMMUNITY COLLEGE

POSITION DESCRIPTION

Position Title:	Classification:		
Assistant Librarian	Staff		
Organizational Unit:	Reports To:	Date:	Rev. # & Date
Academic Services	Director of Library Services	12-18-91	1/15/1999

I.   Narrative General Description

Under the direction of the Director of Library Services, the Assitant Librarian performs reference and circulation desk duties, requests from other libraries materials not available in the BCCC Library, fills similar requests received from other libraries, supervises student workers.

II.   Functional Responsibilities

A. Locate and order by mail, FAX or electronic mail any books or articles not available in the BCCC library
B. Fill requests for books and articles received from other libraries
C. Orient and supervise work-study and college employment students.
D. Assist patrons with on-line searching.
E. Supervise the check-in of newspapers and periodicals received each day.
F. Perform designated circulation duties at the circulation desk when necessary.
G. Create displays for the lobby display case
H. Track ILL statistics and data for reporting purposes
I. Assists with other library and information requests as necessary to provide information services to the college community.
J. Perform other such duties as may be assigned by the Director of Library Services and any other appropriate level of administration.
K. Provide reference services to students, faculty, staff, administration and the general public.
L. Keeps statistics on library usage.

III.   Consulting Tasks

A. With Director of Library Services, provides reports as necessary for the college
B. Work with the Director of Library Services in tracking and claiming missing periodical issues.
C. Work with all library staff to facilitate the schedules and work assignments of all student employees.

IV.   Supervises the Following Staff

A. All Student employees, and facilitates the work of student

employees for the other library staff

V.   Required Knowledge, Skills

A. Knowledge of computer programs required to process ILL requests
B. Knowledge of library of Congress classification system

    C. Knowledge of serials operations
    D. Knowledge of basic library resources and information sources to provide reference assistance when required
    E. Knowledge of library circulation procedures
    F. Ability to communicate effectively with students, faculty, and staff to serve as a liaison between the library, other ILL cooperating libraries, library patrons, and the rest of the campus and the community.
    G. Ability to compile and type reports and information reports such as bibliographies, faculty requests for information, etc.
    H. Ability to supervise paraprofessionals and student help.
    I. Ability to work under the pressures of deadlines.
    J. Creative ability to prepare displays and promotional materials.

VI. Required Experience

    A. At least one to three years library experience required, preferably at the community college level. Some required skills could be obtained through on the job training.

VII. Required Educational Background

    B. A Masters in Library Science preferred. A bachelors degree or substantial work towards completion of a bachelors degree in an appropriate field is acceptable if combined with extensive and proven library and information services experience.

VIII.Exemption Status _____ Exempt _X_ Non-exempt

JK:71896:000060

COLUMBUS STATE COMMUNITY COLLEGE
Job Description

PAY GRADE: _____

DATE WRITTEN: _____

DATE REVISED: _____

POSITION: _____

WRITTEN BY: _____

TITLE: Catalog Librarian

SUMMARY: Responsible for the classifying and cataloging of all materials (print and non-print) for the Educational Resources Center collection.

RELATIONSHIP: Reports to the Director of Educational Resources and receives direction from the Technical Services Coordinator. Interfaces regularly with other ERC staff members, employees of the College, and students.

**DUTIES AND
RESPONSIBILITIES:**

1.   Classifies and catalogs materials in all media for the ERC collections according to the appropriate classification scheme, and assigns appropriate Library of Congress subject headings;

2.   Assigns cutter numbers according to Cutter-Sanborn table;

3.   Assigns and verifies call number of each title to be added to collection;

4.   Searches and catalogs materials not found in OCLC database using bibliographic information found in other authoritarian sources;

5.   Catalogs all new materials using the OCLC terminal system and is responsible for input and revision of records contained in the OCLC database and CS/Link database;

6.   Submits monthly statistics of materials cataloged to the Director of Educational Resources;

7.   Serves as CS/Link/OhioLINK Coordinator/Head Implementor, under direction of Director of Educational Resources, and maintains the hardware and software for

the online system, in conjunction with Data Center personnel, Innovative/Interfaces, and OhioLINK support staff.

8.   Participates in the selection of materials for the general collection;

9.   Performs updates/changes and maintains the serials union listing functions;

10.   Prepares materials for, and maintains college archives housed in, the ERC;

11.   Assists with other library services operations as needed;

12.   Executes the general responsibilities common to all employees of the College;

13.   Performs other duties and projects as may be assigned by the Technical Services Area and the ERC, as well as specific guidelines established by the Director of Educational Resources.

AUTHORITY: Operates within the procedures and methods of the Technical Services Area and the ERC, as well as specific guidelines established by the Director of Educational Resources and Technical Services Coordinator.

DAWSON COMMUNITY COLLEGE

POSITION DESCRIPTION

APRIL 1999

POSITION: Assistant Librarian

DEPARTMENT: Library

ACCOUNTABLE TO: Library Director

SUMMARY OF WORK: Position develops, maintains, and provides access to and instruction in library resources and information at Dawson Community College. Provides information services to faculty, administration, students, staff, and community.

JOB CHARACTERISTICS:

Nature of Work: This position performs administrative and technical duties requiring accuracy and attention to detail in the operation of the college library. Position is required to work a split shift which results in evening and sometimes weekend work. Must be flexible to cover additional hours usually working over 40 hours per week. Fills in when the Library Director is absent. Must be able to lift and shelve books and have access to upper and lower library shelves. Maintains confidentiality of sensitive information.

Personal Contacts: Continuous contact with library patrons including students, staff, administrators, faculty, and the community.

Supervision Received: Position is mainly self-directed with special or immediate assignments from the supervisor.

Supervision Exercised: Supervision of from 6-12 work study students per year; each averages nine hours per week. Trains students in the various library functions. Disciplines and terminates, if necessary.

Essential Functions: Position requires ability to: communicate orally and in writing; supervise and train work study students; read written material; order and process books and materials; apply computer knowledge including current word processing software and Internet searching; maintain catalog; maintain circulation database; complete inter-library loan requests; keep library organized and tidy; calculate; maintain records; type and file; assist users; and operate office machines.

AREAS OF JOB ACCOUNTABILITY AND PERFORMANCE:

--Implement and provide assistance in accessing learning resources to patrons.

--Provide technical services including database management of automated catalog, circulation system and OCLC/WLN service; Interlibrary Loan services and periodical management.

Cataloging:

--Generate, classify, and process orders for new acquisitions.

--Physically process all new acquisitions.

--Maintain cost account of all acquisitions.

--Transfer and edit electronic records to and from OCLC/WLN, Library of Congress (LC) and the local database while maintaining integrity and accuracy of authority records.

Circulation:

--Maintain and update circulation database and resolve related problems.

--Train student assistants to follow established circulation policies and procedures.

--Set up report modules to print overdue notices and other reports and statistics.

OCLC/WLN (Online Computer Library Center):

--Submit accurate and consistent holding records for all new acquisitions to the OCLC/WLN network and attach our call number; send quarterly.

--Make corrections and/or update our holdings records.

Interlibrary Loan:

--Directs all inter-library loans from patron request through loan completion and maintains records.

--Produces required reports for statistics and state reimbursement.

--Uses bibliographic and other electronic databases to effect the interlibrary loans.

--Chooses appropriate, cost-effective and timely sources for meeting ILL needs; uses and supervises the use of computer equipment, copies and fax.

Periodicals:

--Receipts and processes journals, newspapers and other periodicals.

--Maintains physical periodical collection; replaces damaged and missing materials.

--Assists users in the use of periodicals.

--Assists with Internet accessible journals and indexing.

--Maintains periodical records in the shared database and WLN.

Other duties:
--Assists in development, review and evaluation of library resources, policies and procedures.

--Maintains statistics of library operations for internal and external reporting.

--Attend training as technology changes.

--Assists with answering the telephone in the evenings for the college.

--Manages the faculty reserve shelves.

--Oversees and assists with equipment use, videos, and rentals.

--Does book repair.

--Orders and processes materials and supplies for the Library.

--Handles materials and some tests for the Distance Learning Center.

--Assigns work study duties, trains, and supervises.

--Performs other related duties as required.

JOB REQUIREMENTS:

Knowledge: This position requires a knowledge of: modern practices and procedures for researching, accessing and maintaining library materials and resources; computerized library systems; use of office machines and AV equipment; and current word processing programs.

Skills: This position requires skills in use of: computers, office machines, A/V equipment, and skills in maintaining databases and critical thinking skills.

Abilities: This position requires the ability to: organize and prioritize duties; be self-directed; supervise and train students; work evening hours; be on call when work study students work evening hours; solve people and computer problems; do research; communicate effectively orally and in writing; follow verbal and written instructions; work with numerous interruptions; learn complex database systems; handle stress; sit for long periods of time at computer; establish effective working relationships with fellow employees, students, supervisors, and the public.

EDUCATION AND EXPERIENCE:

The above knowledge, skills, and abilities are typically acquired through a combination of education and experience equivalent to:

--A minimum of an Associate degree in library science preferred.

--Two or more years of experience working in a library.

--Experience with computers and office machines.

--Must be certified by the state in interlibrary loan procedures.

JOB PERFORMANCE STANDARDS:

Evaluation of this position will be based primarily upon performance of the preceding requirements and duties. Examples of job performance criteria include, but are not limited to, the following:

--Performs assigned duties.

--Demonstrates knowledge of modern library practices and procedures.

--Keeps abreast of new technology related to library functions.

--Capably provides library services to patrons.

--Capably trains and supervises work-study students.

--Competently maintains computerized records and databases.

--Capably assists patrons to find information and materials.

--Capably assists with phones and other duties for the college.

--Provides for an organized, tidy library.

--Maintains accurate and timely records.

--Prepares and submits accurate and timely reports.

--Deals tactfully and courteously with the public.

--Observes work hours.

--Demonstrates punctuality.

--Maintains strict confidentiality regarding library usage and faxes.

--Establishes and maintains effective working relationships with fellow employees, supervisors and the public.

EDISON COMMUNITY COLLEGE
Learning Resource Faculty

Position Function:

This position is responsible for providing professional quality work as a non-teaching faculty member.

Supervision:

Employees in this class are directly responsible to and work under the general supervision of the District Director of Learning Resources who reviews work through conferences and reports.

Responsibilities:

Provides Reference Service and Bibliographic instruction.

Assists in all aspects of the Learning Resources circulation, reference, acquisition and cataloging.

Works closely with other faculty in developing and in teaching techniques for Bibliographic Instruction.

Assists the District Director of Learning Resources in planning and implementing the policy and procedure recommendations relating to Learning Resources.

Assists the District Director of Learning Resources in monitoring expenditures, maintaining budget integrity and providing data for monthly institutional charges for the area.

Assists the District Director of Learning Resources in a periodic review of stack conditions and the total systems of user accessibility to the collection in all media formats.

Assists the District Director of Learning Resources in recommending materials to be ordered for, or withdrawn from, the collection in the Learning Resources.

Conducts in-service training of staff.

Assists the District Director of Learning Resources with workshops, seminars, and classes in the Learning Resources area.

Assists the District Director of Learning Resources in supervision of the Learning Resources Technical Assistants and Learning Resources Assistants within the Learning Resources area.

Assists the Learning Resources Technical Assistants in preparing statistical reports as required.

Participates in appropriate meetings and serves on committees as elected or appointed.

Assists the District Director of Learning Resources in determining and developing sources of external funding.

Pursues opportunities for professional growth.

Performs other duties and responsibilities as required by the District Director of Learning Resources

Minimum Requirements:

Must possess a master's degree from a regionally accredited institution of higher education in the field of library science and/or media.

Must possess the ability to perform duties in each area of the Learning Resources.

Must demonstrate proficiency in oral and written communications.

Must demonstrate ability to communicate effectively with and maintain a positive working relationship with students, peers, supervisors and staff.

Demonstrated belief in and concern for community service.

Demonstrated high ethical and moral character.

Personal and educational philosophy compatible with the goals, objectives, and mission of the College.

FLORIDA KEYS COMMUNITY COLLEGE
HUMAN RESOURCES OFFICE

JOB DESCRIPTION

JOB TITLE: ASSISTANT LIBRARIAN

GENERAL DESCRIPTION

This is highly specialized professional work assisting in the supervisory functions and all phases of library operations. Work is performed under the general direction of the Librarian.

ESSENTIAL JOB FUNCTIONS

1.   Provide reference and research assistance to the students, faculty and staff.

2.   Assists with development of library orientation program.

3.   Helps coordinate collection development activities.

4.   Serves as media and interlibrary loan liaison.

5.   Helps supervise, train and evaluate Library Specialists, Library Audio/Visual Specialist, Senior Library Specialist, and part-time Library Specialist

6.   Provides full range of reference services, including computer-assisted searches.

7.   Conducts library orientations and bibliographic instructional sessions for classes when required.

8.   Serves as back-up to Librarian with management of federal depository program.

9.   Assists as needed in the full range of other library/learning resources activities, including statistical record keeping, collection development, circulation, management/manager of bibliographic data base, interlibrary loan, acquisitions and audiovisual support.

10.   Assists with LINCC and other library automation activities.

11.   Assists in various other outreach, planning and evaluation duties. Assists with special projects as directed.

12.   Recommends policies and procedures for effective library operations.

13.   Evaluates library services and recommendations for improvement.

14.   Serves in community liaison activities.

(These essential job functions are not to be construed as a complete statement of all duties performed. Employees will be required to perform other job related marginal duties as required.)

Florida Keys Community College

ASSISTANT LIBRARIAN
Page 2

MINIMUM QUALIFICATIONS

KNOWLEDGE, ABILITIES AND SKILLS:

- Knowledge of the principles, practices and methods of library science, development and administration as it pertains to the library at a college.
- Knowledge of library materials and methods.
- Knowledge of media and electronic services including teleconferencing, video production, etc.
- Ability to plan, organize and direct library programs and activities.
- Ability to interpret college interests and needs and plans for library services.
- Ability to establish and maintain effective work relationships with other employees and college groups.
- Ability to work in a stressful and rapidly changing technological environment.
- Ability to communicate effectively both orally and in writing.
- Ability to analyze facts and exercise judgement in decision making.
- Ability to supervise effectively.
- Ability to access, input and retrieve information from a computer.

EDUCATION AND EXPERIENCE:

- A Master's Degree in Library Science from an ALA accredited institution.
- Familiarity with OCLC and other library automation activities, including microcomputer applications packages.
- Three (3) years experience working in a library setting.
- Supervisory experience and other relevant work experience will be helpful.

(A comparable amount of training, education or experience may be substituted for the above minimum qualifications.)

LICENSES, CERTIFICATIONS OR REGISTRATIONS:

- None

ESSENTIAL PHYSICAL SKILLS:

- Acceptable eyesight (with or without corrections).
- Acceptable hearing (with or without hearing aid).
- Ability to place materials on six foot shelves.
- Walk, bend, stoop, and reach materials.
- Push loaded book truck.
- Ability to lift up to 35 pounds and stand for long periods of time.

ENVIRONMENTAL CONDITIONS:

- Works inside in an office environment.

(Reasonable accommodations will be made for otherwise qualified individuals with a disability.)

Gulf Coast
Community College

TITLE	Job Description Assistant Librarian, Library Instruction	NUMBER	2.8
DATE	April 1998	PAGE	1 of 1

JOB TITLE: Assistant Librarian, Library Instruction

REPORTS TO: Director of the Library and Instructional Technology

BASIC FUNCTION: Coordinate Library Instruction

CLASSIFICATION: Support Staff, twelve month personnel

DUTIES AND RESPONSIBILITIES:

- Responsible for the development of library instruction.

- Work closely with faculty in the coordination of the delivery of library instruction.

- Design and produce library handouts as needed.

- Assist in staffing of Reference Desk.

- Manage at least one collection in reference, circulating books, serials, archives or web site.

- Select materials in subject specialties.

- Serve as a member of the professional management team assisting in the management of the library as a whole.

- Perform other duties as may be assigned.

MINIMUM QUALIFICATIONS:

Master's Degree in Library Science from an ALA accredited program.

POSITION ANNOUNCEMENT

TITLE: LIBRARIAN II

The Librarian II reports to the Director of Library Services.

RESPONSIBILITIES:
Essential:
1. Maintain, build, and control serial collection, i.e., journals, microforms, and newspapers. The serial collection contains 364 titles and more than 63,000 microfiche.
2. Manage and maintain CD-Rom technology.
3. Assist users with circulation, reserves, Interlibrary Loan, and ready reference services.
4. Assist in MARC cataloging using Bibliofile cataloging system.
5. Assist in collection development.
6. Assist with bibliographic instruction.
7. Maintain exhibits and displays.
Secondary:
8. Manage special collections, such as FAA and grants.
9. Perform other duties as assigned by the Director of Library Services.

QUALIFICATIONS:
1. Master in Library Science degree required.
2. Two years recent experience in an academic or community college library required.
3. Reference service, Internet, periodical and microform, and CD-Rom experience preferred.
4. Ability to accept supervision and to establish and maintain effective working relationships with other employees, subordinates, and the general public.
5. Willingness to learn and work with an automated system.
6. Microcomputer and keyboarding skills preferred.
7. Knowledge of MARC cataloging preferred.
8. Physical and mental requirements ...

SALARY: Current salary is $23,520.
Commensurate with qualifications. This is a 12 month annual position. Some evening and weekend duties. Fringe benefit options available.

HUTCHINSON COMMUNITY COLLEGE - AREA VOCATIONAL SCHOOL IS AN EQUAL OPPORTUNITY AFFIRMATIVE ACTION EMPLOYER

POSITION ANNOUNCEMENT

TITLE: LIBRARY TECHNICIAN

The Library Technician reports to the Director of Library Services.

RESPONSIBILITIES:
Essential:
1. Manage, build, and develop reference collection. The reference collection contains 2000-3000 volumes and includes the legal library.
2. Develop reference service programs, perform online database searches, search the Internet, and assist users with ready reference services.
3. Supervise and attend circulation, reserves, and Interlibrary Loan.
4. Manage and maintain circulation system, i.e., issue fines, overdues, establish calendar, and other related tasks.
5. Hire, schedule, evaluate and supervise 7-10 student assistants.
6. Prepare records and statistics of library operation and library book inventory.
7. Provide evening bibliographic instruction to HCC students.
8. Assist with MARC cataloging using Bibliofile cataloging system.
9. Assist in collection development.
10. Perform other duties as assigned by the Director of Library Services.

QUALIFICATIONS:
1. Master's Degree in Library Science required..
2. Experience in an academic and community college preferred.
3. Reference and Internet experience preferred.
4. Willingness to learn and work with automated circulation system.
5. Ability to accept supervision, instruction and and to develop and maintain effective work relationships with many people.
6. Previous Library and Media Center experience, microcomputer and typing skills preferred.
7. Experience with computer operation preferred.
8. Knowledge of MARC cataloging preferred.
9. Physical and mental requirements ...

SALARY: Current salary is $19,189.
    Commensurate with qualifications.
    12 month annual position; will work Sunday through Thursday evening, with schedule variations during semester breaks and summer. Fringe benefit package available.

APPLICATION:

Submit application materials to:
PERSONNEL OFFICE, ROOM 26, LOCKMAN HALL
HUTCHINSON COMMUNITY COLLEGE
1300 NORTH PLUM, HUTCHINSON, KS 67501, 316-665-3522.

HUTCHINSON COMMUNITY COLLEGE - AREA VOCATIONAL SCHOOL IS AN EQUAL

Hutchinson Community College

REFERENCE and INSTRUCTION LIBRARIAN

BASIC FUNCTION

Provides general reference service for students, faculty and staff.

Plans and coordinates library instruction activities.

Provides research, bibliographies, publications, reference collection development, interlibrary loan, and other services related to the Reference Department.

Participates in library policy and procedure development and budget development.

Coordinates scheduling of Information Desk coverage.

PRINCIPAL DUTIES AND RESPONSIBILITIES

1. Serves 17 - 20 hours per week as librarian on duty at the Information Desk.

2. Provides library instruction for classes and other groups; develops library instructional programs and materials.

3. Prepares literature searches for faculty and staff, using print, computer-based, and Internet resources.

4. Schedules library professional staff for continuous coverage of Information Desk.

5. Coordinates selection and subject control of pamphlet collection, including input of subject headings into the online catalog.

6. Purchases government publications and assigns locations.

7. Participates in policy and procedure development/implementation and budget planning with other reference staff and the director.

8. Maintains reference and career collections; selects new reference and career materials; arranges material to meet user needs; inventories the collection and reorders needed materials.

9. Provides backup interlibrary loan service (one day per week).

10. Supervises paraprofessional, clerical staff and student aides in the performance of any reference service activities.

11. Supervises library service when only librarian on duty.

12.   Participates in campus-wide and departmental committees, as appropriate.

13.   Participates in local, state, and national organizations and committees as appropriate.

14.   Strives for continuing professional growth through reading of professional journals and attendance at workshops and training sessions whenever possible.

15.   Contributes ideas for improvement of library service.

16.   Other duties and activities as assigned by the library director or his/her designee.

ORGANIZATIONAL RELATIONSHIPS

Reports to the Director of Library Services.

Supervises paraprofessional, clerical, and student aides as needed.

QUALIFICATIONS FOR APPOINTMENT

Required: MLS from an ALA-accredited library school program; strong oral communication skills.

Desirable: Previous academic library experience.

1/23/95
Revised 7/6/95

NORTH IDAHO COLLEGE

Position Description

Learning Resources Administrative Team Coach/Technical Services Librarian

Name of Person Currently Holding Position: Johnston, Ann T.

Department/Office: Learning Resources/Molstead Library
Percent Time: 100%   Number of Months: 10   FTE: 1
Is Supervised by (Name & Title):   Vice President of Instruction
Supervises: Assistant Technical Services Librarian (1)
IT full-time personnel (2)
Library Assistants (4)
Student Assistants and part-time employees (5 - 6 FTE)
Learning Resources Senior Secretary

Position Summary:

In the capacity of a member of the Learning Resources Administrative Team, this position reports to the Vice President of Instruction and is responsible for the administration, planning and development of a community college comprehensive learning resources program. The position provides leadership in the operation, coordination, supervision, and evaluation of the library and instructional technology and their integration into instruction across the curriculum. The person filling this position ensures that the Learning Resources program is responsive to the needs of the college and community-at-large, Idaho State Law, Idaho Administrative Code, policies of the Board of Trustees and procedures established by North Idaho College. In the capacity of Technical Services Librarian, this person is responsible for overseeing all functions of the Technical Services Department which include serials, acquisitions, cataloging, and physical processing and preservation of library materials.

Minimum Requirements:

*M.L.S. from ALA-accredited institution
*Minimum of one year of experience in technical services and cataloging

Special Training or Experience Required:

*Working knowledge of AACR2 and LCSH
*Knowledge of WLN, OCLC, or equivalent system
*Supervisory experience
*Word processing and Internet experience
*Ability to lift fifty (50) pounds
*Team-based management experience (one year)
*Ability to work collaboratively with various campus and community constituencies
*Good communication skills, both written and oral

*Experience working within a community college learning resources environment
*Experience with collaboratively developing and overseeing a departmental budget

Other Desirable Background/Training/Education:

*Knowledge of WLN, CARL, and OCLC
*Reference and bibliographic instruction experience
*Knowledge of strategic planning and facilities planning and management
*Training in team-based organizational processes and structures

Technical Services Librarian Position Description:

1. In collaboration with Learning Resources Administrative Team members, and/or other Learning Resources staff, develops and administers policies and procedures governing the acquisition, organization, bibliographic control, automation, physical processing and preservation of library materials.

2. Manages the activities of the Technical Services Department, including the establishment of departmental policies and procedures, as well as the distribution of work-flow.

3. Responsible for overall bibliographic maintenance of CARL and the library's holdings on WLN/OCLC.

4. Oversees personnel matters relating to the Technical Services Department, including selection, training, supervision and evaluation of the Technical Services staff. Supervises Library Assistant II, Technical Services, Cataloging, and Processing, as well as, student and part-time assistants. In conjunction with the Assistant Technical Services Librarian, supervises Library Assistant II, Technical Services, Acquisitions and Continuations.

5. Provides leadership in identifying and achieving strategic goals related to the Technical Services Department.

6. Provides appropriate channels of communication within the Technical Services Department, and provides the Technical Services liaison to the Learning Resources Administrative Team and the Public Services Department.

7. In conjunction with the Learning Resources Administrative Team, collaborates with the Assistant Technical Services Librarian in the development of the library's collections by developing and implementing collection development policies.
>   a. Liaison with faculty members involved in materials selection.
>   b. Gift and exchange programs.
>   c. Selection of appropriate materials for the collection.

8. Participates in professional development activities.
    a. Demonstrates awareness and understanding of current developments in librarianship and library management.
    b. Is involved in campus and community service activities.
    c. Is active in statewide/regional library activities.
    d. Actively participates in the life of the campus faculty community by serving on faculty committees and attending Faculty Assembly.

9. Serves as backup Reference Librarian for Public Services.

10. Special projects, as assigned.

Learning Resources Administrative Team Member Position Description:

1. In collaboration with the Vice-President of Instruction and the Learning Resources Administrative Team members, directs Learning Resources in its operations.
    a. Supports and assists Learning Resources department personnel in the performance of their duties.
    b. Promulgates and codifies Learning Resources policies and procedures which should be developed in accordance with the college mission, strategic plan, facilities plan, the Learning Resources statement of purpose and the departmental strategic plan.
    c. Helps set goals for Learning Resources on a yearly basis.

2. In collaboration with the Vice-President of Instruction and the Learning Resources Administrative Team, oversees Learning Resources personnel matters.
    a. Completes yearly self-evaluation and evaluates both individual Team member's performance and the overall performance of the Administrative Team as a unit.
    b. Makes recommendations on salaries, raises, position reviews, hiring, firing, etc.

3. In collaboration with the Vice President of Instruction and Learning Resources Administrative Team members, provides leadership in identifying and achieving strategic goals.
    a. Develops and administers a staff and budget proportionate in size to the mission of Learning Resources and ensures the efficient use of human and material resources.
    b. Represents and advocates the best interest of Learning Resources to the college administration and other appropriate organizations.
    c. Involves Learning Resources staff and committees in the strategic planning process.
    d. Directs the planning and development of Learning Resources to meet the challenges of growing enrollment, changing curriculum, and innovative curriculum delivery systems.

4.   Provides channels of communication.
      a. Encourages and promotes the free exchange of ideas within Learning Resources with the goal of continually improving the department's operations.
      b. Encourages and promotes communication and cooperation between Learning Resources staff, college staff, students, and college administrators.

5.   In collaboration with the Vice President of Instruction and the Learning Resources Administrative Team, is responsible for Learning Resources' funding.
      a. Develops the Learning Resources' budget to adequately meet the needs of users.
      b. Actively seeks to acquire additional funding through grants, gifts, and endowments.

6.   In collaboration with the Learning Resources Administrative Team, is responsible for the appropriate use of technology within Learning Resources.
      a. Provides the appropriate balance between acquisition of and access to information sources.
      b. Facilitates opportunities needed for the campus community to learn to use information resources.
      c. Plans and implements technologies, in conjunction with appropriate campus departments that bring educational opportunities to the college's service areas.

7.   In collaboration with the Learning Resources Administrative Team and appropriate NIC departments
      a. Develops instructional and training components for faculty, staff and students
      b. Provides instructional programming to meet the aims and objectives of the general education competencies, particularly as they apply to information literacy.
      c. Provides appropriate services for NIC's extension programs, as well as other institutions' extension programs located on NIC's campus.

8.   As a member of the Learning Resources Administrative Team, serves as a rotating member of the Learning Resources Advisory Committee (LRAC).

9.   Participates in professional development activities.
      a. Demonstrates awareness and understanding of current developments in librarianship, instructional technology, library automation, and management.
      b. Participates in campus and community services and activities.
      c. Participates in statewide/regional/national professional activities when appropriate.

10.   Serves on any campus committees as assigned by the Vice President of Instruction, appropriate faculty committees and shared assignments among other members of the Learning Resources Administrative Team.

North Idaho College

11.   In collaboration with members of the Learning Resources Administrative Team, is responsible for forming and charging Learning Resources departmental teams when appropriate.

12.   In collaboration with members of the Learning Resources Administrative Team, arranges for the training of Learning Resources staff in the areas of team-based work models and Senge's learning organization concepts.

13.   In collaboration with Learning Resources Administrative Team members, oversees the work of, evaluates, and assigns tasks to the Learning Resources Administrative Team Senior Secretary.

_____   _____
Employee Signature/Date   Supervisor Signature/Date

Updated January, 1999

NORTHLAND PIONEER COLLEGE
Position Description

TITLE: Librarian

DEPARTMENT: Library

CLASSIFICATION: Exempt

GENERAL RESPONSIBILITIES:

The Librarian assists the Head Librarian to oversee library operations, services, and resources; develop policies, procedures and new services; interfaces with colleagues and collaborators; participates in local, state and national professional organizations; provides acquisitions and cataloging services. Integrates Library services with the College's mission, Strategic Plan, and educational objectives. In addition he/she provides reference and circulation services at the Painted Desert Campus.

ESSENTIAL JOB FUNCTIONS:

Assist with the short- and long-range planning activities for the library.
Assist with management of library operations, including book and journal collections, information technology, reference and library instruction, budget and facilities, through initiative, coordination and delegation.
Assist with coordination and supervision of the library staff.
Assist with development and administration of library policies and procedures in collaboration with library staff.
Serve as acquisitions and cataloging librarian.
Assist customers with locating information.
Oversee customers and their use of the library.
Assist with collection development
Continuously develops a strong knowledge of the library collection and materials and how to find information using the best access methods.
Monitor tests and delivers class materials for audio, video and distance classes.
Prepares statistical and other reports regarding library operations and use.
Perform related work as required.

KNOWLEDGE, SKILL AND ABILITY:

Strong knowledge of the principles and practices of library work, and of the library's electronic systems.

Ability to identify library needs in relation to state and national standards and College mission, initiate and develop policies, procedures and programs to meet the needs and monitor performance.

Ability to identify customer needs and requirements and meet their needs.

Works in a pleasant and effective manner with customers, co-workers, other departments and agencies.

Ability to supervise while establishing and maintaining effective working relationships with superiors, subordinates, other employees and customers.

Ability to work cooperatively and collaboratively.

PHYSICAL REQUIREMENTS:

Assists library customers in their use of the library performing work, which is moderately physically demanding and accesses the library collection wherever materials may be located including obtaining and replacing books from shelving, walking and standing for extended periods of time (two to four) hours and carrying a reasonable selection of materials between places.

Able to communicate effectively orally, in writing and by listening in the modes of public speaking, providing instruction and direction, preparing notes, memorandum, correspondence and reports. This includes the direct use of computers.

Able to receive, understand, interpret and carry out library policies and procedures.

Able to hear normal sounds, distinguish sound as voice patterns and communicate through human speech.

Ongoing intellectual effort to maintain current knowledge of library resources.

QUALIFICATIONS:

Masters degree in Library Science or Library/Information Service from an institution accredited by the American Library Association; minimum of three (3) years of increasingly responsible library experience, including management; familiarity with use and management of computerized library resources; affinity for cooperation and collaboration.

REPORTS TO:
Head Librarian

(The above description is illustrative. It is intended as a guide for personnel actions and must not be taken as a complete itemizing of all facets of any job.)
April 2000

Northland Pioneer College

Position Opening – Nunez Community College, Chalmette, LA

JOB DESCRIPTION: Librarian—Reference and Instruction
POSITION OPENS: January 5, 1999
REPORTS TO: Head of Public Services
DESCRIPTION OF POSITION:
Supports the instructional program by assisting students, faculty, and staff in the use of library services and resources. This includes reference and research assistance, library orientation and instruction, computer maintenance, interlibrary loan, and some collection development responsibilities. Active member of the library's management and planning team.
DUTIES:
- Works with faculty to provide course-integrated library instruction; works with faculty to help students achieve information literacy competencies.
- Provides orientation to the library through class presentations, tours, and individual instruction.
- Assists students, faculty, and staff in the use of library materials and equipment.
- Assists in developing, maintaining, and evaluating the collections to support the instructional programs, particularly for assigned subject areas.
- Prepares bibliographies and other learning aids independently and in conjunction with faculty for specific classes.
- Obtains materials through interlibrary loan.
- Oversees and maintains the library PCs and printers, including patron and staff Internet access and the CD-ROM tower.
- Participates in professional development and continuing education to develop and expand expertise in areas of responsibility and in library information science in general.
- Submits required reports to the Head of Public Services. Reports to the Head of Public Services any difficulties experienced by staff and users of various areas.
- Represents the library by serving on college committees, by serving as library liaison with departments and individual faculty and staff, and by participation in local and statewide consortia.
- Supervises support staff and student workers as directed.
- Performs other duties as required.
SALARY: $27,000-$30,000
FACULTY RANK: Instructor, may be promoted to tenure track rank; 12 month contract.
REQUIRED QUALIFICATIONS:
- Master's degree in Library Science from an ALA accredited institution.
- Experience in basic PC hardware and software troubleshooting in a networked environment.
- Understanding and commitment to Equal Access/Equal Opportunity.
- Ability to work in the diverse environment of a community college and commitment to the college's mission.
- Excellent oral and written communications skills in English. Ability to use a standard keyboard, mouse, and computer monitor; to move books onto and off of shelves; to move a book truck.
PREFERRED QUALIFICATIONS:
- Experience in reference and/or teaching.
- Experience with NOTIS LMS.
- Experience with OCLC searching and interlibrary loan functions.

Send application letter and resume to: Carol McLeod, Director of Human Resources, Nunez Community College, 3710 Paris Road, Chalmette, LA 70043. No later than 11/15/99. (E-mail: cmcleod@nunez.cc.la.us)

Nunez Community College, located 20 minutes from downtown New Orleans, is a member of the Louisiana Community and Technical College System. The library is a member of LOUIS: The Louisiana Library Network. An ADA/Equal Opportunity Employer. http://www.nunez.cc.la.us/library/ncclib.htm

9/24/99

Nunez Community College

PRAIRIE STATE COLLEGE
CLASSIFICATION DESCRIPTION

POSITION TITLE: Librarian (Faculty)

PURPOSE OF POSITION: To provide professional librarian and learning resources services for students, faculty, and staff of the College, making provisions for learning materials and services that support the programs, courses, educational services, and operations of the College and the information needs of the College community.

OVERALL PROFESSIONAL RESPONSIBILITIES AND OBLIGATIONS: Librarians are expected to fulfill professional workload responsibilities of thirty-five (35) hours per week and, as per the Faculty Federation/Board of Trustees collective bargaining contract, Librarians are required to work no more than seven (7) hours per day. These normal workload responsibilities are exclusive of any teaching assignment unless the affected Librarian and supervisor mutually agree as to how the teaching duties shall be equated for purposes of determining workload.

Librarians fulfill additional professional obligations and commitments within or outside of the thirty-five hour workload for professional contributions to the College and in accordance with the Librarian's interests and abilities.

REPORTING AND SUPERVISORY RELATIONSHIP(S):

1.   Direct reporting relationship to the Dean of Learning Resources and Telecommunications.

DISTINGUISHING RESPONSIBILITIES:

Workload and Professional Obligations:

1.   Evaluates and selects materials for the Learning Resources Center, including books, periodicals, audio-visual materials, and vertical file acquisitions.

2.   Cooperates with faculty in selecting materials and in planning for their effective use.

3.   Provides formal orientation and instruction in the use of the Learning Resources Center.

4.   Encourages and promotes use of the Learning Resources Center and its materials and services.

5.   Participates in the development and improvement of instructional methods, materials, and resources.

6.   Maintains appropriate records and reports on library and learning resources services utilization and effectiveness.

Prairie State College

Librarian (Faculty)
Page 2

7. Guides students, faculty, staff, and citizens in locating and using learning resource materials.

8. Researches materials and compiles bibliographies.

9. Provides interlibrary loan services.

10. Assists in student outcomes research and institutional evaluation and effectiveness measurement.

11. Participates and serves on committees and task forces of the College.

12. Attends college-wide convocations and participate in Commencement and other academic events and ceremonies.

13. Assists in the development and implementation of the College's mission, goals, and strategic plan.

Professional Commitments:

1. Maintains an active interest in and knowledge of current practices and discoveries that affect learning resources.

2. Participates in professional growth and development opportunities.

3. Provides advice and support to student clubs and organizations and to other activities that help promote student involvement.

4. Participates in public and community service activities.

5. Participates in the professional advancement of the discipline or field of study.

6. Upholds the ethical standards and principles particular to learning resources, and contribute toward advancement of the College.

Revised 9/1/94

St. Petersburg Junior College

POSITION DESCRIPTION

POSITION TITLE: **Information Services Librarian**

DEPARTMENT: **Educational and Student Services** SITE: **Various**

SALARY SCHEDULE: **Instructional** - GRADE: **N/A**

BASIC FUNCTION:

Assures library service in support of the college mission.

RESPONSIBILITIES:

Primary responsibilities, 25-30 hours weekly

Reference, Individual Istruction, and Public Service Duties
Provide instruction and assistance to students, staff, and public

- Advise patrons in researching and organizing information
- Recommend reference resources and assist with use
- Use telephone and email to assist patrons
- Assist with preparation of assignments, including documentation
- Answer questions of all kinds
- Provide referrals or ILLs when appropriate
- Make patrons feel welcome
- Assist with computer programs used for research, word processing andother applications
- Help patrons with copiers and AV equipment
- Assure a comfortable study atmosphere in library
- Troubleshoot and maintain library equipment

Teaching

- Provide classroom/individual instruction to students and staf
- Prepare and deliver workshops
- Maintain website or other electronic resources
- Prepare study aids or bibliographies
- Collaborate with instructors in teaching specialized topics

Secondary
Secnary responsibilities, 10-15 hours weekly

Supervisory or Support Duty
Oversee support staff in a particular departmental area

- Training
- Troubleshooting
- Evaluations
- Goal setting, scheduling, and prioritizing
- Policy evaluation

St. Petersburg Junior College

- Encourage employee development
- Foster cooperation among staff
- Coordinate budget and supplies
- Recruit, orient, and evaluate Adjunct Librarians
- Coordinate services for aparticular site, or college wide in areas such as:
- Acquisitions / Collection Development
- Bibliographic Instruction
- Resource Sharing
- Archives
- Periodicals
- Circulation

Administrative Duty

Collection development assistance

- Faculty Liaison
- Selection
- Development planning and budgeting
- Weeding
- Evaluation of services
- Participation in library, college campus, state and national committees
- Library policy formulation
- Cooperative ventures with other libraries/institutions

EDUCATIONAL REQUIREMENTS:

Master's degree in Library or Information Science.

EXPERIENCE REQUIREMENTS:

Demonstrated success in providing library public services, preferably in higher education.

KNOWLEDGE/ABILITIES/SKILL REQUIREMENTS

Strong written and oral communication skills. Instruction skills. Knowledge of library electronic resources and services and use of the internet.

SOUTH FLORIDA COMMUNITY COLLEGE
POSITION DESCRIPTION

POSITION TITLE: Evening/Center Librarian

CLASSIFICATION: Non-instructional Faculty

REPORTS TO: Director, Library Services

SUPERVISES: Library Staff

SUMMARY: Full-time, ten-month, professional faculty position to serve as the evening working supervisor of the library.

DUTIES AND RESPONSIBILITIES:

1. Supervises evening functions of the main campus library and Learning Lab.

2. Provides information services to Center library users.

3. Assists Director in the development of all SFCC Library collection.

4. Maintains safety and security standards.

5. Recommends revisions and updates to operating procedures.

6. Maintains data and prepares reports on Center libraries.

7. Makes recommendations for improvement of libraries.

8. Maintains a cooperative and effective working relationship with College personnel, as well as students and the general public.

9. Instructs others in the proper use and handling of library materials and equipment.

10. Makes progress toward meeting the goals and objectives of the Accountability Plan and Equity Update Report.

11. Acts in accordance with College policies and procedures.

12. Performs other duties as assigned.

EDUCATIONAL
REQUIREMENTS: Master's degree in Library Science, or 18 graduate hours in Library Science with a Master's degree in a related field, required. Must meet and maintain SFCC Professional Certification Standards.

EXPERIENTIAL
REQUIREMENTS: Minimum of two years library experience required. Library supervision experience preferred.

OTHER
REQUIREMENTS: Computer skills preferred. Must be willing to work evenings and some Sundays.

I understand and accept the duties
and responsibilities of this position. _____
Employee Signature   Date

CTRLIB.PD
01/31/97

South Florida Community College

UMPQUA COMMUNITY COLLEGE
JOB DESCRIPTION

<u>JOB TITLE</u> **REFERENCE LIBRARIAN**	<u>LEVEL</u> **XVI**
<u>DEPARTMENT</u> **LIBRARY**	<u>CLASSIFICATION</u> **Classified**

<u>RESPONSIBLE TO:</u>   Director of Library Services

<u>GENERAL DESCRIPTION:</u>
Assists with all aspects of library service: provides direct service to students, faculty, staff, and the public; assists in materials selection, cataloging, and weeding; instructs groups in the use of the library, especially it's electronic resources; cooperates and communicates with faculty in developing assignments, providing instruction, and maintaining their areas of subject expertise.

<u>EXAMPLES OF DUTIES:</u>
   Essential Functions:
- Provides excellent public service to library users.
- Works well with an innovative and flexible staff.
- Answers reference questions from the college community and the public.
- Provides library orientations to classes, including the use of print and computer-based research tools.
- Learns new technologies quickly and provides training to others in their use.
- Cooperates with faculty to develop library and research assignments.
- Develops bibliographies and tutorials both in print and online.
- Develops projects and completes them independently.
- Teaches Use of the Library, a 2 credit elective course, each term.
- Trains college staff in the use of library resources.
- Provides back-up assistance at the Circulation Desk.
- Catalogs all types of library materials.
- Participates in the development of the library collection and services.

<u>TYPICAL PHYSICAL DEMANDS AND WORK ENVIRONMENT:</u>
- Hearing alarms, hearing voice conversation, lifting/carrying 0-14 pounds, reaching, sitting, standing, standing long periods, stooping, walking, crouching, kneeling, reading fine print and faint labels on books, exposure to dust or pollen, work in crowded areas occurs in this job daily.
- Lifting/carrying 15-34 pounds, pushing occurs regularly but not daily.
- Climbing ladders, crawling occurs rarely within the work year.

<u>QUALIFICATIONS:</u>
REQUIRED:
- Baccalaureate Degree and work experience indicating possession of the knowledge and abilities to perform the essential functions of the position.
- Thorough knowledge of print and electronic library and research tools appropriate to a community college library.
- Ability to teach library & research skills to individuals and to groups, including students, faculty, staff and/or campus community.
PREFERRED:
- Master's Degree in Library Science.
- Experience with automated library systems (the UCC library uses Data Research).
- Experience teaching bibliographic instruction and use of the Internet.
- Basic knowledge of HTML and web page design.
- Dewey decimal cataloging experience.
- College teaching experience.

Umpqua Community College

VILLA MARIA COLLEGE

INFORMATION LITERACY LIBRARIAN

The Information Literacy Librarian is responsible to the Director of the Library. This position combines both reference duties and bibliographic instruction. The responsibilities of the Information Literacy Librarian are as follows:

To provide reference and research assistance using traditional and electronic formats;

To participate in the development and implementation of the College's Information Literacy Program;

To collaborate with faculty to develop, present and evaluate course-related instruction in information retrieval and analysis;

To design and implement library workshops appropriate to College information literacy needs;

To develop print and Web-based instructional materials;

To assist with selection of new reference resources and deselection of outdated reference resources;

To collect, collate, and analyze user statistics pertaining to reference and bibliographic instruction;

To maintain and update Library web pages;

To participate in college functions and serve on committees of the college;

To assist and participate in any other activities related to library services;

To assist the Director of the Library in assessing the effectiveness of the Library.

Part-Time Librarians

Assistant Librarian (Evening & Weekend Supervisor)
Assistant Librarian, Weekend
Evening/Center Librarian
Hourly Reference Librarian
Learning Resources Part-Time Faculty
Part-time Librarian

COLUMBUS STATE COMMUNITY COLLEGE
Job Description

PAY GRADE: _____

DATE WRITTEN: _____

DATE REVISED: _____

POSITION: _____

WRITTEN BY: _____

TITLE: Hourly Reference Librarian

SUMMARY: Responsible for providing the full range of reference services, including providing bibliographic instruction.

RELATIONSHIP: Reports to the Director of Educational Resources and receives direction from the Reference Librarian. Interfaces regularly with ERC staff and Columbus State students and employees.

DUTIES AND RESPONSIBILITIES:

1. Provides bibliographic instruction classes and orientation programs for students, faculty and staff on the use of ERC collections, services and facilities;

2. Provides individual and group guidance and instruction to students in methods of research, including use of the online catalog;

3. Performs computerized information searches for students, faculty and staff;

4. Participates in the selection of materials for the general collection in response to users needs;

5. Assists students, faculty and staff in locating information;

6. Maintains reference usage stats and submits monthly reports to Reference Librarian;

7. Maintains reference loose leaf services and other reference serials including checking-in, processing, and filing in a timely manner.

8. Executes the general responsibilities common to all employees of the college;

9. Performs other duties and projects as may be assigned by the Director of Educational Resources.

AUTHORITY: Operates within the procedures and methods of the Educational Resources, as well as specific guidelines established for the reference area.

RESPONSIBILITIES OF LEARNING RESOURCES
PART-TIME FACULTY

1. Minimum Qualifications For The Position:

    a. Earned Master's degree from a regionally-accredited institution of higher education in the field of library science and/or media.

    b. Ability to perform duties in each area of the Library.

    c. Personal and educational philosophy compatible with the goals, objectives, and mission of Edison Community College.

2. The Learning Resources Faculty is responsible to the Director for Learning Resources for the following areas:

    Specific/General

    a. Provides Reference Service and Bibliographic Instruction.

    b. Coordinates all aspects of the LR circulation, reference, acquisition and cataloging.

    c. Coordinates minor servicing of instructional equipment, copy machines, security system, and other accessory equipment and tools related to the circulation process.

    d. Recommends materials to be ordered for, or withdrawn from, the collection in the LR in a specific subject area.

    e. Attends workshops in LR area when possible.

    f. Pursues opportunities for professional growth.

    g. Performs other duties and responsibilities as requested by the LR DD.

10/5/98

TITLE	Job Description Assistant Librarian, Weekend	NUMBER	2.9
DATE	April 1998	PAGE	1 of 1

JOB TITLE: Assistant Librarian, Weekend

REPORTS TO: Director of the Library and Instructional Technology

BASIC FUNCTION: Weekend Reference Service

CLASSIFICATION: Support Staff, twelve month personnel

DUTIES AND RESPONSIBILITIES:

Provide professional library reference assistance on weekends in all areas of the library.

Conduct weekend library instruction classes.

Supervise all other weekend staff.

Be responsible for the building opening and closing on the weekends.

Assist the other librarians in selection of materials for purchase.

Perform other duties as may be assigned.

MINIMUM QUALIFICATIONS:

Master's Degree in Library Science or Media Specialists

Job Description
WESTERN OKLAHOMA STATE COLLEGE

Job Title: **Assistant Librarian (Evening & Weekend Supervisor)**

Qualifications
    Education: Master's Degree in Library Science from an ALA accredited graduate program.

    Credentials: None

Special Knowledge, Skill, or Ability: Must be familiar with computer aided referencing, CD ROM, and related software. Must be able to operate computers and know how to assist students with all facets of learning center. Must have knowledge of public and technical services, bibliographic instruction, and how to supervise personnel.

Training or Experience Required: None

Reports to: Director of Learning Resources Center

Performance Expectations: The incumbent/ employee will be responsible for the following:

- Be customer focused to resolve problems effectively

- Manage human resources and diversity while promoting productivity and efficiency; employee training and development, empowerment, and appraisal

- Manage resources with fiscal responsibility while maintaining proper accountability of records

- Manage information and communications with staff and public effectively

- Conduct short and long-range planning to set and/or attain college goals and objectives

- Demonstrate leadership by being a good role model to reinforce productive and customer-focused behavior; use creativity, innovation, and initiative to identify solutions to problems

- Be a team player with co-workers, subordinates, other managers, and community leaders to accomplish college objectives or goals

- Contribute to quality of college programs including extracurricular programs; Be involved in personal growth and development

Job Goal (Purpose of Position): Performs supervisory and administrative-level duties under general supervision to provide leadership, supervision, and coordination over learning resources center including supervision of LRC personnel; provides cataloguing, reference, acquisition and selection services; provides instruction in the use of the library and library resources. Works with faculty and staff to ensure the college's mission is accomplished effectively.

86 Assistant Librarian
      Evening & Weekend Supervisor

An incumbent in this position will utilize discretion, ingenuity and independent judgment due to the complexity of the job. Since there may be several ways to solve a problem, an incumbent is free to choose the solution.

Contact with Others: An incumbent in this position has regular contact with persons outside the college which requires tact and diplomacy and independent judgment, problem solving; making formal presentations; interpreting policies and procedures based on experience. May be required to make formal presentations and reports.

Essential Job Functions/ Performance Responsibilities:

1. Oversees and supervises part-time and student personnel including orienting, training, scheduling, and assigning work.

2. Oversees and performs cataloging of books, periodicals, and other materials for the college.

3. Performs reference services.

4. Assists with collection development including books, periodicals, microfiche/microfilm, and other library material.

5. Performs system administrator duties pertaining to the library automation system and the library network.

6. Provides bibliographic instruction and library use to support instructional programs.

7. Completes reports, maintains records, and handles necessary correspondence as required.

8. Assists with ordering and accounting, purchasing and requisition functions.

9. Performs circulation duties such as checking materials in and out, shelving materials, reading shelves, sending overdue notices, and maintaining records as required.

10. Assists with all aspects of Learning Resources Center administration.

11. Acts as LRC supervisor in the absence of the Director of Learning Resources Center.

12. Serves on institutional committees as needed.

13. Performs other duties as assigned.

Supervision exercised: An incumbent serves as supervisor to a small staff of employees, responsible for training, assigning and reviewing work, as well as performing similar work approximately 50% of the time. Approximately 50% of the time is performing higher level work or in supervision. Has additional responsibility of performance evaluation and may assist with hiring, discipline, and other such responsibilities for other LRC personnel.

Physical/Mental Requirements and Working Conditions: Other than those physical/mental requirements included in the essential functions, employee must be able to communicate on the telephone and in person; must be able to work with little supervision to accomplish goals of position.

SALARY RANGE:

EVALUATION: Performance of this job will be evaluated in accordance with Board policy.

Western Oklahoma State College

Computer Related Positions

The education and experience requirements vary greatly for these positions. Some also require a library degree. Some positions are related to distance learning, others focus on computer systems within the library.

Assistant Director and Systems Librarian
Collaborative Learning Librarian
Coordinator of Instructional Technology Design
Distance/Collaborative Learning Librarian
Distance Learning Department Manager
Distance Learning Technician
Education Technology Coordinator
Facilitator of Instructional Technology (Faculty)
Information Services Librarian
Instructional Technology Specialist
Learning Resources Administrative Team Member/Coordinator of Learning Resources
      Technologies
Learning Resources Assistant/Distance learning Technician.
Learning Resources Automation Coordinator
Learning Resources Systems Manager
Learning Resources Systems Specialist
Learning Resources Technical Coordinator
LRC Computer Specialist
LRC Instructional Computer Analyst
Manager Distance Learning
Manager, Instructional Technology
Manger, Library Systems
Systems Coordinator
Systems Technician
Technology Services Librarian
Web and Multi-Media Support Position

EDISON COMMUNITY COLLEGE
Instructional Technology Specialist

Position Function

This is advanced responsible technological work in the Learning Resources/Distance Learning. Work includes organizing and managing College-wide instructional design application and delivering instructional technology. Work also involves helping instructional personnel incorporate learner centered, multimedia, and distance learning instructional methods into the curriculum.

Supervision

Work is performed under the leadership and general direction of the District Director of Learning Resources who reviews work through conferences, reports, and results obtained.

Responsibilities

Works with faculty to transform lecture-based instruction into other forms of instruction to include student-based learning multimedia, computer-based modeling and demonstration, collaborative and distance learning.

Determines competency levels and training needs of faculty and instructional staff.

Develops and presents training sessions and programs to faculty and instructional staff regarding web courses, distance learning, techniques, and computer-assisted instruction.

Advises the Library Coordinator on significant matters relating to instructional technology, and in the day-to-day operations in distance learning.

Advises the Learning Resources District Director of problems arising between students and faculty regarding delivery of instruction.

Plays a major role in development of compressed video operations, instructional telecasting, CCTV, website functions, and asynchronous distance learning.

Works with faculty members on strategies to infuse technology into curriculum and instruction.

Consults with individuals regarding software and media availability, development and applications that support curriculum revisions.

Seeks grant funding to augment resources in conjunction with the Library Coordinator.

Performs other related duties as assigned.

<u>Minimum Requirements</u>

Bachelor's degree, with a specialization related to the position. A Master's degree is preferred.

Experience in instructional design and multimedia.

Ability to deliver instructional and curriculum design and implementation whenever necessary.

Thorough knowledge in diverse learning and teaching styles.

Ability to work closely with faculty in instructional technology projects.

Strong computer skills including knowledge of LAN's, distance learning, multimedia, and of programming in at least one language or instructional construction package (e.g., Toolbox, Authorware, or Director).

Ability to interact effectively with people from all levels of the College.

Working knowledge of a variety of personal computers, software and operating systems.

Basic understanding of LAN/WAN topologies, including Windows for Workgroups.

Has some knowledge of programming in third or fourth generation languages.

Understanding of distance learning systems and hardware.

Successful experience in educational technology.

Successful record of responsible work in education; post-secondary educational experience in a community college preferred.

Effective oral and written communication skills.

Personal and educational philosophy compatible with the mission, goals and objectives of the College.

Approved: 11/4/96; revised 3/4/99

EDISON COMMUNITY COLLEGE
Learning Resources Assistant/Distance Learning Technician

Position Function

This is routine and technical library support work. Employees in this classification perform a series of specialized tasks critical to the operation of the Learning Resources (LR) in accordance with prescribed policies and procedures. Work requires meeting with students and the public in the course of assigned duties, as well as providing limited supervision to student assistants. Included in these specialized tasks is operation and maintenance of the Distance Learning equipment to include interactive video. The assistant will also be responsible for examination duplication, storage, and proctoring as listed by the telecourse and interactive video schedule.

Supervision

Employees work under the general supervision of a professional Librarian who assigns work and reviews work through conferences and results obtained. Specific instructions are received from a supervisor when exceptions arise or new work routines are established. Primary supervision is the responsibility of the District Director of LR. The Campus Directors will jointly define duties and responsibilities with the District Director of the Learning Resources.

Responsibilities

Checks out print and non-print materials at the circulation desk, using the on-line computerized circulation module; registers patrons and issues user cards; checks in materials; shelves; maintains shelves; ensures security of area and resources; mails overdue notices; and assists in maintaining reserves for faculty and students. Duplicates, files, and proctors distance learning examinations as per the published schedule.

Assists patrons with the use of machines including copiers, microfilm copiers, audio visual equipment; distributes and operates audiovisual service and video systems equipment; performs other task-oriented duties; and trouble-shoots problems with machines as necessary. Operates and maintains distance learning equipment.

Performs other related duties as assigned.

Minimum Qualifications

High School graduation or equivalent.

Ability to establish and maintain effective working relationships with associates and patrons of the LR.

Knowledge of over all LR operations and policies is preferred.

Ability to learn and adapt to servicing patrons of both print and non-print media at the university, community college and community levels in manual and automated modes.

10/6/98, 2/26/99

Edison Community College

 **Gulf Coast**
Community College

TITLE	Job Description Coordinator of Instructional Technology Design	NUMBER	2.12
DATE	April 1998	PAGE	1 of 1

JOB TITLE: Coordinator of Instructional Technology Design

REPORTS TO: Director of the Library and Instructional Technology

BASIC FUNCTION: Instructional Technology

CLASSIFICATION: Support Staff, twelve month personnel

DUTIES AND RESPONSIBILITIES:

Provide professional leadership in the creation, integration and utilization of emerging technologies, in the classroom and through the Internet.

Instruct faculty and staff in the use of various programs and technologies either one on one or through formal workshops.

Work with departments on the implementation of technology based instruction.

Maintain the college's Homepage.

Assist with the creation of departmental home pages.

Provide the Director with all necessary statistics and reports.

Assume responsibility for the maintenance of all computer software in Instructional Technology.

Stay abreast of new technologies and advise librarians as to acquisitions to support the Resource Center.

Perform other duties as may be assigned.

MINIMUM QUALIFICATIONS:

Master's degree in library science, instructional technology, instructional design or related field and two years of experience in some phase of technology management and development and implementation of both media and interactive instructional systems.

HILLSBOROUGH COMMUNITY COLLEGE

JOB DESCRIPTION

Position Title:	Learning Resources Automation Coordinator	**Date:**	10/1/96
Position Level: G	**FLSA Status:** Exempt	**Class Code:**	P2210

GENERAL DESCRIPTION

Manages and coordinates Learning Resources/library automation operations and serves as a district resource for Learning Resources automation issues.

KEY RESPONSIBILITIES	% OF TIME
1. Trains Learning Resources staff in the use of library and office automation software and hardware; regularly schedules training sessions and provides assistance in solving problems.*	25%
2. Installs, tests, maintains and troubleshoots software and hardware utilized in Learning Resources computer applications.*	20%
3. Researches and recommends for purchase hardware and software upgrades and enhancements.*	15%
4. Writes user documentation and develops guidelines, procedures and training material for office and library automation.*	15%
5. Works closely with the Technical Services Manager, Audio Visual Manager, and Associate Vice President for Learning Resources Services in a variety of matters.*	5%
6. Serves as Systems Manager for the College for the state-wide library automation project.*	5%
7. Serves as College Center Library Automation (CCLA) hardware contact and serves on the CCLA Standing Committee for Circulation.	5%
8. Maintains a computer equipment inventory for all Learning Resources areas.	5%
9. Maintains hardware and software vendor contact.	5%
10. Performs other similar and related duties as assigned.	

* Indicates an "essential" job function.

Position Title:	Learning Resources Automation Coordinator	Class Code: P2210	Position Level: G

KEY JOB REQUIREMENTS

Education:	Associate's Degree or Two Year College equivalent required.
Experience:	3 years to 5 years prior related work experience required.
Planning:	Plans events that are expected to occur in the next one to three months or on a quarterly basis. The primary scope of planning activities in this position affects the campus.
Impact of Actions:	*Operating Budget Responsibilities:* Provides supportive advice, analysis, or related services which impact the expense or revenues but with no authority to actually spend the budget. May collect or process revenues/expenses. *Grant Fund Responsibilities:* Provides incidental services indirectly related to the use or misuse of the expense or revenues. *Revenue Generating Impact:* No impact on revenues.
Impact of Decisions:	Moderate responsibility for making recommendations or decisions which usually affect the assigned department, but may at times affect operations, services, individuals, or activities of the assigned campus.
Complexity:	Work is complex and varied, and requires the selection and application of technical and detailed guidelines.
Decision Making:	Supervision is present to establish and review broad objectives relative to basic position duties or departmental responsibilities. Independent judgment is required to study previously established, often partially relevant guidelines.
Problem Solving:	Problem solving involves identification and analysis of diverse problems; answers are usually found by reviewing standard technical manuals and administrative procedures and modifying them for unusual situations.
Communication with Others:	Regular contacts to carry out programs and to explain specialized matters. Also requires continuing contacts with officials at higher levels on matters requiring cooperation, explanation and persuasion. Occasionally requires personal contact with the public.
Supervision of Others:	Provides limited supervision for one or more functions within a department. Formally plans, assigns, directs, and coordinates the work of these functions. Typically responsible for performing some non-supervisory duties in addition to supervisory responsibilities. Nature of work supervised in primarily technically oriented or complex, and requires a working knowledge of unit or departmental activities.
Job-Related Knowledge:	Requires extensive knowledge of a distinct trade or technical function. Knows policies and procedures, and can recommend a course of action based upon guidelines, modifying existing methods, procedures or forms as necessary. May work with software applications and data retrieval.
Innovation/ Creativity:	Work requires developing imaginative and complex methods, procedures, products or systems. This is an important part of the job and results generally affect a campus within the College.
Working Conditions/ Physical Effort:	Work requires only minor physical exertion and/or physical strain. Work environment involves only infrequent exposure to disagreeable elements.

APPROVALS

Department Head:

Name: _____   Signature: _____   Date: _____

Director of Human Resources:

Name: _____   Signature: _____   Date: _____

Hillsborough Community College

HILLSBOROUGH COMMUNITY COLLEGE

JOB DESCRIPTION

Class Title:	Learning Resources Technical Coordinator	*Date:*	June 22, 1998
Level: G	*FLSA Status:* Exempt	*Class Code:*	E0731

GENERAL DESCRIPTION

Manages and coordinates the Learning Resource Library/library audiovisual operations and serves as a resource for Learning Resources audiovisual issues.

	KEY RESPONSIBILITES	% OF TIME
1.	Serves as resource person for the audio visual area, including liaison with vendors, College personnel and the community.	15%
2.*	Prepares and maintains LRC budget process for audio/visual equipment, repairs and supplies.	20%
3.	Investigates new sources of AV hardware and software. Researches and recommends new equipment to be purchased by the College.	10%
4.*	Trains, supervises, and disseminates work assignments for assigned staff.	10%
5.*	Installs and maintains equipment. Coordinates with vendors for parts and services exceeding in-house capabilities. Troubleshoots and repairs AV equipment.	15%
6.*	Writes, reviews, and updates LRC and College policies and procedures; reviews forms and recommends changes.	5%
7.	Coordinates the acquisition and distribution of AV equipment and supplies. Establishes rapport with the library faculty and assists them in preparing materials and providing professional support.	20%
8.	Serves on College, regional and statewide committees. Keeps abreast of new developments for learning resources and/or technical services.	5%
9.	Performs other similar and related duties as required.	

* Indicates an "essential" job function.

Class Title: Learning Resources Technical Coordinator	Class Code: E0731	Level: G

KEY JOB REQUIREMENTS	
Formal Education:	Bachelor's Degree required.
Work Experience:	3 to 5 years.
Planning Scope:	Four to Twelve Months: Plan events that will occur during the year, and have some effect on the department's annual expenditures, and or revenues.
Planning Level:	The primary scope of planning activities in this position affects the department or equivalent.
Budgets Impact:	Recommending/Contributory: Have a strong, but not controlling voice in decisions on the budget; can authorize or recommend expenditures within an approved budget. Actions may have a direct contribution on the methods used to generate revenues.
Grant/Revenue Impact:	No impact on grant funds or revenue.
Impact of Decisions:	Makes recommendations or decisions which typically affect the assigned department, but may at times affect operations, services, individuals, or activities of my campus.
Complexity:	Varied: Work is complex and varied and requires the selection and application of technical and detailed guidelines. Moderate analytic ability is needed to gather and interpret data where results/answers can be found after analysis of several facts.
Decision Making:	Analytic: Independent judgment is required to study previously established, often partially relevant guidelines; plan for various interrelated activities; and coordinate such activities within a work unit or while completing a project.
Problem Solving:	Problem solving involves identification and analysis of diverse problems; answers are usually found by reviewing standard technical manuals and administrative procedures and modifying them for unusual situations.
Internal Communications:	Regular contacts to carry out programs and to explain specialized matters, or occasional contacts with officials at higher levels on matters requiring cooperation, explanation and persuasion.
External Communications:	Regular external contacts to carry out organization programs and to explain non-specialized matter, or work requiring continuing personal contact with the public involving the enforcement of laws, ordinances, polices and procedures.
Level of Supervisory Responsibility:	Provide limited supervision for one or more functions within a department. Formally plans, assigns, directs, and coordinates the work of these functions.
Nature of Work Supervised:	Nature of work supervised is primarily technically oriented or complex, includes additional administrative responsibilities, and requires a working knowledge of unit or departmental activities.
Job-Related Knowledge:	Entry Professional Skills: Requires entry-level knowledge of theories and practices of a professional field. This level is reserved for an individual with a four-year degree or with high-level vocational skills demonstrated by a number of years of on-the-position experience. Writes reports using technical data requiring considerable interpretation, developing new methods and procedures. Frequently applies knowledge to practical issues.
Innovation/Creativity:	Work requires using original and creative thinking to develop new, moderately complex results. The results generally impact several work groups, a large project or an extended customer base.
Working Conditions/ Physical Effort:	Work requires only minor physical exertion and/or physical strain. Work environment involves only infrequent exposure to disagreeable elements.

Hillsborough Community College

Title of Position: Assistant Director and Systems Librarian

Salary: _____   **Type of Appointment:** _____ 10 months
                                                          _____ 12 months

Functions of the Position

The Assistant Director and Systems Librarian, reports to the Director of the Library. The Assistant Director's general responsibility is to work with the Library Director in providing appropriate, quality library services to the college community. As System Librarian, this individual is charged with the smooth and effective operation of the library system, networks and access to electronic information. The Assistant Director works with the faculty, staff and service providers at the college to achieve and advocate the goals and objectives of ETS: Libraries, the division and the college; works in a team-centered environment to plan and define the current and future directions of ETS: Libraries. This person serves on the reference desk in a limited role.

Example of Duties

- Works collaboratively with library faculty and staff to provide high quality library services
- Works with the director to monitor and assess the effectiveness of ETS: Libraries operations and planning
- Oversees and coordinates ETS: Libraries automated system, computer applications and access to network resources
- Serve as liaison to campus support and statewide services for the library system, network and computing needs.
- Coordinates projects as assigned by director
- Assists in budget planning and coordination
- Researches and recommends library technology and service innovations
- Represents the library on the divisional, campus, local, regional and national meetings, conferences and events
- Participates in the planning and development of web gateways
- Serves on the library reference desk
- Supervises ETS: Libraries during the absence of the Director
- Promotes library awareness to the campus
- Performs other duties as assigned by the Library Director

Required

M.L.S Degree from an A.L.A. accredited institution
3 years experience in library setting (academic preferred)
Experience with integrated Library Systems, computer applications and networked environment (preferably in a coordinating role)
Administrative experience preferred

Preferred qualities

A highly motivated, positive thinking, experienced and innovative professional librarian, with strong communication skills, and the desire and ability to work well in a team environment.

Monroe Community College

Title of Position: Distance/Collaborative Learning Librarian

Salary: Type of Appointment: 12 month tenure track

Function of Position:

The Distance/Collaborative Learning Librarian will be responsible for investigating, planning and implementing projects to enhance the role of the library in distance learning efforts at MCC. The individual in this position will also act in a liaison and advocacy role with faculty.

Example of Duties:

Promote library services to faculty, working to enhance communication with academic departments and seeking feedback on faculty and department library needs and issues to strengthen the library position within the College community. Coordinate the development of appropriate library support for distance learners, via the use of electronic resources, technology and other appropriate means to ensure that all other library services are available. Participate in the implementation of remote user access to library resources. Assist in the development and maintenance of the Distance Learning component of the ETS Libraries' web page. The Distance/Collaborative Learning Librarian will have regularly scheduled public service hours at the reference desk and will be expected to work evenings or weekends as needed. Provide research assistance, library instruction, reference collection development, interlibrary loan and other services related to the Research and Instruction Services Department. Supervise clerical staff and student aides in the performance of distance/collaborative learning service activities. Supervise library service when the only librarian on duty. Contribute ideas for improvement of library services. Participate in MCC, local, regional, state, and national committees and meetings.

Performs other duties and responsibilities as assigned by the Director.

This person reports to the Research and Instruction Services Team Leader.

Qualifications:

Required: ALA-accredited M.L.S., excellent oral and written communication skills, familiarity with electronic resources, experience with web page design.

Preferred: One to two years experience in an academic library setting, including experience in reference, library instruction and interlibrary loan operations.

New Position

NICOLET AREA TECHNICAL COLLEGE
Position Description

Name: **Department:** Richard J. Brown Library

Position Title: Web and Multi-Media Support Position

Pay Grade: **Reports To:** Dean of Transitional College
                                                                                          Learning Resources

---

Position Summary:

Under the direction of the Coordinator of Audio Visual Services, this position provides primary support for web design, coordination, and maintenance, and provides support for distance learning, video and multi-media production.

Duties/Responsibilities:

The following duties are normal for this position. These are not to be construed as exclusive or all-inclusive. Other duties may be required and assigned.

- Coordinates institutional web design and works directly with departmental personnel in developing and maintaining departmental web pages.

- Develops and maintains multi-browser compatible web sites in compliance with ADA requirements.

- Works directly with faculty in developing and using web based instruction.

- Mounts web-based courses, builds infrastructure for on-going student/faculty web-based dialog and classes.

- Assists faculty in development of multi-media course material.

- Assists AV Coordinator in providing a broad range of instructional support services to the campus.

- Assists in maintaining and troubleshooting ITV system, video home study, and downlinking of telecourses and teleconferences.

Nicolet Area Technical College

Position Description
Page 2 of 2

Qualifications:

Ability to deal with students, faculty, administration, and institutional partners in a professional manner. A high level of skill using current web design and computer multi-media technology. Knowledge of various operating systems and software, computer operations and repair, and troubleshooting strategies.

Training and Experience:

Associate Degree in an appropriate area and substantial advanced training and/or equivalent experience with designing and maintaining web sites and with using multimedia technology in business or educational settings.

In evaluating candidates for this position, Nicolet may consider a combination of education, training, and experience which provides the necessary knowledge, skills, and abilities to perform the duties of the position. Normally, education may be substituted for experience, or experience substituted for education, on a year for year basis.

POSITION DESCRIPTION

Learning Resources Administrative Team Member/Coordinator of Learning Resources Technologies

Name of Person Currently Holding Position   Finney, Andrew W.
                                                    Last   First   MI

Department/Office: Learning Resources/Molstead Library
Percent of Time: 100%   **Number of Months:** 12   **FTE:** 1
Is Supervised by: Vice President of Instruction
Supervises: 100% Reference Librarian
                       IT full-time personnel (2)
                       Library Assistants (4)
                       Student Assistants and part-time employees (5-6 FTE)
                       Learning Resources Senior Secretary

Position Summary:

In the capacity of a member of the Learning Resources Administrative Team, this position reports to the Vice President of Instruction and is responsible for the administration, planning and development of a community college comprehensive learning resources program. The position provides leadership in the operation, coordination, supervision and evaluation of the library and instructional technology and their integration into instruction across the curriculum. The person filling this position ensures that the Learning Resources program is responsive to the needs of the college and community-at-large, Idaho State Law, Idaho Administrative Code, policies of the Board of Trustees and procedures established by North Idaho College. In the capacity of Coordinator of Learning Resources Technologies, this person is responsible for the maintenance and operation of information technologies, network connectivity within Learning Resources which includes CARLWeb, INLAN, WLN, and Internet.

Minimum Requirements

I.   Bachelor's Degree or equivalent job related technical experience.

II.   Experience in Web Centered Learning Resources technology environments.

III.   Experience with Integrated Library Systems.

IV.   Experience with Electronic Information Resources including Web Centered Internet/Intranet/Extranet connected environments.

V.   Experience with Microcomputer based hardware and software environments.

V.   Experience in teaching or training.

VI.   Good communications skills, both oral and written, including the ability to listen, explain, and discuss technology in non-technical terms.

VII.   Ability to lift 50 lbs.

Special Training and/or Experienced Required:

I.   Team management experience (1 year)

II.   Knowledge of UNIX and/or Windows NT servers.

III.   Knowledge of HTML, JAVA, and TCP/IP.

IV.   Knowledge of DOS, Windows, and Macintosh OS.

V.   Knowledge of Internet/Intranet/Extranet and Ethernet software and hardware.

VI.   Knowledge of CD-ROM technology applications.

VII.   Knowledge of Microsoft applications including Word, Excel, Access, Power point, and FrontPage.

VIII. Knowledge of WordPerfect, Photoshop, and PageMaker.

Other Desirable Background/Training/Education

I.   Master's Degree in job related area.

II.   Experience in complex applications and computer workstation client support.

III.   Experience in multimedia hardware and software set up and support applications.

IV.   Experience in graphics, scanning, and desktop publishing hardware and software for Web centered Internet/Intranet/Extranet applications.

V.   Interpersonal communication skills including ability to listen, to explain and discuss technology in non-technical terms, and willingness to adapt to the end-user's needs.

Coordinator of Learning Resources Technologies Position Description:

1.   Responsible for supporting, maintaining, and upgrading the 50+ computer terminals within Learning Resources while demonstrating an ability to work effectively in a Learning Resources team environment having college-wide impacts.

2.   Primary liaison with INLAN in the development and implementation of Learning Resources' CARLWeb catalog.

3. Works in close collaboration with the Director of Computer Services and his staff, and complies with established college network and system standards.

4. Aware of current trends and applications in the field of Learning Resources and information technologies in community college setting.

5. Committed to improving access to the Library's services and collections for campus and distance education staff and students.

6. Provides instruction to the faculty in MS FrontPage for the development of web based distance learning courses.

7. Researches, recommends, bids, procures, installs, configures, maintains, troubleshoots, and upgrades computer hardware and software for Learning Resources and related instructional applications areas within college policies.

8. Sets-up, upgrades, and maintains Web sites and Internet/WWW access for Learning Resources and related instructional applications areas.

9. Assists clients on database design, development, deployment, systems applications, and Internet/Intranet/Extranet connectivity for Learning Resources and related instructional supported applications areas.

10. Provides technical support for Learning Resources and related instructional support applications using computers, printers, modems, codecs, and scanner hardware and software applications.

11. Sets up, upgrades, maintains CARL access for Learning Resources and related instructional applications areas.

12. Creates training tools for applications; training staff, faculty, and students in Internet/Intranet/Extranet operations; other computer based CD-ROM applications; and supports on-line learning and instructional resources for Learning Resources.

13. Staffs the Information Desk for approximately two hours each day which includes reference and research services and general supervision duties.

14. Represents Learning Resources on campus committees and professional organizations dealing with instructional technologies and computer educational topics.

Learning Resources Administrative Team Member Position Description:

1.   In collaborations with the Vice-President of Instruction and the Learning
        Resources Administrative Team members directs Learning Resources in its
        operations.
        a.   Supports and assists Learning Resources department personnel in the
                performance of their duties.
        b.   Promulgates and codifies Learning Resources policies and procedures
                which should be developed in accordance with the college mission,
                strategic plan, facilities plan, the Learning Resources statement of purpose
                and the departmental strategic plan.
        c.   Helps set goals for Learning Resources on a yearly basis.

2.   In collaborations with the Vice-President of Instruction and the Learning
        Resources Administrative Team, oversees Learning Resources personnel matters.

        a.   Completes yearly self-evaluations and evaluates both individual Team
                member's performance and the overall performance of the Administrative
                Team as a unit.
        b.   Makes recommendations on salaries, raises, position reviews, hiring,
                firing, ect.

3.   In collaborations with the Vice-President of Instruction and the Learning
        Resources Administrative Team members provides leadership in identifying and
        achieving strategic goals.
        a.   Develops and administers a staff and budget proportionate in size to the
                mission of Learning Resources and ensures the efficient use of human and
                material resources.
        b.   Represents and advocates the best interest of Learning Resources tot he
                college administration and other appropriate organizations.
        c.   Involves Learning Resources staff and committees in the strategic
                planning process.
        d.   Directs the planning and development of Learning Resources to meet the
                challenges of growing enrollment, changing curriculum, and innovative
                curriculum delivery systems.

4.   Provides channels of communication.
        a.   Encourages and promotes the free exchange of ideas within Learning
                Resources with the goal of continually improving the department's
                operations.
        b.   Encourages and promotes communication and cooperation between
                Learning Resources staff, college staff, students, and college
                administrators.

5.   In collaborations with the Vice-President of Instruction and the Learning
        Resources Administrative Team is responsible for Learning Resources' funding.

North Idaho College

    a.   Develops the Learning Resources' budget to adequately meet the needs of users.

    b.   Actively seeks to acquire additional funding through grants, gifts, endowments.

6.   In collaborations with Learning Resources Administrative Team responsible for the appropriate use of technology within Learning Resources.

    a.   Provides the appropriate balance between acquisition of and access to information sources.

    b.   Facilitates opportunities needed for the campus community to learn to use information resources.

    c.   Plans and implements technologies, in conjunctions with appropriate campus departments that bring educational opportunities to the college's service areas.

7.   In collaborations with the Learning Resources Administrative Team and appropriate NIC departments

    a.   Develops instructional and training components for faculty, staff and students

    b.   Provides instructional programming to meet the aims and objectives of the general education competencies, particularly as they apply to information literacy.

    c.   Provides appropriate services for NIC's extension programs, as well as other institution's extension programs located on NIC's campus.

    8.   As the Learning Resources Administrative Team coach, serves as a member of the Learning Resources Advisory Committee (LRAC)

9.   Participates in professional development activities.

    a.   Demonstrates awareness and understanding of Current developments in librarianship, instructional technology, library automation, and management.

    b.   Participates in campus and community services and activities.

    c.   Participates in statewide/regional/national professional activities when appropriate.

10.   Serves on any campus committees as assigned by the Vice President of Instruction, appropriate faculty committees and shared assignments among other members of the Learning Resources Administrative Team.

11.   In collaboration with members of the Learning Resources Administrative Team, responsible for forming and charging Learning Resources departmental teams when appropriate.

12.   In collaboration with members of the Learning Resources Administrative Team, arranges for the training of Learning Resources staff in the areas of team-based work models and Senge's learning organization concepts.

13.   In collaboration with members of the Learning Resources Administrative Team members, oversees the work of, evaluates, and assigns tasks to the Learning Resources Administrative Team Senior Secretary.

_____   _____

Employee Signature/Date   Supervisor Signature/Date

January, 1999

PORTLAND COMMUNITY COLLEGE
Class Description

TITLE: LRC Computer Specialist
CLASS: Classified
EXEMPT STATUS: Non-exempt
GRADE: 20

NATURE AND SCOPE OF WORK:

Under the direction of LRC management, coordinates specific computer activities for the LRC department. Installs and maintains all library information systems, maintains all LRC computer systems at the Cascade campus, and performs specific computer services for all LRCs. Works with the LRC Instructional Computer Project Analyst, Information Technology Services staff, other LRC staff and vendors. Job requires highly effective human relations skill to communicate complex and technical information, and to train others who may be unfamiliar with the subject matter. Incumbent's contribution is key to ensuring the best LRC computing resources and compatibility with existing PCC computing systems. Responsible for performing technical journey-level work output on an independent basis.

PRINCIPAL ACCOUNTABILITIES:

1. Provides technical expertise for electronic library systems:

A. Helps install and maintain software for integrated library system (Dynix) including modules for purchasing, accounting, serials control, collection description and inventory, the public on-line catalog, reserves and circulation.

B. Installs and maintains software for electronic indexes and full-text services to which the LRC subscribes including services such as Academic ASAP, a remote database that combines a magazine indexing product with access to full-text of magazine articles.

C. Installs and maintains software for informational programs on the LRC's CD-ROM LAN and stand alone CD stations. Programs include software that runs in either DOS or Macintosh environments such as multimedia encyclopedias, indexes and interactive histories.

D. Installs and maintains software for access to PORTALS' services. Works with LRC Instructional Computer Project Analyst and Instruction to maintain viable communication links with PORTALS.

2. Works with library system vendors to understand and diagnose the systems' health, and build reports for supervisor and other LRC staff. Helps research needs to upgrade systems. Installs and tests new library information systems.

3. Works with Information Technology Services to ensure effective interfaces with college information systems.

4. Works with LRC Instructional Computer Project Analyst to ensure stable telecommunications for library systems.

5. Provides technical documentation for library systems and provides user training and basic recovery procedures for those systems.

6. Selects and maintains computer supply inventory for the LRC system-wide.

7. Coordinates repair of LRC Macintosh computer equipment and peripherals. Performs basic diagnosis

and repairs.

8. Provides maintenance and problem diagnosis on all systems (library and instructional) for the Cascade LRC.

9. Provides backup for the LRC Instructional Computer Project Analyst.

10. Performs other related duties as assigned.

WORK ENVIRONMENT:

Coordinating a variety of activities and/or responding to peak work load periods can result in periods of high pressure. Incumbent is generally able to regulate own schedule, work flow, etc. Regular exposure to video screens, electrical and electronic equipment.

PHYSICAL REQUIREMENTS:

Learned physical skill required to perform keyboarding functions. Regular lifting of equipment/materials for installations, troubleshooting, repairs, etc.

MINIMUM QUALIFICATIONS:

High school diploma or equivalent. Associate's degree or two years of college-level coursework or training in a computer-related discipline. Experience performing the duties of the job may substitute for the post-secondary education or training on a year-for-year basis.

Two years of experience which demonstrates a good working knowledge of computers is required. Must have knowledge of relational databases, client-server architecture, DOS, Windows, Macintosh software and operating systems, the Internet, TCP/IP protocol, ethernet and mainframe operations.

Excellent interpersonal skills with the ability to work as a team member with a variety of people. Ability to communicate technical information and train staff on a one-to-one basis. Good recordkeeping and problem solving skills. The ability to work independently is essential. Must have the ability to effectively coordinate and perform multiple tasks/projects concurrently.

NEW: 08/15/96

PORTLAND COMMUNITY COLLEGE
Class Description

TITLE: LRC Instructional Computer Analyst
CLASS: Classified
EXEMPT STATUS: Non-exempt
GRADE: 22

NATURE AND SCOPE OF WORK:

Under the direction of LRC management, plans, organizes, coordinates and documents installation of LRC and special instructional computer systems, LAN's and educational software applications. Plans and designs networks and ensures integration of all instructional network resources with the campus wide area network. Conducts orientations, demonstrations, presentations and training sessions for LRC staff and/or faculty and students. Coordinates with vendor representatives to document installations. Incumbent interacts with a diverse set of individuals including the LRC Director, the Instructional Computing Facilitator; and other LRC staff; and staff from Information Technology Services (ITS), campus computing teams, vendors and other educational institutions. Job requires highly effective human relations skill to communicate complex and technical information and to train others who may be unfamiliar with the subject matter. Incumbent's contribution is key to ensuring the best LRC computing resources and compatibility with existing PCC computing systems. Responsible for producing technical journey-level work on an independent basis and works with minimum guidance. Leads and reviews work of LRC Computer Specialist when tasks are not specific to library applications.

PRINCIPAL ACCOUNTABILITIES:

1. Researches, selects, installs, configures, operates and maintains LAN's for the LRC including student and administrative LAN's in each LRC and the CD-ROM LAN for the district. Works with ITS to ensure the LRC systems are compatible with PACE. Provides security, metering and virus protection.

2. Works with ITS to ensure stable network and Internet connections for the LRC. Installs and maintains Internet software for the LRC.

3. Researches and recommends hardware/software purchases to support the LRC and special instructional computing projects. Ensures licensing compliance.

4. Assists vendor representatives with installations and problem resolution of non-library LRC and special instructional projects.

5. Designs and implements a disaster recovery plan for project computer systems and LAN's.

6. Designs and monitors student labs in the LRC's and serves on the LRC computer committee to assist in setting policy/services, and helps train student lab assistants.

7. Assists the AV Coordinator in building an effective faculty production area wherever computers are used and in maintaining equipment/software in LRC meeting rooms.

8. Coordinates repair of LRC DOS/Windows computer equipment and peripherals. Performs basic diagnosis and repairs.

9. Provides technical documentation for network and instructional systems and provides user training and basic recovery procedures for those systems.

10. Represents the LRC on the college's Network Advisory Committee and the Computer Lab Managers

110   Instructional Computer Analyst

Council.

11. Assists the Instructional Computing Facilitator with projects relevant to academic computing at a district level.

12. Provides maintenance and problem diagnosis on all LRC systems for the Rock Creek LRC.

13. Serves on the LRC committee to design and maintain an LRC home page.

14. Leads and reviews the work of LRC Computer Specialist when tasks are not specific to library applications.

15. Provides backup for the LRC Computer Specialist.

16. Performs other related duties as assigned.

WORK ENVIRONMENT:

Coordinating a variety of activities and/or responding to peak work load periods can result in periods of high pressure. Incumbent is generally able to regulate own schedule, work flow, etc. Regular exposure to video screens, electrical and electronic equipment.

PHYSICAL REQUIREMENTS:

Learned physical skill required to perform keyboarding functions. Regular lifting of equipment/materials for installations, troubleshooting, repairs, etc.

MINIMUM QUALIFICATIONS:

High school diploma or equivalent. Associate's degree or two years of college-level coursework or training in a computer-related discipline. Experience performing the duties of the job may substitute for the degree requirement on a year-for-year basis.

Relevant experience implementing and managing a variety of microcomputer applications. Experience with Novell, Ethernet, DOS and WIndows software, Macintosh computers and mainframe integrated systems. Knowledge of client-server architecture, the Internet and TCP/IP protocol

Excellent interpersonal skills with ability to work as a team member with a variety of people. Ability to communicate technical information and train staff on a one-to-one basis. Good recordkeeping and problem solving skills, and ability to work independently essential. Ability to effectively coordinate and perform multiple tasks/projects concurrently.

REV: 03/11/98
REPLACES: LRC Automation Coordinator, Gr. 22, 08/23/96

Portland Community College

PORTLAND COMMUNITY COLLEGE
Class Description

TITLE: Manager, Instructional Technology
CLASS: Management
EXEMPT STATUS: Exempt
GRADE: 29

NATURE AND SCOPE OF WORK:

Under the direction of the Director of Learning Resources, provides leadership and coordination to the college's instructional technology program which includes both academic computing and audiovisual services. Assists the college learn about, plan for and implement an effective program for using instructional technology in the teaching/learning processes and helps coordinate student labs and campus support services. Areas of accountability include delivery of classroom services, LRC labs for students and staff, faculty development, support staff development, interfacing academic and administrative computing, and the management of human and financial resources for the areas of accountability.

PRINCIPAL ACCOUNTABILITIES:

1. Facilitates the planning, organization, coordination and evaluation of instructional technology at Portland Community College. Provides leadership, advocacy and coordination.

2. Works with campus administrations, district departments responsible for technology, and LRC staff to assure student and faculty access to equipment, software, user support and training.

3. Supervises LRC staff who are responsible for audiovisual and computing services to include faculty development in instructional technology, classroom delivery and LRC electronic labs.

4. Manages a budget for instructional technology and works with the PCC Foundation, grant writers and college administrators to seek funding from industry or government agencies for model projects.

5. Helps develop policies, practices and standards which facilitate and enhance the use of instructional technology. Works with Information Technology Services, Purchasing and other stakeholders in setting those policies.

6. Helps the college interpret advances in technology and adopt systems which are both effective and efficient. Advises departments and campuses.

7. Works as part of the Learning Resources team to provide quality service and learning resources for the college campuses.

8. Serves as the college liaison for vendors and organizations relevant to instructional technology.

9. Performs other related duties as assigned.

WORK ENVIRONMENT:

Work pressure and some irregularities in work schedule require adaptation. Generally good working conditions with little or no exposure to safety or health hazards. Work is generally performed in an office environment, although periodically it is necessary for the incumbent to be in lab or classroom environments. Must be able to stay abreast of continually changing technologies related to job assignment.

PHYSICAL REQUIREMENTS:

Portland Community College

Learned physical skill required to perform keyboarding. Minimum physical exertion required to perform job duties.

MINIMUM QUALIFICATIONS:

Master's degree in Education, Instructional Technology, a computer related discipline, or related field. Experience performing job related duties may substitute for the degree requirement on a year-for-year basis.

Five years of progressively responsible experience in instructional technology; at least one year performing supervision of staff. Expertise in the use of computers, networks, software and audiovisual equipment is required. Coursework and/or experience in instructional design is required. Must possess strong communication skills including the ability to influence others toward a stated objective.

NEW: 02/20/97

**PRAIRIE STATE COLLEGE
POSITION DESCRIPTION**

POSITION TITLE: Assistant Professor/Facilitator of Instructional Technology (Faculty)

PURPOSE OF POSITION: To support faculty in their efforts to enhance the integration of instructional technology throughout the curriculum.

OVERALL PROFESSIONAL RESPONSIBILITIES AND OBLIGATIONS: The Assistant Professor/Facilitator is expected to fulfill professional workload responsibilities of thirty-five (35) hours per week and, as per the Faculty Federation/Board of Trustees collective bargaining contract, the facilitator is required to work no more than seven (7) hours per day. The Assistant Professor/Facilitator fulfills additional professional obligations and commitments within or outside of the thirty-five (35) hour workload for professional contributions to the College and in accordance with the facilitator's interests and abilities.

REPORTING AND SUPERVISORY RELATIONSHIP(S):

1. Direct reporting relationship to the Associate Vice President of Academic Affairs/Dean of the Learning Resources and Distance Learning.

SPECIALTY AREAS:

The Assistant Professor/Facilitator has an assigned speciality area and related functions in Instructional Technology.

DISTINGUISHING RESPONSIBILITIES:

1. Provide assistance and resources to faculty and staff in development of materials and pedagogy for technology-based instruction.

2. Develop strategies that extend the use of technology-assisted instruction into the mainstream classroom.

3. Manage the Teaching and Learning Center.

4. Develop and facilitate a comprehensive plan for the implementation of computer technology/Internet applications for instructional programs.

5. Work one-on-one with faculty members on hardware/software issues.

6. Develop short and long range goals for the academic computing and interactive learning activities of the College.

7. Teach/train faculty and staff in computer software applications.

8. Plan, write curricula, schedule and prepare materials and deliver workshops.

9. Prepare and disseminate information about computer technology to faculty and staff.

10. Serve as academic liaison to Management Information Systems and Service.

11. Assist Associate Vice President in development of grant proposals, budget and reports.

12. Maintain an active interest in the knowledge of current practices and discoveries that affect the area of expertise.

13. Participate in professional growth and development opportunities.

MINIMUM QUALIFICATIONS:

1. Bachelor's degree with coursework in instructional design or academic computer applications.

2. Classroom teaching experience.

3. Knowledge of standard Internet information delivery systems and communications tools, i.e. www, FTP, e-mail, asynchronous and real time text-based/audio-video conferencing and streaming audio and video.

4. Experience in the use of computer-based instructional materials and with web-based course development.

5. Ability to work collaboratively with faculty and staff.

6. Excellent analytical, oral, written and interpersonal skills.

PREFERRED QUALIFICATIONS:

1. Master's degree in instructional technologies or related field with coursework in instructional design theory and practices.

2. Experience with instructional technology tools, currently used at Prairie State College such as Web CT, Blackboard, Real Media, Adobe Photoshop, etc.

3. Experience teaching or learning in a totally online environment.

4. Experience working with culturally diverse faculty and staff.

5. College teaching experience; preferably in a community college.

Revised 11/02/99

Prairie State College

STANDARD JOB DESCRIPTION
Exempt

Date: Oct. 1995 Job Code:
Position Title: Learning Resources Systems Manager
Department : Learning Resources
Incumbent Name:

POSITION PURPOSE: Responsible for:
Design, development, operation, maintenance, and expansion of Learning Resources computer network and telecommunications systems, including integrated library systems, Local Area Networks, CD-ROM networks, Internet services, and other specialized regional, national, and international online information systems
Working with other instructional technology and College Computing Services personnel to maintain, improve, and expand the College's computing and telecommunications capacities.

REPORTING RELATIONSHIP:
REPORTS TO: Director of Learning Resources
AS DO: 1 Librarian, Admin. Services (E); 1 Librarian Systems/Tech. Services (E); 1 Librarian, Media Services (E);
              1 Director of TV Production (E); 1 Librarian, Branch Campus (E); 1 Administrative Assistant (N).
POSITIONS REPORTING DIRECTLY TO THIS POSITION: 1 Learning Resources Systems Specialist (NE); work-study students.

JOB DIMENSIONS:

Annual Technology Budget	Annual Payroll	Annual revenues, accounts
100,000 (est)	$25,000	Indeterminate

Other relevant figures: Responsible for operation of system of more than 70 personal computers and associated peripherals and approximately 30 CD-ROM databases and other online services. Responsible for maintaining full system operations at multiple sites, including Redwood and South City campuses, Sandy and Millcreek Centers, and other physical and distance learning instructional sites. Services provided to approximately 20,000 students, all full-time and part-time faculty and staff, and off-campus users through Utah Academic Library Consortium (UALC) and community user programs.

POSITION SUMMARY:

ESSENTIAL

Manage Learning Resources integrated library system (including circulation, public catalog, cataloging, acquisitions, media scheduling and reservations, and serials modules) in a multi-site environment so as to provide smooth error-free operation for multiple simultaneous users at all college instructional sites as well as off-site users utilizing Internet or other remote access network connections.

Manage Learning Resources LAN (Local Area Network) and CD-ROM network in a multi-site environment so as to provide smooth error-free operation for multiple simultaneous users at 2 College campuses, 2 centers, and multiple instructional sites as well as off-site users utilizing Internet or other remote access network connections.

Manage Learning Resources system connection to national OCLC (Online College Library Center) library system in a multi-site environment so as to provide smooth error-free operation for multiple simultaneous users at 2 College campuses in both dedicated line and Internet remote access modes.

Manage Learning Resources Internet connections so as to provide smooth error-free operation for multiple simultaneous users at 2 College campuses, 2 centers, and multiple instructional sites.

Manage system connections between AMX College media distribution system and library integrated system in a multi-site environment so as to provide smooth error-free operation for multiple simultaneous users at 2 College campuses, and (eventually) 2 centers.

Analyze student, faculty, and staff information needs so as to plan and design enhancements to current systems capabilities; provide custom programming in support of needed system enhancements or modifications.

Coordinate system operations with College Computing Services and College "instructional technology managers" in order to meet or anticipate user needs and assure compliance with College technology policies.

Coordinate system operations with library system managers for Utah Academic Library Consortium (UALC) members and Utah Public Library Network (ULN) members so as to assure smooth error-free linking and operation of College online and statewide shared database resources.

Salt Lake Community College

116 Systems Manager

9. Provide direct input in technology budget planning for Learning Resources.

10. Supervise others including full-time and part-time staff and work-study students; establish work schedules and assignments, monitor work flow and conduct performance evaluations, and provide training for technical support staff.

MARGINAL:
11. Counsel and advise; which may include helping users improve knowledge and skills, providing direction, or suggesting system or resource utilization techniques.

12. Other duties as assigned.

DIFFICULT AND COMPLEX PROBLEMS OR CHALLENGES:
Maintaining current knowledge of College technology systems and infrastructure. Designing and maintaining complex integrated College-wide and statewide systems. Meeting and anticipating needs of a wide variety of student, faculty, staff, administrative, and community users. Providing technical solutions and rapid technical response for all areas of technology used by Learning Resources staff and patrons. Performing custom programming to integrate local databases with local and statewide library integrated systems.

MAJOR PROBLEMS NORMALLY REFERRED TO SUPERVISOR OR OTHERS:
Funding requests to maintain state-of-the-art technology and equipment and solve specialized infrastructure problems.. Major system changes. Network problems throughout the college. Problems with staff or patrons that cannot be resolved at this level. Developing personnel issues.

PRINCIPAL ACCOUNTABILITIES:
1. Provide smooth operation of multiple Learning Resources integrated systems (including local and state integrated library systems, Novel LAN, CD-ROM network, OCLC national library system, and AMX media distribution system) by continuous system monitoring, planning for system expansion or enhancements, and coordinating with College, state , and national technical and systems personnel in technology planning.
2. Coordinate and represent Learning Resources technology needs and interests in statewide and national arenas by active participation in Dynix CODI(Customers of Dynix, Inc.) and other integrated library system user groups and by statewide UALC Systems Committee assignments.
3. Meet Learning Resources staff and patron needs by staying current with technological advances in computer, telecommunications, and networking technologies needed by Learning Resources and by maintaining state-of-the art knowledge of current technology processes and applications unique to Learning Resources.
4. Assure Learning Resources compliance with College or other applicable technology policies by coordination with College instructional technology managers and specialists.

SPECIFIC TYPES OF KNOWLEDGE, SKILL, AND EXPERIENCE REQUIRED FOR THIS POSITION:
Knowledge of: Computer operating systems including UNIX, DOS, OS/2, MAC OS, or other operating systems
Network operating systems including Novell NetWare or other LAN systems
Library integrated systems including Dynix Classic and Dynix Horizon (windows-based)
Client-server architecture operations
CD-ROM system design, development, implementation, and administration
Programming languages appropriate to Learning Resources needs
Internet operations and protocols
Ability to: Design, develop, and administer complex integrated systems
Diagnose and repair system problems
Communicate effectively with faculty, staff, students, and technical personnel
Maintain integrated system security, integrity, and reliability
Organize schedules and staff so as to provide smooth system operation
Research and analyze data

MINIMUM QUALIFICATIONS:
1) Associate degree required (Bachelor's degree or 4 years experience as a network manager preferred)
2) Three years related full-time work experience in management of library technology applications
    Substitution may occur as follows:
    *Additional appropriate work experience may be substituted on a one-for-one year basis for education
    *Additional related education/training may be substituted on a one-for-one year basis for work experience

Prepared By:	Date: 11.13.95	Edited by:	Date:
Supervisor Approval:	Date: 11-13-95	Evaluation:	Date:
VP Approval	Date:		

Salt Lake Community College

SALT LAKE COMMUNITY COLLEGE

OSITION DESCRIPTION
    Non-Exempt
)o not use more than
lotted space.)

Date: January , 1998   Job Code: 11
Position Title: Learning Resources Systems Specialist
Department: Learning Resources
Incumbent Name: Open at present

OSITION PURPOSE: Responsible for assisting faculty, students, and staff with use of software applications available in Learning :sources. Also responsible for assisting in installing, monitoring, repairing, and maintaining Learning Resources computer network and ecommunications systems, including integrated library systems, Local Area Networks, CD-ROM networks, Internet services, and other ecialized regional, national, and international online information systems.

EPORTING RELATIONSHIP:
    REPORTS TO: Learning Resources Systems Manager
    AS DO: 1 Learning Resources Assistant Systems Manager (N)
    POSITIONS REPORTING DIRECTLY TO YOUR POSITION: None

ESPONSIBILITIES AND DUTIES:

rder of portance	% of Total Time (Monthly)	Duties
SENTIAL		
	35%	Provides assistance to faculty, students, and Learning Resources staff with use of computer software applications available through Learning Resources, including Ameritech Horizon integrated library system software, AMX Synergy media retrieval system software, standard applications programs, e-mail systems, networking software, and other specialized library and media applications software programs.
	35%	Assists in installing, upgrading, and maintaining Horizon integrated library system client software, AMX Synergy media system client software, Learning Resources CD-ROM network, and Ariel document delivery system.
	20%	Is on-call for technical support and accountable for systems maintenance and repair during regular working hours as well as after hours and at any time Learning Resources systems are in operation.
	5%	Troubleshoot and maintain other Learning Resources electronic equipment.
ARGINAL		
	5%	Other duties as assigned.
	100%	

PORTANT INFREQUENT DUTIES
nual computer inventory.
FFICULT AND COMPLEX PROBLEMS OR CHALLENGES:
ponding to emergency requests for assistance; performing system diagnostics to locate causes of failure; determining when to refer problems .earning Resources Systems Manager for resolution.
FFICULT DECISIONS:
ritizing repairs and assistance.
.JOR PROBLEMS NORMALLY REFERRED TO SUPERVISOR OR OTHERS:
:ision to install or upgrade system software or operating system; major software problems, major equipment or system problems.

Y REPORT PREPARATION:

Report Title	Compile?	Do You Prepare?	Write?	User
omputer inventory		yes		Learning Resources Director

Salt Lake Community College

118   Systems Specialist

EQUIPMENT OPERATED:

Equipment	% Of Total Time Operated (Monthly)	Maintain?	Do You Service?	Repair?
FAX Machine		no	no	no
Computers/Printers/Peripherals		yes	yes	yes
CD-ROM Drives and Players		yes	yes	yes
Electronic Instruments/Tools		yes	yes	yes

PRIMARY CONTACTS:

Contact	Purpose of Contact	Times/Monthly
* Library Patrons, including students, faculty and staff, and the general public	Assist with system operation, resolve problems	Daily
* Library Staff	Assist with system operation, resolve problems	Daily
* Systems and Computer Staff at Other Libraries and at SLCC	Coordinate systems operations	Weekly
* Computer vendors	Discuss hardware specifications	Weekly

WORKING ENVIRONMENT:

Climatic/Atmospheric Conditions	Access to Worksite/Mobility Barriers	Other Environmental Conditions
Normal	Lift & handle computer equipment and peripherals	

SPECIFIC TYPES OF KNOWLEDGE AND SKILLS REQUIRED FOR THIS POSITION:

Knowledge of:
* Computer operating systems including UNIX, DOS, OS/2, Windows, Mac OS, or other operating systems
* Network operating systems including Novell NetWare or other LAN systems
* Specialized library and media computer systems such as Dynix, Ameritech Horizon, AMX Synergy, and specialized CD-ROM databases and software
* Internet tools and protocols
* Electronics
* Standard applications programs and e-mail

Ability to:
* Maintain computer hardware and software
* Locate and determine equipment problems
* Read equipment manuals and troubleshoot
* Communicate effectively and instruct others in use of computer applications
* Design and present software training sessions
* Work well with others
* Read schematic diagrams
* Ability to document procedures
* Ability to prepare technical manuals preferred

MINIMUM QUALIFICATIONS:

1) Associate's degree in a related field
       AND
2) One year related paid full-time work experience
       Or substitution may occur as follows:
       * Additional appropriate work experience may be substituted on a one-for-one year basis for education
       * Additional related education/training may be substituted on a one-for-one year basis for work experience

Prepared by:	Date:	Edited by:	Date:
Supervisor Approval:	Date:	Evaluation:	Date:
VP Approval:	Date:		

Salt Lake Community College

Audiovisual Services

Assistant Librarian, A-V Services
A-V Assistant
Audio-Visual Coordinator
Audio-Visual Equipment Technician
Audio-Visual Specialist/Engineer
Audio-Visual Specialist/Videographer
Audio-Visual Technician
Audiovisual Supervisor
Closed Caption Technician
Coordinator of Audiovisual Services/Electronic Learning Systems
Coordinator of Media Services
Coordinator, Satellite/EDNET Services
Director Media Production Services
Director Television Production
Editor/Camera Operator/Production Worker
EDMET Coordinator
Graphics and Photography Technician
Graphic Artist
Instructional Technology Media Specialist
ITV Facilitator/Library Aide
Learning Resources Technical Coordinator
Library/Media Specialist
Library/Media Technician
Manager, Technical Operations
Media Equipment Technician
Media Production Technician
Technician
Media Support Services Coordinator
Media Specialist
Media Scheduler
Media Technician
Operations Engineer
Photographer
Photo Media Specialist
Site Facilitator
Slide and Gallery Technician
Supervisor Media Distribution Services
Supervisor Media Operations
Supervisor TV Productions
Technician, Media Services
Technician, Studio Media
Technical Operations Engineer
Technical Operations Manager
TV Studio Specialist
Video Production Specialist

Carl Sandburg College

Job Description

Position Title: Coordinator of Audiovisual Services/Electronic Learning Systems

Classification: Mid-Management

Level: IV

Supervises: Student Workers

Reports To: Dean of Learning Resource Services

Principal Working Relationships: Dean of Learning Resource Services, Faculty and Student Workers

Purpose: To coordinate and maintain the functions of the Audiovisual Services and Electronic Learning Systems. Participate in and support the college Risk Management Program in a capacity appropriate to this position. This includes, but is not limited to, monitoring conditions, events, and circumstances present in the college operation and communicating observations to the appropriate supervisor and/or Risk Management Committee.

Essential Functions

Major Responsibilities

1. Exercise delegated management functions for the following Learning Resource Services:

   A. Audiovisual Equipment Services

   B. Audiovisual Production Services

   C. Telecommunications Services

      1. Distance Learning Systems using cable, wire, fiber or radio frequency

      2. Satellite equipment

   D. Media utilization facilities in classrooms and designated special sites (Learning Resources Center, Lecture Room C-123, the gymnasium, etc.).

   E. Telecourses and other media-based instructional activities with respect to materials, equipment and systems support.

2. Make recommendations to the Dean of Learning Resource Services regarding program planning, organization, budget and personnel.

Coordinates

1. Activities of student assistants.

2. Security arrangements for audiovisual, computer and telecommunications equipment.

Assists With

1. College marketing activities that require audiovisual support.

2. College activities requiring photographic, television or audio support.

3. Other duties as assigned by the Dean of Learning Resource Services.

LOSS PREVENTION →

Minimum Necessary Skills, Experience, and Educational Background

1. Bachelor's degree, 120 semester hours, or specialized related training with 4 years related experience required.

2. Experience in the field to include working knowledge of:

   a. Audiovisual production

   b. Graphics production

   c. Telecommunications technology

   d. Maintenance and minor repairs of AV equipment.

3. Valid drivers license required.

Physical Requirements to Perform Job Functions

1. Vision and hearing necessary to assure satisfactory completion of audiovisual production projects.

2. Ability to bend, reach, and lift at least 50 pounds.

12/April 1997

This position is declared security sensitive and will require a background check as a pre-employment qualifier.

LOSS PREVENTION/REDUCTION

1.

2.

3. Secures audio visual and telecommunications equipment against damage or theft.

CENTRAL FLORIDA COMMUNITY COLLEGE

JOB DESCRIPTION

JOB TITLE: AUDIO-VISUAL SPECIALIST/ENGINEER

PAY GRADE: 214

OVERTIME STATUS: NON-EXEMPT

MAJOR RESPONSIBILITY:

Responsible for operation of specialized equipment and for production or reproduction of original materials from one form to another. Responsible for repair and maintenance of equipment.

PREREQUISITES FOR POSITION (Qualification Standards):

1.   Education or training: Associate degree or two years technical school training beyond high school.

2.   Years of experience in field: Minimum of three years work experience in area(s) related to audio-visual production.

3.   Special skills or abilities related to position: Should possess technical skills in electronics, stage and video lighting, photography, video production, and multi-image production. Ability to coordinate skills or technical knowledge with service requirements. Ability to perform preventative maintenance and repairs.

ESSENTIAL JOB FUNCTIONS:

Note: Media technicians have a variety of specialty assignments. The following duties are either shared or split among technicians and do not necessarily reflect the job of one person.

1.   Instruct individuals and groups in usage/operation of multi-image, photographic, and video equipment.
2.   Set up and operate multi-image shows.
3.   Maintain and repair audio-visual equipment including 16mm, 35mm and 8mm projectors, overhead and opaque projectors, record players, amplifiers, cassette recorders, microcomputers, video production, and distribution equipment.
4.   Supervise overall operation of the College's closed-circuit television distribution system and satellite network system.
5.   Make recommendations on purchase of equipment and supplies.
6.   Supervise junior technicians and student assistants in distribution and use of equipment and supplies.
7.   Assist with technical needs for productions and activities in the college auditorium.

09/17/98

Central Florida Community College

ESSENTIAL JOB FUNCTIONS:

8.   May serve as campus photographer. Provide on-site photography, copy work, slide duplication, and processing and printing of color and black & white slides and prints.
9.   Supervise transparency production.
10. Maintain records and inventories of production.
11. Maintain stock of all supplies needed for production.
12. Assist with production and reproduction of video tapes.

(These essential job functions are not to be construed as a complete statement of all duties performed. Employees will be required to perform other job related marginal duties as required.)

ESSENTIAL PHYSICAL SKILLS:

- Acceptable eyesight (with or without correction).
- Acceptable hearing (with or without hearing aid).
- Ability to communicate both orally and in writing.
- Heavy (45 pounds and over) lifting and carrying.
- Walking.
- Standing.
- Bending.
- Distinguish colors.

ENVIRONMENTAL CONDITIONS:

- Works inside in an office environment.
- Electrical energy and equipment.

(Reasonable accommodations will be made for otherwise qualified individuals with a disability.)

PRIMARY LOCATION OF JOB: Building 3, Ocala Campus

SUPERVISOR OF POSITION: Learning Resources Director

09/17/98

CENTRAL FLORIDA COMMUNITY COLLEGE

JOB DESCRIPTION

JOB TITLE: AUDIO-VISUAL SPECIALIST/VIDEOGRAPHER

PAY GRADE: 214

OVERTIME STATUS: NON-EXEMPT

MAJOR RESPONSIBILITY:

Routine work in delivering, setting up and retrieving audio-visual equipment, including preventive maintenance of equipment.

PREREQUISITES FOR POSITION (Qualification Standards):

1.   Education or training: High school diploma or equivalent required.

2.   Years of experience in field: One year of experience in the handling, operation and repair of A-V equipment.

3.   Special skills or abilities related to position: Knowledge of equipment required relating to audio-visual needs. Knowledge of the operation and repair of a variety of audio-visual and related equipment. Knowledge of the method of repairing equipment used. Knowledge of machine use and film and video care. Knowledge of the campus distribution system. Knowledge of camera usage. Knowledge of the general use of computer equipment.

Ability to learn new equipment features and use. Ability to read and understand repair manuals, diagrams and schematics. Ability to use tools involved in repair of equipment and to diagnose malfunctions. Ability to make limited repairs and adjustments. Ability to establish and maintain effective working relationships with other employees.

Ability to lift large television sets (45 pounds or more).

ESSENTIAL JOB FUNCTIONS:

1.   Deliver, set up and retrieve television sets, projectors, slide carousels, public address systems, record players and other types of players, screens, and other audio-visual equipment and supplies.
2.   Provide instructors and other users with information regarding proper use of equipment.
3.   Maintain inventory of equipment and materials. Provide preventive maintenance for equipment.
4.   Clean, repair and maintain films and videos through use of inspecting and cleaning equipment. Check and process all new equipment received, for completeness of order and proper functioning of all features. Check equipment for correct tagging, carding and storage.

09/17/98

ESSENTIAL JOB FUNCTIONS: (Continued):

5.   Operate television distribution system which involves programming to proper locations through a systems controller and computer terminal. Check video and audio levels with appropriate modulator.

6.   Process new video tapes by viewing and recording programs.

(These essential job functions are not to be construed as a complete statement of all duties performed. Employees will be required to perform other job related marginal duties as required.)

ESSENTIAL PHYSICAL SKILLS:

■   Acceptable eyesight (with or without correction).
■   Acceptable hearing (with or without hearing aid).
■   Ability to communicate both orally and in writing.
■   Heavy (45 pounds and over) lifting and carrying.
■   Walking.
■   Standing.
■   Bending.
■   Distinguish colors.

ENVIRONMENTAL CONDITIONS:

■   Works inside in an office environment.
■   Electrical energy and equipment.

(Reasonable accommodations will be made for otherwise qualified individuals with a disability.)

PRIMARY LOCATION OF JOB: Building 3 (Learning Resources Center)

SUPERVISOR OF POSITION: Learning Resources Director

09/17/98

Central Florida Community College

COLUMBUS STATE COMMUNITY COLLEGE
JOB DESCRIPTION

PAY GRADE _____   DATE WRITTEN _____
POSITION _____   DATE REVISED \---------
                                                    WRITTEN BY _____

TITLE: Media Production Technician

SUMMARY: Responsible for participating in the design and production of media projects
                    that include computer generated graphics, photography, transparency making,
                    dry mounting, and lamination.

RELATIONSHIP: Reports to the Director of Educational Resources, coordinates activities of
                    hourly student assistants, and receives directions from Video Production
                    Specialist.   Regularly interfaces with other members of the ERC staff,
                    employees of the college, and students.

DUTIES AND
RESPONSIBILITIES:

1. Fulfills request for graphic support, design and media duplication
    services for staff, faculty, and students. Includes the design and
    production of graphics for classroom presentation and campus display
    functions. Includes computer-based projects and traditional design
    and production techniques. Also includes photo services such as slide
    production and outsourced film processing;

2. Produces graphics, which includes signs, labels, displays, bulletin
    boards, and handouts for ERC functions and services;

3. Assists faculty and staff in using new media and web-based software
    for classroom presentations;

4. Completes audio tape duplication projects;

5. Maintains service desk in Media Production;

6. Inventories supplies and submits requisitions for replenishing supplies;

7. Assists the Video Production Specialist with video production
    projects;

8. Assists the A/V Video Technician in labeling and inventory of
    equipment.

Columbus State Community College

Media Production Technician
Job Description
Page 2

9.   Collects and compiles statistics for Media Services, which includes production projects, video duplication, and teleconferences.

AUTHORITY: Operates within the policies and procedures of the college and the ERC, as well as, specific guidelines established by the Director of Educational Resources.

Columbus State Community College
Job Description

PAY GRADE: _____   **DATE WRITTEN:** _____

                                        DATE REVISED: _____

POSITION: _____   **WRITTEN BY:** _____

TITLE: Media Equipment Technician

SUMMARY: Schedules and distributes audiovisual equipment, performs minor repair
                    and assistance in using equipment, and assists with the annual equipment
                    inventory.

RELATIONSHIP: Receives direction from the Coordinator of Media Support Service and
                    reports to the Director of Educational Resources. Interfaces regularly
                    with ERC staff and Columbus State employees and students.

**DUTIES AND
RESPONSIBILITIES:**

1. Provides for circulation of equipment so that faculty and staff are
    supported with efficient and prompt services;

2. Diagnoses equipment as needing major repair and refers this
    equipment to the Library Equipment Technician for further action;

3. Trains the employees of the college in the proper operation and
    utilization of circulating equipment;

4. Trains the ERC staff in the operation of equipment and in the
    circulation procedures for the equipment;

5. Assists with media production projects when needed.

6. Performs light repair and maintenance on equipment;

7. Assists in the annual equipment inventory as needed;

8. Answers the telephone, and receives people who come to the office
    for services;

9. Assists the ERC Supervisor in the overall ERC operation as
    needed;

10. Executes the general responsibilities common to all employees of the College;

11. Performs other duties and projects as may be assigned by the Director of Educational Resources.

AUTHORITY: Operates within the procedures and methods of the Library Services area an the ERC, as well as specific guidelines established by the Director of Educational Resources.

10/99

Columbus State Community College
Job Specifications

POSITION: _____   **DATE WRITTEN:** _____
                                              DATE REVISED: _____

TITLE: Media Equipment Technician

EDUCATION: Prefer an associate degree in the field of audio-visual services or
                    equivalent work experience in the audio-visual area.

**SKILLS AND
EXPERIENCE:**

1.   Must have the ability to communicate effectively with co-workers,
      Faculty, and staff.

2.   Must demonstrate the ability to carry out an effective equipment
      circulation service in an academic setting.

3.   Must demonstrate the ability to perform light maintenance of audio
      Visual equipment.

4.   Must demonstrate ability to perform A-V software inspection.

5.   Prefer at least one year experience working with an equipment
      circulation service.

6.   Must have the ability to make mature and sound judgements.

7.   Some library and computer experiences are desirable.

10/99

COLUMBUS STATE COMMUNITY COLLEGE
JOB DESCRIPTION

PAY GRADE _____
POSITIONS _____

DATE WRITTEN _____
DATE REVISED _____
WRITTEN BY _____

TITLE: Video Production Specialist

SUMMARY: Responsible for the designing and production of instructional video modules.

RELATIONSHIP: Reports to the Director of Educational Resources and directs the efforts and assigns tasks to Media Production Technician and hourly employees in the work group. Regularly interfaces with other ERC staff, employees of the college, and students as well as members of off-campus agencies; i.e. HECC, Educable, OPSTC, etc.

DUTIES AND RESPONSIBILITIES:

1. Assists faculty and students in the design and production of instructional video modules;

2. Creates and produces audio, graphic, and print materials for the instructional video modules;

3. Coordinates telecourse and Satellite programs.

4. Presents workshops and seminars to faculty demonstrating the use of instructional video modules;

5. Evaluates production projects based upon established guidelines;

6. Reports on cost, time, and supply elements of production projects;

7. Advises the Director on the purchase of hardware and software;

8. Executes the general responsibilities common to all employees of the college;

9.   Performs other duties and projects as may be assigned by the Director of Educational Resources

AUTHORITY: Operates within the policies and procedures of the College and the ERC, as well as specific guidelines established by the Director of Educational Resources.

Updated 9/97

COLUMBUS STATE COMMUNITY COLLEGE

JOB DESCRIPTION

PAY GRADE _____   DATE WRITTEN _____
POSITIONS _____   DATE REVISED _____
                                              WRITTEN BY _____

TITLE: Media Support Services Coordinator

SUMMARY: Coordinates the Media Support Services unit of the ERC, which includes PC support, AV equipment delivery and set-up, and other media support.

RELATIONSHIP: Reports to the Director of Educational Resources. Directs the efforts and assigns tasks to the Evening AV/Video Equipment Technician and part-time employees.

DUTIES AND RESPONSIBILITIES:

1. Supports ERC PC's for staff and students, which includes PC installation and operation, printers, software loading, trouble-shooting, and other PC related assistance;

2. Serves as liaison between ERC and Data Center for PC support;

3. Oversees the delivery and set-up of equipment, monitors and maintains the inventory of ERC AV equipment.

4. Diagnoses AV equipment as needing repairs and refers equipment to the AV/Video Specialist for further action;

5. Performs minor repair and maintenance of equipment;

6. Trains employees of the ERC and college in the operation and utilization of AV equipment;

7. Maintains an inventory of supplies for AV equipment;

8. Directs staff in preparing equipment for delivery, including assembly, labeling, affixing pockets, engraving, painting, and inventorying;

9. Provides technical support for ERC teleconferences, videoconferences, cable television, and video production;

9. Provides technical support for ERC teleconferences, videoconferences, cable television, and video production;

10. Assists in the preparation of purchase requisitions for PC, AV, Video and library equipment;

11. Executes the general responsibilities common to all employees of the college;

12. Performs other duties and methods of the ERC, as well as specific guidelines established by the Director of Educational Resources..

AUTHORITY: Operates within the procedures and methods of the ERC, as well as specific guidelines established by the Director of the ERC. Coordinates the work and provides guidance to full and part-time employees assigned to the Media Services unit.

6/16/99

Ross Library   Cottey College

Job Description: Assistant Librarian, A-V Services

Purpose: To manage all aspects of audio-visual services campus-wide; to assist with cataloging and database management, especially in regard to audio-visual materials.

Reports to: Library Director

Required Qualifications:

1.   Training and experience in the operation and maintenance of audio-visual and multi-media equipment.

2.   Familiarity with online library catalogs. Our library has Sirsi Corporation's Unicorn system.

3.   Ability to lift equipment up to 20 lbs. and to use a cart to transport equipment between locations.

4.   Ability to work effectively with students and faculty to determine and serve their audio-visual needs.

5.   Experience in using computer-based word processing and spreadsheet applications.

Desirable Qualifications:

1.   Library Technical Assistant certificate.

2.   Experience in audio-visual services, including equipment maintenance, scheduling, and selection and cataloging of curriculum materials.

3.   Experience in online cataloging with MARC formats; knowledge of Dewey Decimal Classification.

4.   Familiarity with electronic reference databases.

Duties:

1.   Coordinate the purchase, inventory, use, and routine maintenance of audio-visual equipment and supplies used throughout the campus, including televisions, recording and playback equipment, overhead and other projectors.

2.   Assist with the location, selection, and cataloging of curriculum-related materials in audio-visual formats, including videos, sound recordings, slides, and satellite broadcasts.

3.   Review and edit shared catalog records, create original cataloging, and perform database maintenance, using correct USMARC tagging, the Dewey Decimal Classification, and Library of Congress subject headings.

4.   Share with other staff members in providing circulation and reference service at scheduled times, including evenings and weekends on a rotating basis.

5.   Supervise Library Media Student Assistant.

\nancy\avdesc99.doc

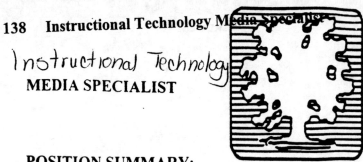

Instructional Technology
MEDIA SPECIALIST

POSITION SUMMARY:

Provide technical and creative assistance with various video and multimedia production techniques and technologies to faculty, staff and students. Responsible for programming and scheduling Channel 8 and campus video network. Reports directly to the Dean of the Learning Resources Center.

ESSENTIAL FUNCTIONS:

- Assist faculty, staff and students with planning, designing and producing Powerpoint and Astound presentations.
- Provide technical and creative support for multimedia production.
- Use image scanning, video/audio capture and CD recording hardware and software.
- Responsible for ENG video production and non-linear editing.
- Responsible for video recording and duplicating.
- Use authoring software, Toolbook II, Authorware and Multimedia Studio 6.
- Responsible for the daily scheduling, programming and calendar update of Channel 8 and programming on campus video network.
- Responsible for satellite down-linking and off-air taping.
- Responsible for media equipment and set-ups.
- Serve on various committees as assigned.
- Perform other work as assigned.

QUALIFICATIONS:

- Excellent communications and interpersonal skills.
- Two-year technical degree in video and multimedia production.
- Demonstrated experience in video and multimedia production.

SALARY: Commensurate with college pay scale.

APPLICATION DEADLINE: Review of applications begins August 14, 1998 and continues until filled.

APPLICANT INFORMATION: Send letter of application, official DSCC application, resume, official transcripts, and three current letters of recommendation to the address below:

**DYERSBURG STATE
COMMUNITY COLLEGE**
Dyersburg State Community College

Personnel Department
Dyersburg State Community College
1510 Lake Road
Dyersburg, Tennessee 38024

07-20-98-467

POSITION: Library / Media Specialist
CLASSIFICATION:
DEPARTMENT: Library
REPORT TO: Librarian

GENERAL JOB SUMMARY

Under limited supervision of the Librarian, will coordinate all aspects of the South Attendance Center Library, perform administration of GED test, record assessment scores, record and prepare reports on equipment use, and administer other tests or exams for the instructional faculty . Customer service is a paramount attribute to the position, requiring the person to be positive and helpful. Availability to work evening hours as needed.

% of TIME	ESSENTIAL DUTIES/RESPONSIBILITIES
1. Constant (67-100%)	1. Act as liaison between public library and college library
	2. Make recommendations to Librarian as to collection acquisitions.
	3. Supervise all full and part-time employees. Develop and implement work schedules
	4. Organize tasks, delegate work activities with follow up for accuracy.
	5. Monitor equipment checkout and prepare periodic reports.
	6. Administer make up exams for faculty
	7. Operate circulation desk in accordance with established procedures.
	8. Supervise and monitor workstudy employees
	9. Assist with cataloging of materials
	10. Answer telephone
	11. Order books through inter/intra library loan system
2. Frequent (34-66%)	1. Administer GED tests to be designated individuals in the Emmetsburg, Algona and Spencer LRC's
	2. Update all information retrieval systems as needed
3. Occasional (10-33%)	1. Update all computer resources as required and needed
	2. Report repair and maintenance needs
	3. Prepare all South Attendance Center reports under the direction of the Librarian
	4. Prepare and send all correspondence relative to center

KNOWLEDGE, SKILLS, AND ABILITIES

1. Full knowledge of and ability to work with necessary computer software such as Office 95
2. Attend conferences/meetings at the local, state, regional and national as needed and required
3. Be willing and able to represent the college in the most positive manner with students, staff and the general

public.

4. Access, input and retrieve information from a personal computer, operate standard office equipment: typewriter, copier, calculator, etc

5. Read and understand written and oral instructions

6. Ability to effectively communicate with students, staff, administration and the general public.

7. Ability to drive a vehicle to travel between campuses and satellite centers

8. Ability to work effectively in an atmosphere of frequent interruptions

Sedentary to medium work. Position involves standing, walking, and sitting with frequent changes from one to another position; exerting up to forty (40) pounds of force occasionally (10-33%). Occasional climbing, balancing, kneeling. Frequent stooping, crouching, reaching, handling, pushing, pulling, lifting, and carrying (34-66%)/ Constant talking, hearing, and viewing (67-100%). Will travel to other campuses and satellite centers.

The statements contained herein reflect general details as necessary to describe the essential functions, job duties/responsibilities, and performance expectations of the position, which should not be considered an all-inclusive listing of work requirements. Individuals may perform other duties as assigned.

MINIMUM QUALIFICATIONS

B.A. degree required, Library Science preferred. Must have training/experience in personal computer use.

SALARY

FRINGE BENEFITS

APPLICATION PROCESS

Iowa Lakes Community College

NICOLET AREA TECHNICAL COLLEGE
Position Description

Name: Kathleen A. Tromp

Department: Richard J. Brown Library/ITV

Position Title: ITV Facilitator/Library Aide

Date:

Pay Grade:

Reports To: Dean of Transitional College
Learning Resources

Position Summary:

Under the supervision of Audio-Visual Technician, responsible for preparing ITV studio and assisting with distance-learning classes. Under supervision of Circulation Desk Manager, responsible for a variety of Inter-library Loan tasks and circulation desk responsibilities.

Duties/Responsibilities As ITV Site Facilitator:

The following duties are normal for this position. These are not to be construed as exclusive or all-inclusive. Other duties may be required and assigned.

- Prepares ITV classroom and studio equipment prior to class. Trouble-shoot for technical problems and check for faxes or other material from

- Provide orientation to participants on classroom equipment, support services, and emergency equipment. Assist two or more students in learning basic functions of instructor control panel and phone/fax machine.

- Distribute and collect course materials as provided; return to instructor by fax or mail as requested.

- Serve as proctor at request of instructor.

Duties/Responsibilities As ITV Site Facilitator:

- Lead library assistant for Saturdays; responsible for opening and closing the library and all related duties.

- Assist with Inter-library Loans and general circulation duties.

- Supervise workstudy students in absence of Department Manager or manager's assistant.

- Assist patrons in the use of library resources, including library tours, locating materials, and providing instruction in the use of online resources.

Nicolet Area Technical College

Position Description
Kathleen A. Tromp
Page 2 of 2

Assist with the sorting, check-in, and filing of materials and microfilms in Library Assistant's absence or as requested.

Work Direction Received:

Works under the supervision of the Audio-Visual Technician and Circulation Desk Manager.

Supervision Exercised:

Supervise work/study students in absence of Department Manager or Assistant.

Decision Making:

Decisions are made independently concerning ITV and Library activities, assisting patrons, students and faculty with problems.

Interaction:

There is significant interaction with faculty, staff, students, and the general public.

Desirable Knowledge and Abilities:

Training and Experience:

In evaluating candidates for this position, Nicolet may consider a combination of education, training, and experience which provides the necessary knowledge, skills, and abilities to perform the duties of the position. Normally, education may be substituted for experience, or experience substituted for education, on a year for year basis.

Nicolet Area Technical College

POSITION DESCRIPTION
Non-Exempt·
(Do not use more than
allotted space.)

Date: June, 1997
Position Title:
Department:
Incumbent Name:

Job Code:
Operations Engineer
Learning Resources

POSITION PURPOSE: Responsible for providing technical engineering services in SLCC TV Productions in support of media/video productions, teleconferencing, and distance learning activities. Oversee maintenance and service programs for equipment and systems related to audio and media productions and communications , including RF, component, composite, digital, microwave, and fiber based systems.

REPORTING RELATIONSHIP:
REPORTS TO: Technical Operations Manager
AS DO: 1 Studio Media Technician (N); various part-time and contract personnel.
POSITIONS REPORTING DIRECTLY TO YOUR POSITION: None

RESPONSIBILITIES AND DUTIES:
Position is responsible for repair and maintenance of:

Order of Importance·	% of Total Time (Monthly)	Duties
ESSENTIAL		
1	35%	Provide engineering support for studio production and distance learning technical operations in order to deliver a quality service that is in compliance with all applicable FCC rules and regulations, Utah Education Network (UEN) and Utah State System of Higher Education (USHE) requirements, and institutional policy.
2	35%	Coordinate quality control and oversight of maintenance of all equipment and systems, including studio audio and video production equipment, UEN state fiber hub and fiber connect installations, distance learning equipment, teleconference room and associated interface equipment, and close caption workstation. Assure that bench stock, test equipment, and tools are available to technical staff as projects require.
3	22%	Provide engineering support for ongoing technical projects and assistance in planning and implementation of future projects for all College locations.
4	5%	Stay current with changes in the telecommunications and broadcast industry and help formulate plans to keep operations in compliance with industry standards and current technology.
MARGINAL		
5	1%	Provide technical information to support grant applications in telecommunication, media/video, and broadcast fields.
6	2%	Other duties as assigned
	100%	

IMPORTANT INFREQUENT DUTIES:
Training instructors on use of interactive rooms and equipment; maintaining technical documentation for equipment and projects.

DIFFICULT AND COMPLEX PROBLEMS OR CHALLENGES:
Maintaining technical equipment in top operating condition at all times; maintaining state-of-the-art technical operation within limited fiscal resources.

DIFFICULT DECISIONS:
Engineering analysis for long-term College projects; coordinating equipment repairs and maintenance with production/use schedules.

MAJOR PROBLEMS NORMALLY REFERRED TO SUPERVISOR OR OTHERS:
Project priorities; budget decisions; actions to be taken when major equipment fails and is needed ASAP.

KEY REPORT PREPARATION:

Do You:

Report Title:	Compile?	Prepare?	Write?	User
Service/Repair requests	Yes	Yes	No	TV Productions
Usage reports and statistics	Yes	Yes	No	Distance Learning
				Learning Resources

EQUIPMENT OPERATED:

Equipment	% Of Total Time Operated (Monthly)	Maintain?	Do You Service?	Repair?
Broadcast video equipment	35%	Yes	Yes	Yes
Broadcast audio equipment	15%	Yes	Yes	Yes
Video/audio test equipment	35%	Yes	Yes	Yes
Fiber/RF/Data systems	10%	Yes	Yes	Yes

PRIMARY CONTACTS:

Contact	Purpose of Contact	Times/Monthly
UEN/datalink engineers/technicians	Fiber hub maintenance and training	5/month
Technical contractors	Wiring/data installation	5/month
Various on-campus technicians	Interface on campus projects	Weekly as required
Studio customers	Completion of requested projects	Daily as required

WORKING ENVIRONMENT:

Climatic/Atmospheric Conditions	Access to Worksite/Mobility Barriers	Other Environmental Conditions
Exposed to extreme temperature conditions	Must be able to assume uncomfortable positions, climb ladders and rigging. Work in awkward and confined areas	

SPECIFIC TYPES OF KNOWLEDGE, SKILL, AND EXPERIENCE REQUIRED FOR THIS POSITION:

Knowledge of:	Basic electrical engineering and electronics
	Television production
	Broadcast engineering and management
	Composite and RF based video/audio delivery systems
	Digital audio & video systems
	LAN/WAN computing technology
Ability to:	Work well under pressure and unsupervised
	Manage multiple projects simultaneously
	Diagnose equipment problems and perform quality repairs on equipment to part level.
	Effectively use required test equipment & tools.
	Deal effectively with a wide variety of people and organizations
	Manage time effectively
	Read and draft system schematics and technical and architectural blueprints
Experience:	5 years experience in broadcast engineering and management (BSEE desirable)
	Current FCC license or SBE certification

===

Prepared by:	Edited by:
(Signature)	Date:
Supervisor Approval:	Evaluation:
Date:	Date:
VP Signature:	Date:

Salt Lake Community College

HR Reviewer/date
Determination
AV Technician
C. Douglas   3/24/98   HR

Tallahassee Community College
POSITION DESCRIPTION

Employee Name:

Position Number: CS4 AVT03

Position Title: Audio-Visual Technician

Department/Division/Section: Library AV Center

Working Hours/Total Hours in Work Week: 40
1 p.m. - 10 p.m. Mon-Thur, (Dinner Break 5 p.m. - 6 p.m.); 1 p.m. - 5 p.m. Friday;
Saturday 9 a.m. - 1 p.m.

Name and title of immediate supervisor: Mr. Albert Spradley, A/V Librarian

Name and titles of employees directly supervised: OPS and College Work Study Students

List machines or equipment used regularly in work. Give estimated percentage of total job time spent in operation of each:

25%	Distance Learning Equipment (Highly technical equipment, IE Document Camera, slide to video transfer units	Overhead Projectors CD Players SFS projectors
8%	VCR's (channel operation)	Turntables
1%	Walkie Talkie Radios	Laserdisc players
5%	Video Projectors and LCD Panels	Caramate projectors
2%	Character Generator	Carousel projectors
2%	IBM personal computers (Equipment inventory)	Audiotape duplicators Laminating machines
25%	Tech Unit (Automated VCR controller) Channel maintenance and operation	Photocopiers Opaque projectors
2%	Scopes and test equipment	Calculators

5%	Other equipment (basically to evaluate for malfunction purposes)
	Satellite unit
	ITV Production equipment
	    16mm projector
	    Audio tape recorders
		Camcorders
		Screens

In addition to the knowledge, skills, and abilities for this position *(see next page),* **it has been determined that the following** minimum training and experience requirements **are necessary for a position in this classification:** *(see class specification)*

Graduation from a standard high school or equivalency diploma and two years of experience in operating and maintaining a wide variety of audiovisual equipment or two years of related experience.

Successful completion of college course work may be substituted at the rate of 30 semester hours on a year-for-year basis for the required experience.

Ability to lift, push or pull up to 70 lbs.

Preference will be given to applicants with a Florida drivers license.

List the knowledge, skills and abilities required to perform the duties and responsibilities of this position:

-Knowledge of basic electronics
-Knowledge of the operational procedures for the various pieces of audio visual equipment owned by the college
-Knowledge of practices and procedures of the Audio Visual Department
-Know of TCC library policies and procedures
-Knowledge of the organization and programs of the Audio Visual Department

-Ability to read and interpret complex manuals and schematics
-Ability to operate and interpret the data from complex test equipment
-Ability to work independently
-Ability to trouble shoot and isolate computer related problems
-Ability to plan, organize, prioritize and coordinate work assignments
-Ability to enter data
-Ability to follow established policies and procedures
-Ability to communicate effectively verbally and in writing
-Ability to make independent judgements
-Ability to establish and maintain effective working relationships
-Ability to work well with faculty, staff and students
-Ability to lift up to 70 lbs, pull, sit, stand, stoop and reach for extended periods of time
-Ability to load (insert into machines) videotapes, monitor channel operation and correct channel related problems
-Ability to learn to operate and monitor distance learning equipment
-Ability to independently operate the AV Center on nights and weekends.
-Ability to learn to operate a video and audio tape dub bay
-Ability to perform time-sensitive and complex tasks
-Ability to operate a motor vehicle safely. May be required to travel to remote campus sites.
-Skill in using complex computer databases
-Skill in using a wide variety of complex electronic equipment
-Skill in troubleshooting computer hardware problems
-Skill in troubleshooting electronic equipment problems

Tallahassee Community College

DUTIES AND RESPONSIBILITIES

DIRECTIONS: Summarize each duty/responsibility including percentage of time spent in area on an average annual basis. Please be succinct in each summary; the majority of positions can be summarized using only this form with no attachments.

Each duty/responsibility must be listed either as an essential or non-essential function. Use as many of the numeric codes listed below as appropriate to justify why each duty/responsibility has been designated as an essential function.

EF CODES: A job function is considered to be essential if:

#1.   The position exists to perform the function.

#2.   There are a limited number of other employees available to perform the function, or among whom the function can be distributed.

#3.   A function is highly specialized, and the person in the position is hired for special expertise or ability to perform it.

% Time	EF Codes	Essential Functions
25%	1,2,3	Monitors the operation of the educational access channel, executing any corrections needed to ensure the efficient operation of the channel; troubleshoots equipment malfunctions, signal failures, etc; monitors voice mail reporting channel problems, identifies causes and reports to the A V Librarian and the Library Services Specialist; creates the tape load schedule and loads the tapes on a daily basis.
25%	1,2,3	Assists Library Technical Assistant I with booting up and monitoring the Distance Learning Classroom equipment; ensures that all DL equipment is performing according to specifications; reports all malfunctions to the Library Services Specialist and AV Librarian.
20%	1,2,3	Maintains the daily inventory functions of the department, accurately tracking more than 1,000 units of Audio Visual Equipment; submits various inventory reports to AV Librarian in a timely manner; completes and submits missing equipment reports to the AV Librarian; using a variety of computer programs updates master files with information concerning equipment; ensures that all equipment is marked with orange-glo paint, engraved with identifying numbers, attached to carts as needed and engraved numbers painted on carts; ensures that copyright warnings are affixed to VCRs and other equipment.
15%	1,2,3	Monitor the operation of the AV Center including but not limited to assisting students and faculty in the center, delivery of equipment and materials to designated sites. assisting with the college work-study and OPS students, performing clerical duties etc.
9%	1,2,3	Dubs the appropriate number of ITV program copies, making and applying the appropriate labels for ITV titles; audits quality of existing tapes and prepares replacements as needed; maintains collection of tapes for educational access channel shelving materials, reading shelves and searching for missing materials; assists with the inventory of video tape stock; notifies the AV Librarian when the tape stock needs

to be replenished.

| 5% | 1,2,3 | Evaluates malfunctioning equipment, recommending to the AV Librarian that it be repaired or surplused; evaluates repaired equipment to determine if it has been satisfactorily repaired and recommends approval of equipment repair invoices. |
| 1% | 1,2,3 | Inputs character generator data into the channel character generator adding and deleting relevant college information; inputs and deletes information provided by library staff, library director, and other college personnel. |

<u>% Time</u>   <u>Non-Essential Functions (if any)</u>

This document is an accurate description of this position as of the signature dates below.

_____   _____
Employee   Date

_____   _____
First Level Supervisor   Date

_____   _____
Second Level Supervisor   Date

_____   _____
Third Level Supervisor (if applicable)   Date

Tallahassee Community College

Paraprofessional & Clerical Staff

Accounting Clerk
Administrative Assistant
Administrative Secretary
Assessment Center Coordinator
Cataloging Clerk
Co-Op Apprenticeship Coordinator
Cataloging/Acquisition Technician
Circulation Clerk
Circulation Department Assistant
Circulation Department Manager/Administrative Assistant
Circulation Desk Supervisor
Circulation Supervisor
Circulation Technician
ERC Reserve Desk
Evening Library Assistant
Fiscal Technician
Information Services Technician
Interlibrary Loan Clerk
Lab Assistant
Learning Resources Assistant
Learning Resources Clerk
Learning Resources Technical Assistant
Learning Resources Technician
Library Acquisitions Technician
Library Assistant I, II, III
Library Circulation Clerk
Library Clerk
Library Clerk/Computer Assistant
Library Clerk/Technical Services
Library Desk Clerk
LMTA I, II, III
Library/Media Technician
Library/Media Technical Periodicals/ILL
Library Media Technician Processing
Library Paraprofessional
Library Records Manger
Library: Serials Technician
Library Services Clerk
Library Specialist
Library Technical Assistant I, II, IIII
Library Technical Media Assistant
Library Technician I, II, III
Library Technician—Technical Services

LRC Technician I, II, III
Media Assistant
Media Specialist/Acquisitions
Office Assistant I, II, III
Paraprofessional I, II, III
Principal Library Clerk
Receiving Clerk/Typist
Reference Assistant
Secretary
Secretary I, II, III
Secretary to Director Learning Resources Center
Secretary to the Dean of Learning Resources Services
Senior Library Assistant
Senior Library Clerk
Shelver
Specialist Circulation
Specialist Reference Assistant
Specialist Reserves
Specialist Interlibrary Loan
Specialist Circulation Cashier
Staff Assistant I, II, III
Student Assistant
Student Worker
Technical Services Processor
Technician

5-00

Ancilla College
Gerald J. Ball Library
P.O. Box 1
Donaldson, IN 46513
(219) 936-8898

POSITION: Library Assistant
SUPERVISOR: Glenda Bockman
EMPLOYMENT DATES:

RATE OF PAY: $5.15 per hour

JOB PURPOSE:
The Library Assistant serves at the circulation/reference desk and provides clerical and
other library related assistance to Librarian.

DUTIES AND RESPONSIBILITIES:
The Library Student Assistant is responsible for providing appropriate responses to
reference questions and other requests for help from students, faculty, and staff. Often
the initial contact a student makes with the library staff determines their future use of our
library. The Assistant is responsible for representing the library in a positive manner.
Duties may include:

> Charging, discharging, and renewing materials.
> Printing and distributing student overdue/fine notices.
> Collecting fines and issuing receipts.
> Entering patron requests for charged items.
> Accepting interlibrary loan requests from patrons.
> Helping faculty and staff with the fax machine.
> Assisting students with searching the Internet, the on-line catalog, and
>   other electronic resources.
> Helping students with the photocopy machine and making change for it.
> Shelving books, magazines, and other materials.
> Taking telephone requests and messages for the librarian.
> Making on-the-fly records for magazines and other library materials.
> Putting reserve materials into the database.
> Delivering faxes and inter-office mail.
> Doing some word processing.
> Basic reference assistance to students, faculty, and staff.

JOB QUALIFICATIONS:
Applicants for Librarian Assistant should meet the following criteria:

Possess good communication skills.
Be able to interact with students, faculty, staff, and guests.
Give attention to accuracy and detail.
Have some computer experience.
Be honest and reliable.

BARTON COUNTY COMMUNITY COLLEGE

POSITION DESCRIPTION

Position Title:		Classification:	
Evening Library Assistant		Staff	
Organizational Unit:	Reports To:	Date:	Rev. # & Date
Academic Services	Director of Library Services	8-6-92	7-29-99

I. Narrative General Description

Under the direction of the director of Library Services, the Evening Library Assistant is responsible for providing general reference and information services to evening students, and faculty, including circulation and bibliographic instruction duties.

II. Functional Responsibilities

A. Provides general reference service to students, faculty, staff and the general public.
B. Assists students in using electronic resources to locate information.
C. Provides bibliographic instruction to individuals and groups as requested or necessary.
D. Performs copy and original cataloging using electronic resources.
D. Performs circulation duties, such as check-in, check-out, circulation data collection, reserve materials, shelving of books , collection of fines and payments, etc.
E. Assists with other library and information requests as necessary to provide information services to the college community.
F. Coordinates the overdue notices.

III. Consulting Tasks

A. Consults with the Director of Library Services and library staff for planning and problem solving.
B. Consults with other library staff for utilization of student workers.
C. Perform other duties related to the library with outside staff as assigned by the Director of Library Services.

IV. Supervises the Following Staff

A. Evening student employees

V. Required Knowledge, Skills

A. Skill in the use of computers for duties related to library functions. Familiarity with basic computer software.
B. Familiarity with standard library resources in electron and print format.
B. Ability to communicate well, both oral and written.
C. Ability to work with minimal supervision and to initiate work on projects independently.
D. Ability to work well with individuals with various backgrounds.

E. Presentation skills necessary to provide bibliographic instruction as requested in the evening.

F. Ability to supervise student employees.

VI. Required Experience

A. Two years computer experience.

B. Experience in library or information services preferred.

VII. Required Educational Background

A high school diploma or its equivalent required. Coursework in information science, library science, computer, or communication areas is desirable, and an AA or BA is preferred.

VIII.Exemption Status _____ Exempt _X__ Non-exempt

JK:71696:000395

BARTON COUNTY COMMUNITY COLLEGE

POSITION DESCRIPTION

Position Title:		Classification:	
Library Technician		Staff	
Organizational Unit:	Reports To:	Date:	Rev. # & Date
Academic Services	Director of Library Services	12-19-91	1/14/1999

I. Narrative General Description

Under the direction and supervision of the Director of Library Services, the Library Technician is responsible for technical duties which relate to library services, including public services and accounting and ordering of acquisitions. The Library Technician shall be responsible for the general operation of the office of the library.

II. Functional Responsibilities

A. Check in and distribute library mail.
B. Keep records of supplies and materials ordered, and order expendable supplies as necessary and directed.
C. Provide clerical support when necessary.
D. Provide support for the TELENET program by answering questions about courses, figuring time sheets for TELENET monitors and processing paperwork for the business office and K-State.
E. Keep accurate and current files of course syllabi.
F. Type documents for Library Services as needed.
G. Keep accurate and current files of minutes of meetings of all organizations and committees on campus.
H. Keep files for all Library correspondence and documents.
I.   Provide assistance to students and staff who need to use the FAX services.
J. Provide general reference services to students, faculty, staff and the general public, and take requests for more in-depth reference needs for the Director of Library Services.
K. Perform circulation duties, such as, check-in, check-out, circulation data collection, reserve materials, shelving of books, collection of fines and payments, etc.
L. Performs acquisition functions. Assist in the total acquisition process by suggesting materials, and checking requests against the existing catalog.
M. Perform other such duties as may be assigned by the Director of Library Services, and any other appropriate level of administration.

III. Consulting Tasks

A. With the Director of Library Services, provides reports as necessary
B. Works with the BCCC Facility Management personnel and State Telenet personnel to insure scheduling of facilities and use of telenet room, equipment and staffing.
C. Perform other duties related to the library with outside staff as assigned by the Director of Library Services

IV. Supervises the Following Staff

A. Student employees as necessary

Barton County Community College

V. Required Knowledge, Skills

A. Knowledge of general office procedures, i. e. filing, organization, etc.
B. Ability to operate a word processor/computer. Familiarity with basic computer software.
C. Ability to communicate well, both oral and written.
D. Ability to keep information confidential
D. Ability to work with minimal supervision and to initiate work on projects independently.
E. Ability to work well with individuals with various backgrounds.
F. Ability to acquire and perform library related skills such as necessary to provide referral to information sources or staff, to provide circulation assistance, etc.

VI. Required Experience

A. At least two years experience performing the duties of a secretary/receptionist
B. Two years experience organizing an office is preferred
C. At least one year experience operating a word processor/computer
D. Appropriate education may be substituted for required experience as deemed suitable to the position by supervisory staff

VII. Required Educational Background

A. A high school diploma or its equivalent required. Associates degree with computer training preferred.

VIII.Exemption Status

_____ Exempt
_X__ Non-exempt

JK:71896:000061

Library Circulation Clerk

Percentage of Time	Duties and Responsibilities
	PURPOSE: The purpose of this position is to provide assistance at the circulation desk of the Bossier Parish Community College Library. The clerk will serve as an overseer in the daily operation of library circulation and will assist in supervising student workers in routine assignments. The clerk will perform related work as required by circumstances or as directed by supervisor. Position descriptions are subject to change with online automation, utilization of work force, and any other factors that may effect the college's need to modify position requirement.
75%	**GENERAL CLERICAL FUNCTIONS:** Arranges for the circulation of library materials, including reserves. Records statistics done a daily, weekly, monthly and yearly basis. Statistics cover such areas as patron count, book count, magazine count, and audiovisuals count, informational and directional queries, typewriter, Internet, and vertical file usage. Reserves audiovisual equipment for faculty and staff. Notifies students of all overdue books, first by phone and then by postcard. Keeps records of all overdues and fines. Clears those fines paid at the Business Office to avoid delay in report card or registration the following semester. Notifies Registrar's Office of all delinquencies.
20%	Assists Head of Public Services in training student workers in library policies and procedures. Library orientations are given for both former and new student workers each semester. Major issues addressed in orientation include punctuality, assisting patrons at circulation desk, dress code, overview of the collection, shelving and reshelving books, procedures for signing time sheets, and consequences involved if negligent on the job. Assists in student evaluation. Reports all student workers information to Financial Aid Office and Business Office. Clears student workers to work the following semester once all financial responsibilities have been met.
5%	**ESSENTIAL NON-ROUTINE FUNCTIONS:** Provides a warm and wholesome environment conducive to learning. Answers phone inquires. Most inquires are directional, or informational.

Minimum Qualifications:

Must have good interpersonal and communicative skills, a working knowledge of the library and audiovisual equipment, as well as typing and computer skills.

Carl Sandburg College

Job Description

Position Title: Secretary to the Dean of Learning Resources Services

Classification: Secretarial Support

Level: III

Reports to: Dean of Learning Resource Services

Principal Working
Relationship: Dean of Learning Resource Services

Essential Functions

Major Responsibilities

1. Site facilitation and administrative support for distance learning system to include:

    a. Ensuring proper distribution and collection of exams and supplementary materials.

    b. Scheduling training of faculty and staff on the system and maintain records of same.

    c. Maintaining schedule of classes and meetings in distance learning rooms and aiding dean in resolving conflicts

2. Provides administrative support to the Dean for faculty development programs to include preparation and distribution of orientation materials and scheduling of activities.

3. Maintain LRC personnel files including routine records and confidential evaluations for LRC staff.

4. Maintains inventory records for LRC equipment.

5. Maintain records and prepare mailings for special projects and extra duties required of Dean such as Sandburg Scholars and ICISP.

6. Maintain calendars of the Dean of Learning Resources.

7. Prepare all correspondence for the office of Dean.

8. Maintain all files in the office of the Dean including and especially pertaining to grants.

9. Produces all reports required of the office of the Dean.

10. Maintain college historical files in Archives Room (i.e. committee meetings minutes, commencement programs, etc.)

11. Other duties as assigned.

Assists With

1. Writing, processing, and monitoring grants.

2. Other duties as assigned by the Dean.

Preventive Risk Management Activities

1. Participate in and support the college Risk Management Program in a capacity appropriate to this position.

2. Monitoring conditions, events, and circumstances present in the college operations and communicating observations to the appropriate supervisor and/or Risk Management Committee

Minimum Necessary Skills, Experience, and Educational Background

1. Associate degree of 60 hours of college credit or a post-secondary secretarial certificate.

2. Working knowledge of computer systems and software, including word processing and spreadsheet programs.

3. Type 45 – 50 wpm and shorthand or speedwriting required.

4. Must be able to work without supervision with some degree of confidentiality.

Physical Requirements to Perform

1. Manual dexterity (computer work and telephone).

2. Some bending and reaching involved with filing documents.

June 9, 1999

Carl Sandburg College

CENTRAL FLORIDA COMMUNITY COLLEGE

JOB DESCRIPTION

JOB TITLE: LIBRARY SPECIALIST

PAY GRADE: 217

OVERTIME STATUS: NON-EXEMPT

MAJOR RESPONSIBILITY:

To perform para-professional work in supervising an area of library operations under the directions of a Professional Librarian or Director of Learning Resource Center.

PREREQUISITES FOR POSITION (Qualification Standards):

1.   Education or training: Graduation from an accredited four year college or university with a degree in area relating to Learning Resources. Completion of Library Science courses.

2.   Years of experience in field: Three years experience in a library or media production work. A comparable amount of training or experience may be substituted for the minimum qualifications.

3.   Special skills or abilities related to position: Knowledge of various library operational areas. Knowledge of library techniques and practices.

      Ability to establish and maintain working relationships with users. Ability to work with faculty and staff. Ability to operate and demonstrate library equipment. Ability to train and supervise staff.

ESSENTIAL JOB FUNCTIONS:

1.   Supervise the circulation of library materials. Keep circulation statistics and prepare statistical reports for the Library Director.
2.   Account for monies received at the circulation desk.
3.   Send notices to faculty members and students and keep accurate records of overdue materials. Prepare a yearly "due date" schedule and be responsible for changing the dates materials are due.
4.   Participate in taking inventory.
5.   Work closely with faculty members in setting up and maintaining a reserve book collection.

09/17/98

Central Florida Community College

ESSENTIAL JOB FUNCTIONS (Continued):

6. Promote the use of library facilities by instructing patrons in how to use the card catalog, how to locate library materials and how to use them. Provide assistance to patrons in the use of equipment, such as microfilm machines and the location of microtext and newspapers.
7. Answers basic reference questions and provides research assistance to patrons. Supervises reading areas.
8. Verify selection made by the faculty and staff.
9. Update editions of annual publications, encyclopedias and directories. Update replacement copies. Check the card catalog for duplications and process book and periodical orders.
10. Hold position of Supervisor of Access Services.
11. Train, schedule, supervise, and evaluate the performance of staff within Access Services.
12. Develop and implement access service (circulation and processing) procedures and systems to ensure the effective access to library materials.
13. Monitor and coordinate the preparation of related statistics, reports, surveys, manuals, and files associated with Access Services.
14. Coordinate the day-to-day activities within Access Services, which includes the former areas of Library Circulation and Technical Processing.

(These essential job functions are not to be construed as a complete statement of all duties performed. Employees will be required to perform other job related marginal duties as required.)

ESSENTIAL PHYSICAL SKILLS:

- Acceptable eyesight (with or without correction).
- Acceptable hearing (with or without hearing aid).
- Ability to communicate both orally and in writing.
- Ability to access file cabinets for filing and retrieval of data.
- Ability to access, input and retrieve information from a computer.

ENVIRONMENTAL CONDITIONS:

- Works inside in an library environment.

(Reasonable accommodations will be made for otherwise qualified individuals with a disability.)

PRIMARY LOCATION OF JOB: Learning Resources Center, Ocala Campus

SUPERVISOR OF POSITION: Learning Resources Director

09/17/98

CENTRAL FLORIDA COMMUNITY COLLEGE

JOB DESCRIPTION

JOB TITLE: SENIOR LIBRARY ASSISTANT

PAY GRADE: 210

OVERTIME STATUS: NON-EXEMPT

MAJOR RESPONSIBILITY:

To perform advanced and para-professional work in a library, including assuming lead responsibility for the automated LINCC Serials module including microfilm and statistics. Serves as CCLA Serials Contact and Serials Printserver operator, and maintains serials and microfilm collections. Provides general Circulation Services to patrons and participates in materials processing.

PREREQUISITES FOR POSITION (Qualification Standards):

1.   Education or training: A.A. or A.S. degree or equivalent. Coursework in library science, instructional media, computer applications, and records management preferred.

2.   Years of experience in field: Three years experience, reflecting increasingly complex work responsibilities, in a library setting, preferably with one or more years experience with an integrated library automation system.

3.   Special skills or abilities related to position: Positive human relations skills. Ability to establish and maintain working relationships with students, faculty, and co-workers. Ability to meet and deal with the public, using poise, tact and courtesy. General Knowledge of library and office practices and procedures. Ability to work independently and with supervisor and co-workers in a changing environment, demonstrating initiative, teamwork and creative problem-solving skills. Knowledge of computers and other equipment commonly used in a library. Proficiency in written and oral communication skills. Ability to understand the role of the Learning Resources Department and its relationship to the college and the community. Willingness to help others achieve their goals and education. Able to work a flexible schedule which includes evening and weekend duty.

09/17/98

Central Florida Community College

ESSENTIAL JOB FUNCTIONS:

1. Assumes lead responsibility for the automated LINCC Serials module including microfilm and statistics. This includes processing current periodicals and microfilm, serving as liaison to CCLA for the Serials Module, identifying missing issues and cooperating with vendor to replace missing issues, monitoring relevant statewide listservs and documentation, training and assisting co-workers in routine use of the module, and trouble-shooting and resolving any unanticipated challenges.
2. Serves as CCLA Serials Printserver Operator, documenting process, maintaining records and assisting with the compilation of relevant statistics.
3. Maintain serials and microfilm collection, participating in their selection, coordinating shelf maintenance, regularly updating the periodical list holdings, receiving and claiming serials (print and microfilm formats), maintaining the serials holdings database, and serving as CCLA Serials Contact.
4. Provides general circulation services including issuing, renewing and receiving materials for patrons, issuing borrower cards and maintaining patron records, handling overdue f fines, and keeping the circulation area orderly.
5. Prepares statistics, reports, surveys, manuals, and files associated with Access Services.
6. Provide assistance to patrons in the use of library equipment, such as microfilm machines, photocopiers and audiovisual equipment. Initiates appropriate signage and publicity.
7. Answers directional questions and provides basic library assistance to patrons.
8. Oversees reading areas, listening/viewing area, and microfilm areas of library. Maintains library collection by shelving and shelf-reading all materials, and by keeping library picked up and orderly.
9. Participates in book, video, and periodicals verification, ordering, receipt, copy cataloging, physical processing, shelving and circulation.
10. Participates in continuous evaluation of Access Services, work toward the overall effectiveness and cooperation of Library and Media Services staff and services, and participates in the total LRD program review and planning process.
11. Performs any and all other duties as assigned by Director of Learning Resources and/or designee.
12. Assumes and participates also in all responsibilities listed in Library Assistant and Senior Library Assistant Essential Job Functions.

(These essential job functions are not to be construed as a complete statement of all duties performed. Employees will be required to perform other job related marginal duties as required.)

ESSENTIAL PHYSICAL SKILLS:

- Acceptable eyesight (with or without correction).
- Acceptable hearing (with or without hearing aid).

COLUMBUS STATE COMMUNITY COLLEGE
JOB DESCRIPTION
ERC - RESERVE DESK

PAY GRADE:_____   DATE WRITTEN:_____

                                    DATE REVISED :_____

POSITION: _____   WRITTEN BY: _____

TITLE: Library Services Clerk (Reserve and Cataloged Collections/A-V Labs)

SUMMARY: Performs all the tasks to maintain the smooth operation of the reserve collection, provides collection maintenance of the cataloged collection, and provides assistance to users in the use of A-V lab equipment, and reserve and cataloged collections.

RELATIONSHIP: Reports to the Director of Educational Resources and provides guidance to any part-time employees assigned to this function. Interfaces regularly with ERC staff and Columbus State students and employees.

DUTIES AND
RESPONSIBILITIES:

1. Responsible for operation/maintenance of Reserve collection including cable courses. ERC materials are accurately processed for reserve shelf within two (2) days of receipt of list according to outline procedures (CSLINK). Reserve shelves are read daily. All reserve materials are shelved immediately after use.

2. Assist with problems in PC lab. Communicates information to director and all library staff of any updates made to PC lab. Also communicates with Data Center on updates and information about PC lab.

3. Responsible for operation/maintenance of equipment - AV lab, viewing rooms, copier. Maintains equipment in proper working order at all times and notifies repairman as needed. Order supplies in a timely manner so that they are available as needed. Troubleshoot problems with A-V equipment.

4. Responsible for overseeing maintenance, shelving, and shelf reading of ERC cataloged circulating collection. Returned and in-house used materials are shelved accurately and according to set procedures within 24 hours. Main collection is read continuously on a daily basis and problem areas are resolved within 24 hours.

5. Responsible for assisting patrons using A-V lab equipment, reserve materials, online catalog, and cataloged circulating collection. Library Services Clerk is available on top floor during assigned times to assist patrons as requested according to ERC established procedures.

6. Responsible for hourly library assistants assigned to the reserve/A-V lab/cataloged collection area (top floor). Library assistants are trained and evaluated according to established time frames and formats. Work of library assistants is planned, guided and monitored so that assigned work and tasks are accurately accomplished on a daily basis.

7. Responsible for reporting usage statistics. Monthly reserve and copier statistics are accurately maintained and submitted to Directors office within two (2) working days after the end of each month.

8. Assists with other library services operations as needed. Maintains top floor areas to provide an atmosphere conducive to study.

9. Responsible for preparing materials for reference telephone directories. Telephone directories are accurately processed for reference collection and filed within one (1) week of receipt.

10. Assists in providing current and relevant ERC resources and services. Reviews professional journals and makes recommendations for appropriate additions to the collection. Participates in the ongoing process of missing and damaged items according to outlined procedures and time frames. Also provides reference librarian with updated copies throughout quarter.

11. Contact person to Human Resources. Responsible for reviewing applicants, interviewing, hiring, and scheduling of student workers for all public service areas. Work closely with Human Resources by completing all necessary forms.

12. ERC tours. Give tours as needed to classes after ERC orientations. Explain use and function of the ERC's various areas.

AUTHORITY: Operates within the procedures and methods of the Library Services Department and the ERC, as well as specific guidelines established by the Director of Educational Resources Directs the work and provides guidance to part-time employees assigned to the reserve and cataloged collections/PC and A-V labs.

TITLE: Library Clerk

<u>Summary Description:</u>

Ensure library materials are properly arranged and executes routine clerical tasks. Performs other related work as required. Reports to the Director, Learning Resource Center. Supervises work study students.

<u>Major Responsibilities</u>

1. Checks books in and out, inspects books and maintains records on library material in circulation.

2. Demonstrates the use of various machines in the facility such as copying, microfilm, facsimile, VCR's and computers.

3. Answers telephone, takes requests and reserves books for faculty.

4. Types cards and other materials as required.

5. Shelves returned books, straightens books or magazines and ensures that they are in proper order.

6. Performs secretarial duties for the Director of the Learning Resource Center.

7. Takes interlibrary loan requests, searches library location, prepares forms and sends out requests.

8. Files cards using standard filing rules.

9. Performs other work as assigned.

<u>Recommended Qualifications</u>

Education/Training

  High School diploma

Background/Experience:

Experience in libraries or offices which deal with the public and where the person has had to pay close attention to detail.

Specific Skills:

1.   Knowledge of modern office machines, methods and equipment, including word processing.

2.   Knowledge of basic filing, indexing, and cross-reference methods.

3.   Ability to type accurately from plain copy or rough draft.

4.   Ability to understand and follow oral and written instructions.

5.   Ability to communicate oral information in a courteous manner.

6.   Ability to establish and maintain an effective working relationship with students, the public , and other employees.

Other: Must be willing to work evenings and week-ends.

FLORIDA KEYS COMMUNITY COLLEGE

Rev. Sept. 18, 1999

JOB TITLE: Library Specialist

GENERAL DESCRIPTION:
The Library Specialist performs paraprofessional work involving detailed knowledge of library and computer operations. Performs all aspects of library services in regards to providing library support for students, staff and the general public. Work is performed under the supervision of the Librarian.

ESSENTIAL JOB FUNCTIONS:
1.   Provides skilled reference assistance in the use of and retrieval from print and electronic resources, e.g. LINCC, Internet, Newsbank.

2.   Manages automated circulation functions, including reserve room, reports, liaison with the College Center for Library Automation (CCLA) and the Business Office, and staff training.

3.   Performs advanced and specialized technical services duties, e.g. cataloging, acquisitions, serials, interlibrary loan, and liaison with CCLA and the Business Office.

4.   Coordinates all aspects of the Federal Government Depository Library Program, including collection development, maintenance of the collection, preparing statistical and other reports, document processing, reference to users (via increasingly electronic means).

5.   Assists all users with general and specialized software and computer systems.

6.   Coordinates donations evaluation, correspondence and processing.

7.   Serves as liaison between the library and staff computer network needs and the Technology Support Services staff.

8.   Assists in evaluation activities such as collection studies, user surveys, and statistical report analysis.

9.   Assists in outreach, instruction, and public relations activities.

10. Supervises work of and trains student workers.

11. Participates in activities for the general good of the library such as circulating and shelving materials,answering telephones, assisting with equipment use.

12. Serves as staff back-up, as needed, for various library functions.

13. Participates in college committees and activities, e.g. switchboard, FACC, Career Council.

MINIMUM QUALIFICATIONS
    KNOWLEDGE, ABILITIES AND SKILLS

* Knowledge of computer hardware and software used in library operations
* Knowledge of principles and practices of library operations
* Knowledge of basic reference tools and skills as they relate to library science
* Knowledge of English, spelling, basic math
* Knowledge of basic office practices, procedures and equipment
* Ability to operate audiovisual equipment
* Ability to establish and maintain effective working relationships with staff, students and the public
* Ability to learn assigned tasks readily and to adhere to prescribed routines
* Ability to work some evenings and weekends
* Organizational skills

EDUCATION AND EXPERIENCE
Graduation from an accredited two year college or two years of library work experience.
    Working knowledge of audio visual equipment (TVS, VCRs, cameras, etc.) and experience in computer use and Internet access.

LICENSES, CERTIFICATION OR REGISTRATION
None

ESSENTIAL PHYSICAL SKILLS
* Acceptable eyesight (with or without corrections)
* Acceptable hearing (with or without aid)
* Moderate (15 to 44 pounds) lifting and carrying
* Pushing, walking and standing for periods of time

ENVIRONMENTAL CONDITIONS
* Works inside in an office environment
(Reasonable accommodations will be made for otherwise qualified individuals with a disablility.)

TITLE	Job Description Administrative Secretary	NUMBER	2.4
DATE	April 1998	PAGE	1 of 1

JOB TITLE: Administrative Secretary

REPORTS TO: Director of the Library and Instructional Technology

BASIC FUNCTION: Advanced secretarial and administrative duties which involves complex and varied work methods

CLASSIFICATION: Career Service (Grade 10)

DUTIES AND RESPONSIBILITIES:

Acts as personal secretary and/or aid to the Director of the Library and Instructional Technology. Perform secretarial duties of considerable variety and complexity with administrative responsibility requiring a mastery of office skills. Interviews office visitors and answers questions regarding the services or operation of the unit.

Completes forms independently and composes letters for supervisor's signature. Is familiar with various dictating/transcribing equipment, as necessary.

Organizes and maintains files related to the upkeep and maintenance of all subject matter pertaining to the respective office. Files letters, reports and related technical information in a prescribed manner. Assembles information for supervisor's use.

Maintains a calendar of appointments, meetings and events for the supervisor. Advises supervisor of important meetings. Receives and screens callers. Refers callers to other employees, officials or departments as needed.

Exercises independent judgement for overall operation of the office. Makes decisions in accordance with departmental and college rules, regulations and policies. Establishes and maintains effective working relationships with employees and the public.

Is proficient in business English and spelling. Takes minutes of conferences, meetings and official functions as required.

Perform other duties as may be assigned.

MINIMUM QUALIFICATIONS:

Graduation from high school or possession of an equivalency diploma. Typing speed of 55 correct words per minute. Four years of secretarial/clerical experience. A comparable amount of training and experience may be substituted for the minimum qualifications.

POSITION: Secretary to Director
                 Learning Resource Center
CLASSIFICATION: O & C II
INCUMBENT:·

SUPERVISOR: Marty Stilwell

_____
                       (Signature)

DATE._____

POSITION PURPOSE AND OBJECTIVE

Provides complete secretarial service and support to the
Director and other assigned professionals in the department.

ESSENTIAL JOB FUNCTIONS

1. Core Secretarial Competencies.

WORKING CONDITIONS

The functions of this position are performed primarily in the
Learning Resource Center (LRC).

MINIMUM QUALIFICATIONS

Post-secondary preparation and two (2) years of secretarial
experience in an automated office. The incumbent must have
good human relations skills to coordinate the Director's
activities and perform duties that require constant contact
with the public.

PRINCIPAL ACCOUNTABILITIES

1. Courtesy and cooperation in dealings with others.

2. Assuring the efficient administration of the office by
    performing full secretarial duties in support of the
    Director and others in the department as assigned. This
    would include sorting mail, phone screening, typing,
    filing, etc.

3. Assuring quality administrative support services
    including compilation of reports, data collection, etc.,
    allowing the Director to concentrate on professional
    matters.

4. Preparing and distributing accurate departmental
    information (reports, etc.) for various end users:
    faculty, students, administration, etc.

5. Supporting telecourse program by: promptly addressing
    questions; monitoring registration of students;
    assembling and updating telecourse packet information;
    mailing telecourse packets; providing information to the
    instructor for purposes of monitoring enrollment and
    student status; assisting with the distribution of
    telecourse tapes to libraries and cable stations; and
    timely preparation of enrollment reports for telecourse
    licensing agencies.

6/98M

Core Secretarial Competencies

1. Communicate with a diverse population of students, College personnel and community by telephone and in person.

2. Operate a personal computer using a variety of software for word processing and information storage and retrieval purposes.

3. Operate general office equipment.

4. Visually examine, interpret and complete documents and forms.

5. Generate correspondence, reports and listings. Open, maintain and close files and databases.

6. Reception: provide customer service, handle inquiries, make referrals and direct visitors.

7. Bend, reach and move files and groups of files to and from desks and file drawers.

8. Travel throughout the campus.

9. Regular attendance.

Revised 11/99

Part-Time Library Technician

This is a part-time library technician position, M-Th, 3:00-8:00. The position reports to the Director of the Library. He/she will be responsible for processing acquisitions, circulation, copy cataloging on and offline, and some ready reference.

Duties and Responsibilities
- Do copy cataloging, both online and offline, meeting OCLC and AACR2 standards.
- Work at the circulation desk, when needed.
- Run circulation reports, using the automated system.
- Perform ready reference as back up to the reference librarians.
- Search in OCLC for inter-library loans.
- Physical processing of acquisitions.
- Linking records in the automated system, as part of the retrospective conversion project.
- Occasional supervision of student workers.
- Other duties as assigned.

Minimum Requirements
- Some keyboard skills (20+ wpm.)
- Associate's degree with experience in college research.
- 1-2 years of library experience, academic library experience preferred.
- Knowledge of OCLC searching, OCLC copy cataloging experience preferred.
- Knowledge of cataloging using Library of Congress call numbers and subject headings and AACR2 preferred.

Job Dimensions
Attention to detail   Technical/professional self development
Dependability   Teamwork
Work standards   Self Reliance
Knowledge of work   Informal communication
Sensitivity

NICOLET AREA TECHNICAL COLLEGE
Position Description

Name: **Department:** Richard J. Brown Library

Position Title: Circulation Department Assistant   **Date:**

Pay Grade: **Reports To:** Dean of Transitional College
                                                              Learning Resources

---

Position Summary:

Under the routine supervision of the Circulation Desk Manager, is responsible for performing a wide variety of circulation desk responsibilities.

Duties/Responsibilities:

The following duties are normal for this position. These are not to be construed as exclusive or all-inclusive. Other duties may be required and assigned.

- Checks returned material and prepares them to be returned to the shelf.

- Maintains overdue and fine notices.

- Files, indexes, and updates information concerning LRC reference materials.

- Shelves LRC periodicals, ensuring they are filed in the proper place.

- Assists patrons, students, and faculty with questions and with locating materials.

- Assists with inter-library loans. Processes requests, locates, material, checks out and sends materials as requested.

- Processes mail as requested.

- Answers telephones and greets visitors.

- Assists in organizing and maintaining reserve materials for faculty members.

- Helps students and faculty run software programs and computer equipment in a very progressive library setting.

- Shuts down all equipment when closing down the library for the night.

Position Description

Page 2 of 3

- Runs reports for the day that are required to keep records for the LRC circulation desk.

- Assists other staff as necessary.

- Edit all library cards.

- Check new materials and ready them for the shelf.

- Type all labels for video sleeves including pricing, rating, and time.

Work Direction Received:

Works under the routine supervision of the Circulation Desk Manager.

Supervision Exercised:

None

Decision Making:

Decisions are made independently concerning daily activities, assisting patrons with problems, and shelving materials.

Interaction:

There is significant interaction with faculty, staff, students, and the general public.

Desirable Knowledge and Abilities:

Knowledge of modern library practices and procedures, office practices and procedures, coding and filing requirements, and general policies and procedures affecting the LRC. Ability to pay attention to detail, file materials, accurately, communicate effectively orally and in writing, and interact effectively with patrons.

Training and Experience:

Graduation from high school, and one-two years of library experience.

Nicolet Area Technical College

Position Description

Page 3 of 3

In evaluating candidates for this position, Nicolet may consider a combination of education, training, and experience which provides the necessary knowledge, skills, and abilities to perform the duties of the position. Normally, education may be substituted for experience, or experience substituted for education, on a year for year basis.

NICOLET AREA TECHNICAL COLLEGE
Position Description

Name:		**Department:** Library
Position Title:	. Circulation Department Manager/Administrative Assistant	**Reports To:** Dean of Transitional College and Learning Resources

Position Summary:
Under the general supervision of the Dean of Transitional College and Learning Resources Center, is responsible for managing the Library Circulation Department.

Duties/Responsibilities:
The following duties are normal for this position. These are not to be construed as exclusive or all-inclusive. Other duties may be required and assigned.

- Writes and implements procedures for circulation of Library materials and Interlibrary Loans.

- Plans and monitors the work flow for the Library Circulation Department. Ensures all work is completed in a timely fashion.

- Assigns duties to Library Circulation Department staff. Instructs and guides personnel in the performance of duties.

- Instructs and assists patrons and staff in the use of the Winnebago Circ/Cat On-line Catalog, CD Rom, and other related online devices.

- Instructs and assists patrons and staff in the use of Library resources.

- Writes and implements procedures for circulation/management of Lakeland Campus Library materials.

- Provides guidelines for Native American Office for circulation of Library material.

- Provides reference assistance as required.

Work Direction Received:
Works under the general supervision of the Dean of the Transitional College Learning Resources.

Supervision Exercised:
Oversees the work of support staff.

Decision Making:
Decisions are made independently concerning activities of the Circulation Department, including policies and procedures, assigning staff responsibilities, processing Interlibrary Loans, and circulation of Library materials.

Nicolet Area Technical College

Interaction:
There is significant interaction with other libraries, other college departments, students, faculty, staff, and the general public.

Desirable Knowledge and Abilities:
Knowledge of library/media operating procedures, modern library principles, methods, practices and technology, audiovisual materials, and policies and procedures affecting the Library Circulation Department. Ability to interpret, use, teach, and explain the use of all library/media facilities, oversee the work of others, communicate effectively orally and in writing, and interact effectively with students, faculty, staff, and the general public.

Training and Experience:
Bachelor's Degree in Library Science or related field, and three-five years of library experience.

In evaluating candidates for this position, Nicolet may consider a combination of education, training, and experience which provides the necessary knowledge, skills, and abilities to perform the duties of the position. Normally, education may be substituted for experience, or experience substituted for education, on a year for year basis.

Nunez Community College

Technical Service Processor
Library Specialist II Duties:

Organizational relationships. The Library Paraprofessional 2 works closely with the chief Cataloging Librarian and is under the general supervision and coordination of the Director of Library Services.

Job Summary. Assists the library staff in the proper utilization, operation, maintenance, and function of the library. Establishes and maintains appropriate working relationships with administrators, faculty, staff, students, and general public. Maintains confidentiality in all matters related to library patrons.

1. 20 %: Search OCLC, LOUIS catalogs, and Library of Congress Catalog for matching bibliographic records for new acquisitions and gift item
2. 20%: Enter brief bibliographic and item records into the library catalog.
3. 20 %: Process new acquisitions (books, videos, audiocassettes, CD-ROM's, computer disks) with appropriate stamps, security strips, typewritten spine labels, pockets and cards. Type new acquisition list for records.
4. 20%: Perform catalog maintenance on ELAINet as needed; search ELAINet for unauthorized headings, importing authority records from LOUIS sites and OCLC as needed.
5. 15%: Check in and stamp monthly state document shipments; send off shipments of Nunez documents to State Library; maintain documents collections and keep finding aid updated. Assist with archives.
6. 5%: Other duties as assigned by the Director of Library Services.

Normal Schedule.   Monday – Friday 8:00 am to 4:30 pm; can be asked to cover any time the library is open in unusual circumstances (open positions; illness, leave of other employees)

(May 15, 2000 updated)

St. Petersburg Junior College

POSITION DESCRIPTION

POSITION TITLE: **Library Assistant**

DEPARTMENT: **Library** SITE: **Various**

SALARY SCHEDULE: **Career** - GRADE: **8**

BASIC FUNCTION:

Performs a variety of library clerical duties in the campus libraries.

RESPONSIBILITIES:

- Performs clerical work at the Circulation Desk.
- Performs a variety of clerical work in library departments, such as periodicals, audiovisuals, acquisitions or media production.
- Assists library professional in carrying out clerical and secretarial functions including preparing purchase orders, budget records, typing, maintaining records and/or log books.
- Performs receptionist duties, handles phone calls and other inquiries and maintains the areas assigned in absence of the library professional.
- Orders books in accordance with professional direction.
- Performs clerical and secretarial duties.
- Operates microcomputer in providing services to other areas.
- Prepares library and departmental statistical data. Compiles circulation statistics.
- Performs related duties as required.

EDUCATIONAL REQUIREMENTS:

Graduation from an accredited high school or possession of an acceptable equivalency diploma.

EXPERIENCE REQUIREMENTS:

Two (2) years of general clerical, secretarial or public service experience.

KNOWLEDGE/ABILITIES/SKILL REQUIREMENTS:

Knowledge of sentence structure. Knowledge of word usage. Skill in reading comprehension. Skill in proofreading. Knowledge of basic mathematics. Ability to keyboard at a prescribed rate of speed and accuracy. Ability to operate a calculator. Ability to operate computer equipment. Ability to lift up to 20 pounds. Ability to reach library shelves. Ability to deal effectively with people.

Revised 5/96

St. Petersburg Junior College

St. Petersburg Junior College

POSITION DESCRIPTION

POSITION TITLE: **Library Paraprofessional**

DEPARTMENT: **Library** SITE: **Various**

SALARY SCHEDULE: **Career** - GRADE: **13**

BASIC FUNCTION:

Performs responsible paraprofessional work in a college library.

RESPONSIBILITIES:

- Supervises a section or unit of a library under the direction of a professional librarian.
- Prepares procedures manuals for the section to which assigned.
- Trains and evaluates clerical staff.
- Performs complex clerical and record keeping functions.
- Performs support activities such as bookkeeping, compiling budget data, statistics, controlling supplies, handling mail, routing correspondence, preparing time schedules, payrolls, etc.
- Assists in the acquisition of library materials.
- Assists in cataloging and classification of materials.
- Maintains audiovisual room. Shows video tapes to students.
- Performs related duties as required.

EDUCATIONAL REQUIREMENTS:

Two (2) years of college-level study; or Associate's degree with or without library technical assistant training; or post-secondary training in relevant skills.

EXPERIENCE REQUIREMENTS:

Three (3) years experience in library work or an equivalent combination of education and experience.

KNOWLEDGE/ABILITIES/SKILL REQUIREMENTS:

Knowledge of library equipment, materials and techniques. Knowledge of library research techniques. Knowledge of sentence structure. Knowledge of word usage. Skill in reading comprehension. Skill in proofreading. Knowledge of basic mathematics. Ability to keyboard at a prescribed rate of speed and accuracy. Ability to operate a calculator. Ability to operate computer equipment. Ability to lift up to 20 pounds. Ability to deal effectively with people. Language arts skills.

Revised 5/96

St. Petersburg Junior College

SOUTH FLORIDA COMMUNITY COLLEGE
POSITION DESCRIPTION

POSITION TITLE: Library Clerk, Technical Services

CLASSIFICATION: Career Service, Level I

REPORTS TO: Director, Library Services

SUPERVISES: Student assistants as assigned

SUMMARY: A part-time, year-round position, responsible for Technical Services.

DUTIES AND RESPONSIBILITIES:

1. Assists in processing new acquisitions.

2. Assists in maintaining LINCC master database.

3. Works the Circulation Desk in charging, discharging, and renewing materials.

4. Answers the telephone and channels calls to appropriate personnel.

5. Assists in covering public service areas as needed.

6. Maintains current knowledge of routines and activities within areas of responsibility.

7. Acts in accordance with College policies and procedures.

8. Performs other duties as assigned.

EDUCATIONAL
REQUIREMENTS: High school diploma or equivalency preferred.

EXPERIENTIAL
REQUIREMENTS: Previous library experience preferred.

SPECIAL
CONSIDERATIONS: Computer literacy preferred. Flexibility in scheduling required.

I understand and accept the duties
and responsibilities of this position. _____
Employee Signature   Date

LIBCLKPT.TECH.PD
06/21/99

South Florida Community College

SOUTH FLORIDA COMMUNITY COLLEGE
POSITION DESCRIPTION

POSITION TITLE: Reference Assistant

CLASSIFICATION: Career Service, Level III

REPORTS TO: Evening/Center Librarian

SUPERVISES: Student workers

SUMMARY: A full-time position responsible for Reference functions of the
                    SFCC library.

DUTIES AND RESPONSIBILITIES:

1.   Responsible for Reference functions of the Library.

2.   Provides reference service to library users.

3.   Assists with Interlibrary Loans.

4.   Supervises student workers as assigned.

5.   Acts in accordance with College policies and procedures.

6.   Performs other duties as assigned.

EDUCATIONAL
REQUIREMENTS: Associate Degree or substantial College level course work
                required. Bachelor's degree preferred.

EXPERIENTIAL
REQUIREMENTS: Three years of library experience required. Related degree work
                may substitute for experience requirement.

I understand and accept the duties
and responsibilities of this position. _____
                                        Employee Signature   Date

REFASST.PD
2/23/95

SOUTH FLORIDA COMMUNITY COLLEGE
POSITION DESCRIPTION

POSITION TITLE: Reference Assistant, Part-time

CLASSIFICATION: Career Service, Level III

REPORTS TO: Evening/Center Librarian

SUPERVISES: Student workers

SUMMARY: A part-time position responsible for the evening and Sunday
Reference and Public Service functions of the SFCC library.

DUTIES AND RESPONSIBILITIES:

1.   Responsible for evening and Sunday Reference functions of the Library.

2.   Provides evening and Sunday reference service to library users.

3.   Assists with Interlibrary Loans.

4.   Supervises student workers as assigned.

5.   Acts in accordance with College policies and procedures.

6.   Performs other duties as assigned.

EDUCATIONAL
REQUIREMENTS: Associate Degree or substantial College level course work
required. Bachelor's degree preferred.

EXPERIENTIAL
REQUIREMENTS: Three years of library experience required. Related degree work
may substitute for experience requirement.

I understand and accept the duties
and responsibilities of this position. _____
                                                          Employee Signature   Date

REFASST.EVE
2/23/95

Tallahassee Community College
POSITION DESCRIPTION

Employee Name:

Position Number: 41405

Position Title: Library Technical Assistant I

Department/Division/Section: Reference Department/Division of Library Services

Working Hours/Total Hours in Work Week: 40
12:00 p.m. - 9:00 p.m. Monday
8:00 a.m. - 5:00 p.m. Tuesday - Friday
9:00 a.m. - 1:00 p.m. Saturday, as assigned

Name and title of immediate supervisor: Janys Barnidge, Reference Librarian

Name and titles of employees directly supervised: Work study and OPS as assigned

List machines or equipment used regularly in work. Give estimated percentage of total job time spent in operation of each:

Personal computer (35%); computer terminals (25%); microformat reader-printers (15%); typewriter (5%); photocopier (2%); calculator (1%)

In addition to the knowledge, skills, and abilities for this position *(see next page)*, **it has been determined that the following minimum training and experience requirements are necessary for a position in this classification:** *(see class specification)*

Graduation from a standard high school or equivalency diploma and four years of progressively responsible sub-professional library experience. Successful completion of college course work may be substituted at the rate of 30 semester hours on a year-for-year basis or 720 classroom hours from a vocational or technical school for the required experience. Ability and dexterity to operate a computer in accessing, inputting, and retrieving information.

Because an employee in this position has access to college funds and confidential records and/or the ability to alter applications programming, any record of prior convictions, pleas or sentences for felonies or third degree misdemeanors may be considered in making a selection.

Tallahassee Community College

List the knowledge, skills and abilities required to perform the duties and responsibilities of this position:

-Knowledge of TCC Library policies and procedures
-Knowledge of Reference Department policies and procedures
-Knowledge of Technical Service policies and procedures
-Knowledge of Circulation Department policies and procedures
-Knowledge of Audio Visual Department policies and procedures
-Knowledge of LINCC and databases available through the Information Gateway
-Knowledge of LINCC circulation module
-Knowledge of all bibliographic and full-text CD-ROM databases, online databases and multimedia CD-ROM databases in the Reference Department
-Knowledge of the operation and maintenance of microformat reader/printers and coin changer machine
-Knowledge of good grammar, vocabulary, spelling and formats of business correspondence
-Knowledge of Library of Congress subject headings and Library of Congress classification
-Knowledge of time and attendance procedures for entering payroll

-Skill in typing a minimum of 35 CWPM with accuracy and speed
-Skill in using complex computer databases and Boolean operators
-Skill in using networked computers on a LAN system
-Skill in operating personal computer software: word processing, databases, spreadsheets, desktop publishing and graphic design
-Skill in troubleshooting computer hardware problems
-Skill in troubleshooting microformat readers and printers and department and division photocopy machines
-Skill in operating multi-line telephone system and facsimile machine

-Ability to plan, organize, prioritize and coordinate work assignments
-Ability to understand and follow oral and written instructions and manuals
-Ability to follow established policies and procedures
-Ability to handle reference queries, complaints, and/or problems in person or by telephone and when to refer the requests, etc. to other personnel
-Ability to communicate effectively with faculty, students, staff, supervisors, and fellow workers
-Ability to perform as part of a public service team
-Ability to communicate effectively verbally and in writing
-Ability to work independently
-Ability to alphabetize
-Ability to train and supervise student assistants
-Ability to instruct others in the use of microformat machines
-Ability to instruct others in the use of online and CD-ROM databases
-Ability to assist and instruct others in basic computer commands for retrieval of information
-Ability to assist and instruct library users with varying technical skills
-Ability to answer the telephone
-Ability to bend, lift, pull, sit, stand, stoop, and reach for extended periods of time
-Ability to push 25 pound book truck and reach 6 foot high shelves
-Ability to handle money, make deposits at Business Office, and maintain statistical records of daily and weekly transactions
-Ability to work in a stressful environment
-Ability to work in a public service area with constant interruptions
-Ability to work in a rapidly changing technological environment
-Ability to audit time sheets and enter them into the computer and follow procedures detailed in notebook

Tallahassee Community College

DIRECTIONS: Summarize each duty/responsibility including percentage of time spent in area on an average annual basis. Please be succinct in each summary; the majority of positions can be summarized using only this form with no attachments.

Each duty/responsibility must be listed either as an _essential_ or _non-essential_ function. Use as many of the numeric codes listed below as appropriate to justify why each duty/responsibility has been designated as an essential function.

EF CODES: A job function is considered to be essential if:

#1.   The position exists to perform the function.

#2.   There are a limited number of other employees available to perform the function, or among whom the function can be distributed.

#3.   A function is highly specialized, and the person in the position is hired for special expertise or ability to perform it.

% Time	EF Codes	Essential Functions
40%	1,2,3	Answers general information, directional and reference questions; assists and instructs students, faculty, and staff in the use of LINCC, online and CD-ROM databases; assists and instructs students, faculty, and staff in the use of microformat reader/printers
15%	1,2,3	Types new and revised bibliographies, guides, and handouts which require use of desktop publishing, graphics, and page layout; trains and supervises student worker in inventory; maintains inventory of all handouts in computer; processes print requests
15%	1,2,3	Prepares order slips using a computer for vertical file materials and serials, consisting of paid, free, and GPO; tabulates total costs and enters data into LOTUS; files slips for vertical file and serial orders; assigns existing subject headings to pamphlets; checks LINCC for call numbers of unsolicited serials; processes vertical file materials; orders free materials preparing letters and postcards; maintains mailing addresses of state agencies
11%	1,2,3	Maintains microformat room including ordering and inventory of supplies and serves as contact person for service problems/maintenance of all machines; counts and submits monies received from reader/printers and coin changer to Business Office; maintains bookkeeping records; trains and supervises OPS and work study students in maintenance, operation and cleaning of machines; troubleshoots problems with machines; develops written procedures for microformat machines, coin changer, and collection of monies and other items as needed
6%	1,2,3	Serves as computer contact person for the department; maintains records for microcomputer job requests; delivers CD-ROM discs to Information Technology and checks database computers to verify successful installation on the LAN; troubleshoots computer hardware problems for LINCC terminals, staff computers, and LAN computers; maintains paper and ribbons for computers
6%	1,2	Types correspondence, supply requests, supply orders, work orders, and other documents required in support of reference service functions; makes routine phone calls soliciting brochures, order information and price quotes; serves as telephone contact person for people calling the department; inventories, orders, and checks in all supplies
5.5%	1,2	Tabulates data necessary for department reports, department statistics and budget information using spreadsheet
1%	1,2	Assists in collection maintenance such as reshelving, shifting materials, inventory of collection, etc.; performs other duties essential to efficient operation and effective service; assumes student worker tasks when necessary; cooperates as team member with other staff performing any duty essential to the achievement of efficient library operations
.5%	2	Trained as backup for auditing time sheets/leave slips for Division personnel; monthly payroll certification for faculty, classified staff, OPS and CWSP. Will perform duties as needed

Tallahassee Community College

Tallahassee Community College
POSITION DESCRIPTION

Employee Name:

Position Number: 44101

Position Title: Library Technical Assistant II

Department/Division/Section: Educational Services/Library Services/Reference

Working Hours/Total Hours in Work Week: 40 hours; 7:15 - 4:15 M-F;
9 - 1 on fifth Saturday
backup person at night

Name and title of immediate supervisor: Janys Barnidge, Reference Librarian

Name and titles of employees <u>directly</u> supervised: 4 - 5 work study students and OPS

List machines or equipment used regularly in work. Give estimated percentage of total job time spent in operation of each:

personal computer (30%); computer terminals (35%);
microformat readers and printers (12%); photocopier (1%)

In addition to the knowledge, skills, and abilities for this position *(see next page)*, **it has been determined that the following <u>minimum training and experience requirements</u> are necessary for a position in this classification:** *(see class specification)*

Graduation from a standard high school or equivalency diploma and four years of progressively responsible sub-professional library experience.

Successful completion of college course work may be substituted at the rate of 30 semester hours on a year-for-year basis or 720 classroom hours from a vocational or technical school for the required experience.

Because an employee in this position has access to college funds and confidential records and/or the ability to alter applications programming, any record of prior convictions, pleas or sentences for felonies or third degree misdemeanors may be considered in making a selection.

List the knowledge, skills and abilities required to perform the duties and responsibilities of this position:

-Knowledge of TCC campus services and programs
-Knowledge of TCC Library policies and procedures
-Knowledge of Reference Department policies and procedures
-Knowledge of Technical Service policies and procedures
-Knowledge of Circulation Department policies and procedures
-Knowledge of Audio Visuals Department policies and procedures
-Knowledge of reference sources
-Knowledge of all bibliographic and full-text databases, online and CD-ROM, in the Reference Department
-Knowledge of LINCC and LINCCWeb
-Knowledge of the operation of microformat machines
-Knowledge of bibliographic records and working knowledge of Library of Congress subject headings and Library of Congress classification, and American Library Association filing rules
-Knowledge of the Internet
-Knowledge of copyright law

-Skill in typing a minimum of 35 cwpm with accuracy and speed
-Skill in using complex computer databases and Boolean operators
-Skill in operating personal computer software: word processing, databases, specialized programs
-Skill in using networked computers on a LAN system
-Skill in troubleshooting microformat readers and reader printers
-Skill in troubleshooting computer terminals and printers
-Skill in using NETCAT to access LC authority files and MFHD (MARC format for holdings data) records

-Ability to plan, organize, prioritize and coordinate work assignments
-Ability understand and follow detailed oral and written instructions and manuals performing work requiring a high degree of detail and accuracy
-Ability to follow established policies and procedures

Tallahassee Community College

-Ability to handle reference queries, complaints, and/or problems in person or by telephone and to know when to refer the requests, etc. to other personnel
-Ability to perform as part of a public service team
-Ability to communicate effectively, verbally and in writing
-Ability to work independently
-Ability to alphabetize and file
-Ability to train and supervise student assistants
-Ability to instruct other in the use of microformat machines
-Ability to instruct others in the use of online and CD-ROM databases and the Internet
-Ability to assist and instruct library users with varying technical expertise
-Ability to use Library of Congress subject headings and Library of Congress classification
-Ability to set up and maintain records
-Ability to answer the telephone
-Ability to bend, lift, stoop or reach and sit or stand for extended periods of time
-Ability to push or pull a 65 pound book truck, reach 6 foot high shelves, and lifT 35 lbs.
-Ability to create new handouts and revise existing ones
-Ability to work with constant interruptions
-Ability work in a rapidly changing technological environment
-Ability to work in a stressful environment

DUTIES AND RESPONSIBILITIES

DIRECTIONS: Summarize each duty/responsibility including percentage of time spent in area on an average annual basis. Please be succinct in each summary; the majority of positions can be summarized using only this form with no attachments.

Each duty/responsibility must be listed either as an essential or non-essential function. Use as many of the numeric codes listed below as appropriate to justify why each duty/responsibility has been designated as an essential function.

EF CODES: A job function is considered to be essential if:

#1.   The position exists to perform the function.

#2.   There are a limited number of other employees available to perform the function, or among whom the function can be distributed.

#3.   A function is highly specialized, and the person in the position is hired for special expertise or ability to perform it.

% Time	EF Codes	Essential Functions
45%	1,2,3	Answers general information, directional and reference questions; assist and instructs students, faculty and staff in the use of LINCC, online and CD-ROM databases, the Internet, microformat readers/printers
32%	1,2,3	Processes and supervises processing of vertical file materials; assigns subject headings to pamphlets, maps, posters, and prints; determines materials needing new subject headings; maintains appropriate files; reviews vertical file job duties of LTA 1; assumes responsibility for maintaining vertical files, including filing, weeding, and revisions; coordinates new and retrospective barcoding of vertical file materials
10%	1,2,3	Researches, verifies, and selects materials for revisions of existing handouts and for developing new handouts; checks selected reference lists and bibliographies to determine library holdings; reviews new reference titles, periodicals, and newspapers for items of interest to faculty and students and for use in revising handouts
10%	1,2,3	OPS and work study students: participates in the interview and selection process; trains and supervises; assigns job duties and prepares work schedules; monitors times sheets
2%	1,2	Checks titles of all new reference books to ensure inclusion of records in LINCC and marks subject heading in CIP area of books; supervises shelving of all new reference books
1%	1,2	Various Tasks: performs various tasks as needed; cooperates as team member with other staff performing any duty essential to the achievement of efficient library operations

Tallahassee Community College

JOB TITLE **PT INTERLIBRARY LOAN CLERK**   LEVEL **III (3)**

DEPARTMENT **LIBRARY**   CLASSIFICATION **Classified**

RESPONSIBLE TO: Director of Library Services

GENERAL DESCRIPTION:
Processes all Inter/Intralibrary Loan transactions, for materials coming into or going out of the UCC library.

EXAMPLES OF DUTIES:
Essential Functions:
- Uses Douglas County/UCC DRA database terminal, OCLC terminal, ORULS, Books in Print, and other tools to locate requested books, journals, films, records or other materials.
- Uses Douglas County/UCC DRA database terminal, OCLC terminal or ALA interlibrary loan forms to request materials.
- Uses InfoTrac and periodical indexes to verify requests.
- Keeps accurate records and statistics of all inter/intralibrary loan transactions.
- Notifies patrons concerning requested materials.
- Prepares, or delegates, inter/intralibrary loan materials for shipping.
- Operates fax machine and keeps log of use. Notifies recipient of incoming faxes.
- Attends library staff meetings.
- Performs other duties as assigned by supervisor.

TYPICAL PHYSICAL DEMANDS AND WORK ENVIRONMENT:
- Bending, hearing voice conversation, lifting/carrying 0-34 pounds, pushing, reaching, sitting, standing, stooping, walking, reading fine print and faint labels on books occurs in this job daily.
- Color identification occurs regularly but not daily.
- Crawling, crouching, hearing alarms, kneeling will occur rarely within the work year.

KNOWLEDGE, SKILLS AND ABILITIES:
- Typing speed 45 wpm.
- Ability to search for and enter data on computer terminals.
- Good oral and written communications skills.
- Accuracy and attention to detail important.
- Ability to distinguish between similar titles and authors.
- Experience using WordPerfect.
- Ability to use different computer terminals and programs.
- Supervisory skills.
- Ability to handle stress.
- Knowledge of format of bibliographic records for books and magazine articles required.
- Knowledge of basic interlibrary loan procedures required.
- Recent experience in an automated library preferred.

QUALIFICATIONS:
- Associate Degree in Library Technology or related field, plus one year of library experience, or at least three years of library experience.

UMPQUA COMMUNITY COLLEGE
JOB DESCRIPTION

JOB TITLE **PT LIBRARY DESK CLERK EVENING**   LEVEL **IV (4)**

DEPARTMENT **LIBRARY**   CLASSIFICATION **Classified**

RESPONSIBLE TO: Director of Library Services

GENERAL DESCRIPTION: Responsible for the Library without direct supervision during evenings, 4:30-9:00, Saturdays, 1:00-4:00pm.

EXAMPLES OF DUTIES:
Essential Functions:
- Performs work essential to evening and Saturday library service.
- Provides basic reference assistance.
- Checks books in and out with the use of a computer.
- Assists patrons in materials search and location.
- Assists patrons in using computers, copy machines, Internet and online databases.
- Keeps order in the library.
- Does routine clerical work.
- Enters information on computer terminal.
- Secures facilities for overnight.
- Counts cash from fines and copier use.
- Regular attendance necessary.
- Checks-in claims, processes and maintains all periodicals.

TYPICAL PHYSICAL DEMANDS AND WORK ENVIRONMENT:
- Bending, hearing alarms, hearing voice conversation, lifting/carrying 0-14 pounds, pushing, reaching, sitting, standing, standing long periods, walking, exposure to dust and pollen occurs in this job daily.
- Color identification, crawling, crouching, kneeling, lifting/carrying 15-34 pounds occurs regularly but not daily.

KNOWLEDGE, SKILLS AND ABILITIES:
- Ability to use computers and application software.
- Ability to troubleshoot library equipment.
- Ability to assist patrons in use of library equipment.
- Ability to communicate well with faculty, students and the general public..
- Ability to use basic reference sources knowledgeably, including online resources.
- Ability to handle routine office procedures.
- Ability to function independently.

QUALIFICATIONS:
- One year of library experience using an automated system required.
- AA degree or two years of library experience preferred.

c:\wp\job.des\libnite5/97

Umpqua Community College

**UMPQUA COMMUNITY COLLEGE
JOB DESCRIPTION**

JOB TITLE **PT LIBRARY DESK CLERK (9 MONTH)**   LEVEL **IV (4)**

DEPARTMENT **LIBRARY**   CLASSIFICATION **Classified**

RESPONSIBLE TO: Director of Library Services

GENERAL DESCRIPTION:
Provides service in all functions of library circulation to students, faculty, and the community from the Library circulation desk.

EXAMPLES OF DUTIES:
Essential Functions:
*Provides public service at a busy desk
*Answers routine reference questions and refers people to librarians as needed
*Troubleshoots library equipment
*Uses automated library system to check library materials in and out
*Assists people in using library catalog terminals, copy machines and online resources
*Registers library borrowers
*Enters fines and fees on library system and AIMS
*Maintains and circulates reserve materials
*Uses WordPerfect and other programs for library projects

TYPICAL PHYSICAL DEMANDS AND WORK ENVIRONMENT:
● Bending, hearing alarms, hearing voice conversation, lifting/carrying 0-14 pounds, pushing, reaching, sitting, standing, standing long periods, walking, reading fine print and computer screens, crawling, crouching, exposure to dust and pollen occurs in this job daily.
● Color identification, kneeling, lifting/carrying 15-34 pounds occurs regularly but not daily.

KNOWLEDGE, SKILLS AND ABILITIES:
*Excellent human relations skills
*Ability to keep accurate records
*Keyboarding skills
*Type 30 wpm
*Knowledge of basic office procedures
*AS or AA degree preferred
*Library experience preferred
*Experience with computers preferred

QUALIFICATIONS:
● High school diploma or equivalent required.

JOB DESCRIPTION
WESTERN OKLAHOMA STATE COLLEGE

JOB TITLE: **LIBRARY TECHNICAL ASSISTANT**

QUALIFICATIONS:

Education: Associates degree required

Credentials: Library Technical Assistant Certificate or equivalent library science coursework

Special Knowledge, Skill, or Ability: Must have knowledge of the Dewey Decimal system. Must have knowledge of MARC record format, OCLC, CD-ROM databases, and various software programs with an emphasis on word processing, spreadsheets, and databases. Must have strong organizational skills. Must have knowledge of many types of office machines and audio-visual equipment. Must have the ability to compose and produce reports, letters, various types of correspondence, statistical reports, and purchase orders. Must possess aptitude for detail work. Must have the ability to interpret policies and procedures in order to make judgments concerning library operations. Must have computer and keyboard skills, including Windows or MacIntosh, word processing and spreadsheet construction. Must have the ability to adapt to new technology quickly and enthusiastically. Must have file keeping ability. Must have the ability to communicate effectively in person, on the telephone, and in writing. Must have the ability to perform circulation duties, stock shelves, locate, and retrieve materials. Must have public speaking skills, ability to plan, organize and execute programs, tours, and meetings. Must be public service oriented and comfortable with varied clientele; comfortable with varied pace, overlapping tasks, pressure, and change.

Knowledge of computers: Ability to use word processing, spreadsheet, database, desktop publishing, the Internet, and other software and application programs, at an intermediate level.

Other office/business machines that are necessary for employees to operate include: Microform machines, copy machines, telefacsimile terminals, computers, CD-ROM, audiovisual equipment, etc.

Training or Experience Required: Minimum of one year library or public service experience.

Reports to: Director of Learning Resources Center

Performance Expectations: Follows health and safety policies and regulations to work safely. Adheres to departmental rules concerning dress, attendance, leave usage, etc. Cooperates with other employees and work units. Ability to interact pleasantly, constructively and cooperatively with library patrons and staff. Must have excellent communication skills, oral and written. Ability to effectively listen to and respond to patron inquiries. Ability to remain calm and composed when dealing with difficult situations or individuals. Ability to pay close attention to detail, meet deadlines, and perform duties without supervision. Willingness to uphold the principles of the First Amendment and the Library Bill of Rights.

Job Goal (Purpose of Position): Has independent responsibility for functions and services of the LRC which requires interpretation of procedures, applications or policies where frequent exercises in judgment are required. This position requires a detailed knowledge of library principles, procedures and systems, to include technical or paraprofessional operations of considerable difficulty in more than one area of librarianship. High accountability in all phases of assigned duties is required.

Contact with Others: This position has regular contact with students, faculty and staff, and members of the community. Positive interpersonal interaction and communication is required.

Supervision Exercised: This position provides supervision to library clerks, part-time and student workers. Includes guidance, training, monitoring, delegating and assigning work as needed.

Physical and Mental Requirements and Working Conditions: Other than those physical and mental requirements included in the essential functions: Must be able to communicate on the telephone and in person. Must be able to get around the Learning Resources Center, climb stairs, locate and retrieve or shelve books or materials. There is constant standing and walking, frequent bending, stooping, squatting, crouching, and reaching above the shoulder to shelve books and standing on step ladder or stool. There is occasional carrying and lifting of up to 40 pounds while receiving and handling book orders, moving damaged equipment, lifting and moving audio-visual equipment, and moving library furniture.

Salary Range:

Evaluation: Performance of this job will be evaluated in accordance with departmental and Board policy.

Approved:

Essential Functions and Responsibilities:

1.   Circulation
    A.   Follows established policies and procedures.
    B.   Responsible for all aspects related to opening and closing the LRC.
    C.   Oversees and performs day-to-day Circulation Desk operations on automated circulation system:
- checks out, checks in and renews library materials to authorized patrons;
- checks out equipment and materials to authorized patrons;
- collects and receipts monies for charges relating to LRC materials or services;
- establishes records for borrowing privileges to authorized patrons according to established policies and procedures;
- performs all necessary checks before approving student withdrawals;
- places and removes holds on materials for authorized patrons;
- places holds on patrons who owe for damaged materials or have overdue items;
- shelves library materials, performs shelf reading, and other assigned duties to library staff;
- processes list of overdue library materials weekly, contacting those persons with overdue materials to remind them they have items out, posts lists of fines and overdue materials each semester.

    D.   Assembles, monitors, and maintains the Reserve collection by placing or removing materials as needed.
    E.   Performs telephone receptionist duties.
    F.   Provides general information and answers questions on library services and basic circulation policies such as loan periods, fines, and holds.

G. Provides patrons with informational and directional assistance in retrieving material from library stacks.
H. Provides training and guidance to library clerks, part-time and student workers as needed.
I. Assists patrons in the use of photocopiers, microform reader/printers, and other equipment/machines.
J. Collects statistics and provides statistical summaries and reports.
K. Performs back-ups of library systems.

2. Acquisitions/Technical Processing
   A. Follows established policies and procedures.
   B. Prepares request cards, verifies bibliographic information and availability through established procedures.
   C. Prepares print and non-print orders and requisitions.
   D. Enters vital information into the LRC acquisition database.
   E. Posts information in current ledger of item(s) received, date received, and price.
   F. Checks shipments when received, correlates with packing slips and invoices, or supervises the process. Posts necessary information in acquisition database, processes invoices, corresponds with vendors on any discrepancies.
   G. Oversees or performs the preparation of materials to be added to the collection, including spine labels, security stickers, pockets and book cards.

3. Interlibrary Loans
   A. Follows established policies and procedures.
   B. Assists patrons in completing appropriate forms.
   C. Submits requests on the OCLC database for materials to be borrowed from other institutions by authorized patrons.
   D. Receives, circulates, and returns interlibrary loan materials borrowed from other institutions.
   E. Processes materials requested by other institutions. Includes receiving requests through OCLC database, checking collection for availability and determining if material can be loaned, processing loan and packaging material for mailing.
   F. Assures return of material by due date, applies, processes, and collects fines or payments for overdue or damaged/lost material.
   G. Maintains records, prepares reports of all interlibrary activities.

4. Reference
   A. Follows established policies and procedures.
   B. Provides reference assistance to students, staff, and public under the guidance of the professional librarians.
   C. Assists users of the LRC in the use of reference books, indexes, and the automated card catalog, to locate needed information and materials.
   D. Provides intermediate/advanced reference assistance to patrons with printed and computerized tools.
   E. Provides intermediate/advanced instruction in the use of the automated card catalog, word processing, electronic databases, the Internet and other computer programs the LRC makes available to its patrons.
   F. Provides bibliographic instruction sessions as needed to individuals or groups.
   G. Creates and conducts mini-classes on the Internet and electronic resources and databases.
   H. Collects statistics and provides statistical reports.

5. Cataloging
   A. Follows established policies and procedures.
   B. Searches on-line databases for matching MARC records for new acquisitions or conversions.
   C. Inputs necessary information, updates and exports records for uploading to local database.
   D. Exports records from local database to library automation system.
   E. Supplies call numbers using the Dewey Decimal Classification schedules and assigns Subject headings according to the Library of Congress Subject Heading Guide.
   F. Adds enhancements to bibliographic records.
   G. Updates and inputs bibliographic information on library automation system to reflect library holdings and formats.
   H. Creates new bibliographic records according to MARC format for items that do not have existing MARC records.
   I. Maintains the library catalog through adding, deleting, and/or editing local data information.
   J. Provides catalog quality control and general catalog database management to insure quality of catalog records.
   K. Deletes catalog records when items are removed from the collection.

6. Technology
   A. Follows established policies and procedures.
   B. Installs and/or updates new and existing software.
   C. Maintains integrity of computer systems.
   D. Maintains computers and peripherals.
   E. Troubleshoots problems with computers, places appropriate signs on malfunctioning units, and makes appropriate contacts for repairs if needed.
   F. Participates in training opportunities to stay on top of technological advancements.

7. Clerical
   A. Follows established policies and procedures.
   B. Oversees and performs mail distribution by collecting, sorting, distributing, and processing mail.
   C. Uses word processing, spreadsheets, and other software packages to create memos, letters, statistical reports, forms, bulletins, and other correspondence pertaining to the LRC.
   D. Provides advanced word processing, spreadsheets and desktop publishing support to other LRC staff as needed.
   E. Creates and maintains an inventory count of materials added to and deleted from the collection.
   F. Assists in producing and maintaining procedures manuals.
   G. Performs backups of LRC computer files.
   H. Performs filing duties.

8. Bindery/Repairs

Western Oklahoma State College

     A.   Follows established policies and procedures.
     B.   Performs routine checks on materials.
     C.   Performs repairs on materials that remain a part of the collection.

9.   AV Equipment/Office Machines
     A.   Follows established policies and procedures.
     B.   Performs routine maintenance checks on equipment.
     C.   Performs repairs on equipment.
     D.   Replenishes copier and computer supplies.
     E.   Troubleshoots problems with equipment, places appropriate signs on malfunctioning units, and makes appropriate contacts for repairs if needed.
     F.   Assures that equipment is available and working for faculty and staff when needed.

10.   Other Responsibilities
     A.   Follows established policies and procedures.
     B.   Responsible for library, including building and equipment, part-time and student workers, during evening and weekend hours, as assigned, without supervision.
     C.   Responsible for helping to maintain the integrity of the collection in designated areas.
     D.   Supervises the maintenance of the Vertical File.
     E.   Oversees or performs the weeding process of old or damaged materials and equipment.
     F.   Supports overall library operations and services through projects and other duties as appropriate and assigned. Actively supports library colleagues, library mission, goals and objectives, and college mission.
     G.   Within parameters of position responsibilities, proposes new or changed policies and procedures to accomplish own responsibilities, related operations, and library mission.
     H.   Assists with planning and implementation of special projects.
     I.   Granite Courier standby.
     J.   Serves on institutional committees as needed.
     K.   Other duties as assigned.

POSITION TITLE: Library Technician – Tech Services

Reports to: Library Manager

POSITION DESCRIPTION: Under the general supervision of the Library Manager, performs copy cataloging for library, data entry for material records into the library's automation system and maintains shelflist and WISCAT. Orders, receives, processes library materials including books, periodical and supplies and verifies purchase orders. Prepares materials for public use. Maintains periodicals collection, including check-in display, periodicals list, claims and storage. Supervises student assistants. Staffs and maintains the Circulation/Reserve desk one night per week and provides coverage during daily and school year breaks. Assists with reserve collection and fine and overdue records; assists library patrons in information queries using the online catalog, CD services, reference and other materials; compiles statistics; and performs minor service on machines in library. Other duties as assigned.

QUALIFICATIONS: Required: Two year, post-secondary degree and two years experience in technical services in an academic or public library or Bachelor's degree and two years experience. Undergraduate course in cataloging.

ESSENTIAL SKILLS AND KNOWLEDGE: A very strong detail orientation. A very strong service orientation towards students, faculty and staff; ability to organize materials for quick and easy retrieval, ability to maintain a service focus despite hundreds of interruptions daily, ability to work cooperatively with other staff; sound judgement; high energy level.

3/29/99

General Description: Describe the most important regular tasks assigned to this position. For C/T positions indicate the approximate percentage of time required for each task listed.

% Time	Task
35%	Performs copy cataloging and data entry for all newly acquired materials for our automated library system except, generally, the reserve collection. Maintains shelflist and WISCAT, corrects catalog errors, updates bibliographic records, processes new acquisitions for patron use (makes labels, installs security, etc.)
15%	Receives all incoming mail; checks-in and prepares periodicals for use; checks-in books and other materials and verifies them against purchase order
20%	Covers circulation desk one night per week plus other times when necessary (during coffee breaks, lunch hours, illnesses, etc., possibly including Saturdays in rotation in the future); checkout materials; answers information and reference questions; maintains copiers and printers; answer telephone; assist patrons in finding information and materials; gives library tours on occasion.
15%	Maintains periodicals lists, current periodical shelves and periodicals storage area and claims periodicals not received.
15%	Assists in book ordering; maintains acquisition statistics,
2%	Repairs and mends library materials
2%	Maintains library supplies and wants lists
2%	Participates in inventory process
2%	Interviews, trains, and supervises work-study employees.
5%	Other library tasks as assigned

Special or Occasional Duties: Describe duties performed occasionally or as special assignments.

Very occasional typing assignments
Library inventory.

Knowledge/experience: What type of experience (position, length of time, type of organization) is required for effective job performance?

Two year, post-secondary degree with two years of experience in technical services in a public or academic library, or,
Library Technician's Certificate and four years library experience, or
Bachelor's degree and two years library experience.

Undergraduate cataloging degree required.

Education: What level of education is required (degree, major, minor)?

Two year, post-secondary degree with two years of experience in technical services in a public or academic library,or
Bachelor's degree and two years library experience.

Training: What is the task difficulty and variability required for this position? How much on-the-job training will it take for a qualified individual to become fully competent in this position?

Western Wisconsin Technical College

Difficulty ranges from moderately complex (interpretations of cataloging rules) to the very simple. (checking in magazines)

Special Skills: Be specific (i.e. computer skills-Lotus; typing - 60 wpm). List only skills an employee must possess when promoted or hired; not skills they will acquire on-the-job.

> Flexibility
> very high level of detail
> inquiring mind
> service orientation
> team player
> value open communications
> general typing skills 60 wpm (accuracy is far more important than speed)
> knowledge of general office equipment
> general windows software skills

Responsibility/decision making: List measurable items upon which this individual will have a direct or indirect impact. Do they manage a budget? If yes, what amount? What revenues are they responsible for, etc.? List all that apply.

> Recommends changes in policy and procedure for technical services.
> No budget/revenue responsibility

Decision making: Give typical examples of the important decisions made.

> The library technician follows moderately detailed policies and procedures in the normal course of their duties though the selection of record to use in copy cataloging often determines how easily and how quickly library materials can be found

> How this position interprets library policies and procedures to students often determines the quality of library service to our students.

> Staff member is expected to recommend improvements in library policies, procedures, and services.

Latitude of decision making: Does this position function independently or under limited or strict supervision? To what degree do policies, procedures or rules control the decisions made?

> This position functions under the direction of the library manager and works with the reference librarian who does the library's original cataloging. The library attempts to follow AACRII cataloging guidelines. This position will determine if a local variation is required and assigns titles for original cataloging to the Librarian. This position, like all library staff, has wide discretionary power in how they assist students.

What degree of feedback does this position receive from the supervisor regarding task results and accomplishments?

> This positions is in almost hourly contact with Library Manager.

What is the scope of decisions made by this position? Do they affect the entire

Wharton County Junior College

POSITION DESCRIPTION
Human Resources

Position Title: **Library: Serials Technician**

Classification: ❏ Admin/Professional   ❏ Faculty   ❏ Support Staff

Factor Evaluations:

Grade	Total									
			D	R	A	F	T			

A.   **Primary Responsibilities:**

The Serials Technician maintains the periodical and newspaper collections in the J. M. Hodges Library, performs clerical duties, assists with activities of the TVM area and assists in providing reader services to library patrons. The position is supervised by the Director of Library Services.

B.   **Functional Responsibilities:**

1. Maintains the periodical and newspaper collection of the WCJC Libraries:
    a. Receives and check-in magazines, journals and newspapers;
    b. Orders new magazines, journals, newspapers and renews subscriptions as directed by the supervising librarian;
    c. Checks on missing issues and corresponds with jobber and/or publisher;
    d. Prepares periodicals for the bindery and exchange offerings;
    e. Enters data and maintains computer files of periodical collection and processes periodical holdings lists;
    f. Trains and supervises student assistants assigned to work with the periodicals and newspapers;
    g. Supervises the maintenance of the periodical collection (shifting, withdrawing, discarding, and adding, etc.)
    h. Maintains records for the annual report.

2. Performs secretarial duties for the WCJC Libraries:
    a. Answers the telephone, takes messages, and provides directional/general information;
    b. Assists the Director in maintaining files and archives;
    c. Assists the Director in maintaining the NRC (Nuclear Regulatory Commission) collection;
    d. Assists with correspondence, maintenance of handbooks, manuals, etc.;
    e. Schedules and manages media programs reserved by faculty;
    f. Prepares the WCJC ANNOUNCEMENTS (the campus bulletin): enters campus news items in the computer format, duplicates and distributes to college personnel.

Position Description: 2

3. Assists with activities of the TVM area of the Library:
   a. Orders and schedules preview materials, returns and maintains records of previews;
   b. Supervises inspection of newly purchased media programs;
   c. Maintains current vendor catalogs and assists in locating order information for audio visual programs;
   d. Maintains records of media and production services and prepares monthly and annual reports of TVM activities;

4. Provides reader services to library patrons:
   a. Performs circulation desk duties which include using the automated circulation system;
   b. Assists with audio visual equipment and materials circulation and photocopy/microform operations;
   c. Provides reader services, including "point-of-need" instruction to users for access of electronic resources;
   d. Supervises reading areas;
   e. Supervises student assistants assigned to public service areas;
   f. Responsible for supervision and operations of the J. M. Hodges Library during evening hours, as assigned.

C.   Additional Functional Requirements

1. Ability to read and interpret departmental policies, procedures and instructions.

2. Ability to hear and communicate with library patrons in person and by telephone.

3. Sufficient manual dexterity to prepare letters, reports, graphics and other data on the computer.

4. Ability to operate equipment.

5. Capable of pushing/pulling and lifting a minimum of 25 lbs, raising hands above the head and climbing stairs.

D.   Supervision and Direction Received

The Serials Technician is responsible and accountable to the Director of Library Services for fulfilling the objectives, standards, and duties listed in this document. Guidance for the performance of duties outline in this job description comes from the policies and regulations of the college and any other applicable federal, state, and local statutes, ordinances, codes, rules, regulations, or directives.

E.   Performance Standards

Performance is considered satisfactory when:

1.   Mutually agreed-upon objectives have been attained within a specified time frame;

2.   Functional responsibilities of the position have been executed at a level consistent with performance requirements;

3.   Effective, cooperative relationships exist with the Director of Library Services, administrative and professional staff, faculty, support staff, and clientele from the community;

4.   Confidential aspects of the position are strictly maintained;

5.   Functioning in the role is related to college goals and mission attainment;

6.   Work is coordinated with the Director Library Services or his/her designee;

7.   Accuracy and high quality of finished work are strictly maintained and completed within established guidelines.

F.   Education and Experience Expectations

1.   Have completed sixty hours of college credit courses;

2.   Minimum of two years of work experience with demonstrated ability to work effectively with colleagues;

3.   Clerical skills must include work processing skills with a high degree of accuracy including keyboarding of 40 WPM;

4.   Demonstrate computer literacy in Windows operating system and Microsoft Word;

5.   Demonstrate good communication skills, both written and oral, and a strong commitment to public service.

_____   _____
Signature of Employee   Date

_____   _____
Signature of Supervisor   Date

College Organizational Chart

Anne Arundel Community College
Bossier Parrish Community College
Carl Sandburg Community College
Dyersburg State Community College
Estrella Mountain Community College
Fl. Keys Community College
Harrisburg Area Community College
Holmes Community College
Horry Georgetown Technical College
Hutchinson Community College
Iowa Lakes Community College
Kellogg Community College
Kirtland Community College
Manatee Community College
Nicolet Area Community College
North Idaho Community College
Northeast Iowa Community College
Navajo Community College
Northwestern Connecticut Community College
Okaloosa Walton Community College
Panola College
Paul Smith's College
Pierce College
Prince George's Community College
Quinebaug Valley Community College
Seminole Community College
South Florida Community College
Technical College of the Lowcountry
Trident Technical College
Umpquia Community College
Western Oklahoma State College
York Technical College

BOARD OF TRUSTEES

PRESIDENT

ASSISTANT TO THE PRESIDENT FOR DIVERSITY AND FEDERAL COMPLIANCE
DIRECTOR OF PUBLIC RELATIONS AND MARKETING
EXECUTIVE DIRECTOR OF INSTITUTIONAL DEVELOPMENT
EXECUTIVE ASSISTANT TO THE PRESIDENT

VICE PRESIDENT FOR ACADEMIC AND STUDENT AFFAIRS

Assistant Dean for Academic Affairs

Assistant to the Vice President for Academic and Student Affairs

Center for the Advancement of Learning and Teaching
Center for the Study of Local Issues
Environmental Center
Honors Program
Student Success
Supplemental Instruction
Women's Institute

Dean of School of Arts and Sciences

American Studies/
Humanities/Philosophy
Art
Astronomy/Chemistry/Physics/
Physical Science
Biology
Communication Arts
Technology
Education
English/Reading/
Communications
Foreign Languages
Geography/Sociology
History/Political Science
Mathematics
Performing Arts
Psychology

Dean of School of Business, Computing and Technical Studies

Architecture
Business Administration
Business Management
Computer Information Systems
Computer Science
Economics
Engineering
Hotel/Restaurant Management
Law Enforcement/Criminal
Justice and Paralegal Studies

Dean of School of Health Professions, Wellness & Physical Education

EMT/Paramedics
Health and Physical Education
Human Services
Integrated Healthcare Education
Nursing (RN & LPN)
Physician Assistant
Physical Therapist Assistant
Radiologic Technology

Dean of Student Services

ACADEMIC ADVISING AND
RETENTION CENTER (Director)
Transfer Services, Special
Populations, Retention, Disabled
Student Services, Vocational
Student Services
Career Planning and Placement
ADMISSIONS AND ENROLLMENT
DEVELOPMENT (Director)
Multi-ethnic Recruitment and
Retention
REGISTRAR
Records, Registration, Transfer
Credit, STARS Systems
STUDENT FINANCIAL SERVICES
(Director)
Scholarships, Grants, Veteran
Affairs, Loans
STUDENT ACTIVITIES AND
LEADERSHIP DEVELOPMENT
(Assistant Dean)
Student Activities, Campus
Recreation, Student Orientation,
Art Gallery, Student Association,
Substance Abuse Education,
Judicial Affairs, Information Center,
Educational Talent Search,
AmeriCorps, Child Development
Center, Health Services
TESTING AND TUTORING CENTER
(Director)
Reading, & Study Skills Lab, Peer
Tutoring, Technology Learning Center,
Testing Center

VICE PRESIDENT FOR CONTINUING EDUCATION WORKFORCE DEVELOPMENT

ASST. DEAN WORKFORCE DEVELOPMENT & BUS. SERVICES

BUS. & INDUSTRY TRAINING (Dir.)
Customized Training, Instructional
Design
COMPUTER TRAINING (Director)
Northrop Grumman
OCCUPATIONAL SKILLS PROGRAMS
(Director)
Apprenticeship, Corrections,
Occupational Training
TEACHER TECHNOLOGY TRAINING
(T-3) (Project Director)
ASSISTANT DEAN, COMMUNITY
EDU. & EXTENDED LEARNING
CHILDCARE TRNG. INST. (Mgr.)
Licensure, Re-licensure, Small
Business
ENGLISH AS A SECOND
LANGUAGE/BASIC SKILLS (Dir.)
ESL, Adult Basic Education
Workplace Literacy
LIFELONG LEARNING (Director)
Vocational, Avocational, Kids
In College, TAG, Seniors
Community Services
BUSINESS EDUCATION
PARTNERSHIPS (Asst Dir.)
Tech Prep., Credit/Noncredit Share
Off-Campus, Administration
MGR. DIV. OPERATIONS/
IMPLEMENTATION MGR. MIS/SIS
State Reporting, Marketing,
Publications, Budgeting Systems,
Contract Processing, Off-Campus
Operations, FOCUS, Divisional
Training, Technical Support
DIRECTOR, PROFESSIONAL
DEVELOPMENT

VICE PRESIDENT FOR FINANCE, PLANNING AND HUMAN RESOURCES

BUSINESS OFFICE (Controller)
CENTRAL SERVICES (Director)
HUMAN RESOURCES (Director)
DIVISIONAL OPERATIONS &
BUSINESS SERVICES (Director)
PUBLIC SAFETY (Manager)

DEAN OF ADMINISTRATIVE SERVICES

Campus Development
Bookstore
Facilities Management
(Director)
Space Allocation Services
Print Shop/Mail Services
Food Services
Risk Management

DEAN FOR PLANNING, RESEARCH AND INSTITUTIONAL ASSESSMENT

Planning
Research
Institutional Assessment

VICE PRESIDENT OF LEARNING SYSTEMS AND TECHNOLOGY

ASSISTANT DEAN INFORMATION TECHNOLOGIES

Applications Development &
Support (Manager)
Help Desk and Customer Services
(Team Leader)
PC Support,
Help Desk, Training, Lab Support
Networking Services (Manager)
Network Management
Operations, Systems
Management, Distributed
Systems

LIBRARY (DIRECTOR)

LEARNING TECHNOLOGIES (DIRECTOR)

Distance Learning
AV/COM
Media Production Services
Instructional Technologies

Anne Arundel Community College

208 College Organizational Chart

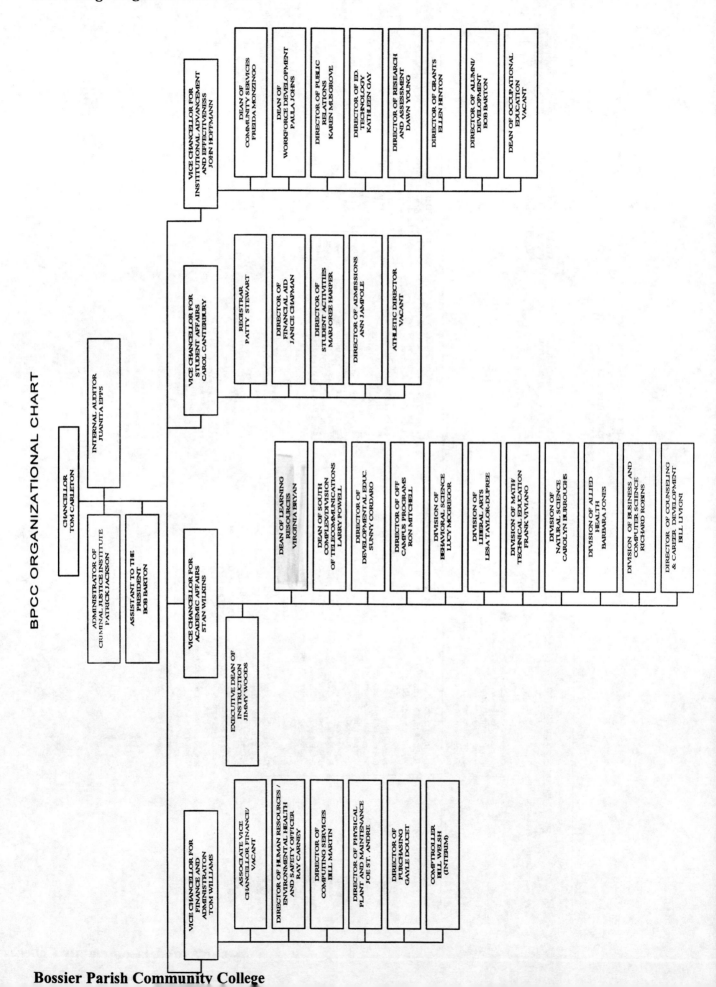

BPCC ORGANIZATIONAL CHART

CHANCELLOR
TOM CARLETON

INTERNAL AUDITOR
JUANITA EPPS

ADMINISTRATOR OF
CRIMINAL JUSTICE INSTITUTE
PATRICK JACKSON

ASSISTANT TO THE
PRESIDENT
BOB BARTON

VICE CHANCELLOR FOR
INSTITUTIONAL ADVANCEMENT
AND EFFECTIVENESS
JOHN HOFFMANN

DEAN OF
COMMUNITY SERVICES
FREIDA MONZINGO

DEAN OF
WORKFORCE DEVELOPMENT
PAULA JOHNS

DIRECTOR OF PUBLIC
RELATIONS
KAREN MUSGROVE

DIRECTOR OF ED.
TECHNOLOGY
KATHLEEN GAY

DIRECTOR OF RESEARCH
AND ASSESSMENT
DAWN YOUNG

DIRECTOR OF GRANTS
ELLEN HINTON

DIRECTOR OF ALUMNI/
DEVELOPMENT
BOB BARTON

DEAN OF OCCUPATIONAL
EDUCATION
VACANT

VICE CHANCELLOR FOR
STUDENT AFFAIRS
CAROL CANTERBURY

REGISTRAR
PATTY STEWART

DIRECTOR OF
FINANCIAL AID
JANICE CHAPMAN

DIRECTOR OF
STUDENT ACTIVITIES
MARJOREE HARPER

DIRECTOR OF ADMISSIONS
ANN JAMPOLE

ATHLETIC DIRECTOR
VACANT

VICE CHANCELLOR FOR
ACADEMIC AFFAIRS
STAN WILKINS

EXECUTIVE DEAN OF
INSTRUCTION
JIMMY WOODS

DEAN OF LEARNING
RESOURCES
VIRGINIA BRYAN

DEAN OF SOUTH
COMPLEX/DIVISION
OF TELECOMMUNICATIONS
LARRY POWELL

DIRECTOR OF
DEVELOPMENTAL EDUC.
SUNNY CORDARO

DIRECTOR OF OFF
CAMPUS PROGRAMS
RON MITCHELL

DIVISION OF
BEHAVIORAL SCIENCE
LUCY MCGREGOR

DIVISION OF
LIBERAL ARTS
LESA TAYLOR-DUPREE

DIVISION OF MATH/
TECHNICAL EDUCATION
FRANK VIVIANO

DIVISION OF
NATURAL SCIENCE
CAROLYN BURROUGHS

DIVISION OF ALLIED
HEALTH
BARBARA JONES

DIVISION OF BUSINESS AND
COMPUTER SCIENCE
RICHARD ROBINS

DIRECTOR OF COUNSELING
& CAREER DEVELOPMENT
BILL LIVIGNI

VICE CHANCELLOR FOR
FINANCE AND
ADMINISTRATION
TOM WILLIAMS

ASSOCIATE VICE
CHANCELLOR FINANCE/
VACANT

DIRECTOR OF HUMAN RESOURCES /
ENVIRONMENTAL HEALTH
AND SAFETY OFFICER
RAY CARNEY

DIRECTOR OF
COMPUTING SERVICES
BILL MARTIN

DIRECTOR OF PHYSICAL
PLANT AND MAINTENANCE
JOE ST. ANDRE

DIRECTOR OF
PURCHASING
GAYLE DOUCET

COMPTROLLER
BILL WELSH
(INTERIM)

Bossier Parish Community College

CARL SANDBURG COLLEGE ORGANIZATIONAL CHART

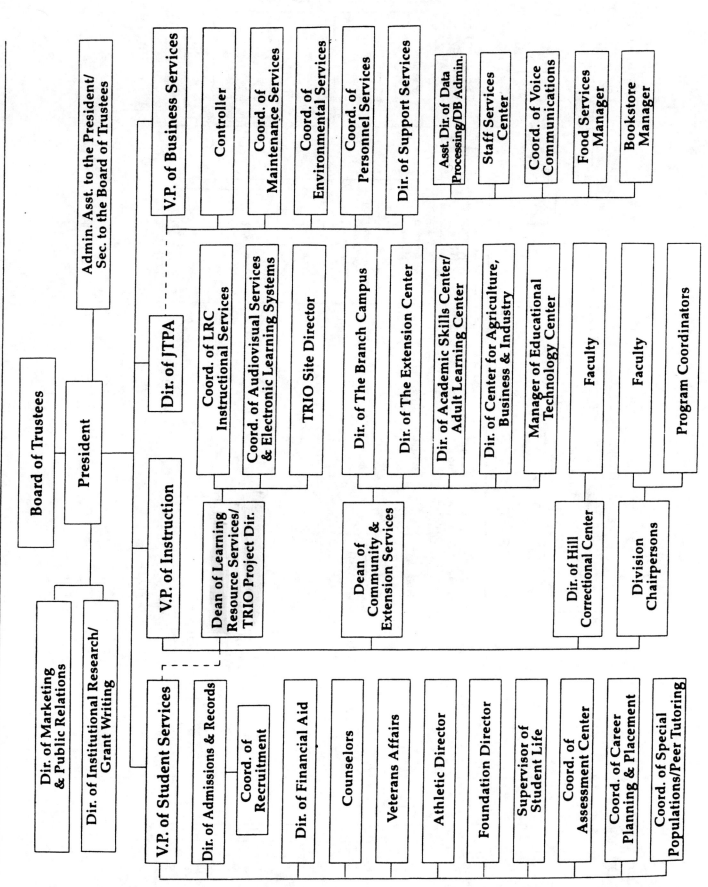

Carl Sandburg College

Dyersburg State Community College
Organizational Chart
1996-1997

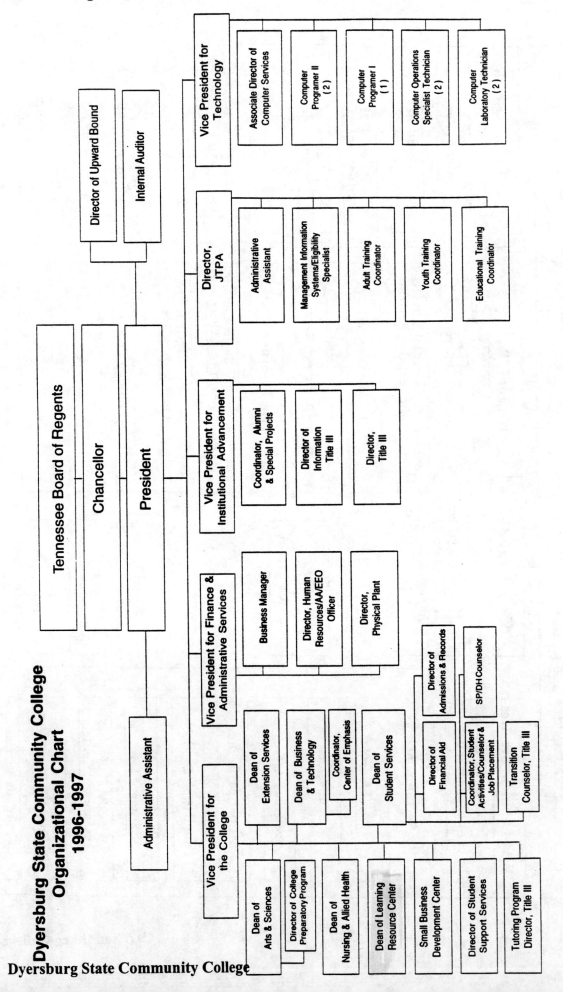

Tennessee Board of Regents	
Chancellor	
President	

Administrative Assistant

Director of Upward Bound

Internal Auditor

Vice President for Technology
- Associate Director of Computer Services
- Computer Programer II (2)
- Computer Programer I (1)
- Computer Operations Specialist Technician (2)
- Computer Laboratory Technician (2)

Director, JTPA
- Administrative Assistant
- Management Information Systems/Eligibility Specialist
- Adult Training Coordinator
- Youth Training Coordinator
- Educational Training Coordinator

Vice President for Institutional Advancement
- Coordinator, Alumni & Special Projects
- Director of Information Title III
- Director, Title III

Vice President for Finance & Administrative Services
- Business Manager
- Director, Human Resources/AA/EEO Officer
- Director, Physical Plant

Vice President for the College
- Dean of Extension Services
- Dean of Business & Technology
- Coordinator, Center of Emphasis
- Dean of Student Services
  - Director of Admissions & Records
  - SP/DH Counselor
  - Director of Financial Aid
  - Coordinator, Student Activities/Counselor & Job Placement
  - Transition Counselor, Title III
- Dean of Arts & Sciences
- Director of College Preparatory Program
- Dean of Nursing & Allied Health
- Dean of Learning Resource Center
- Small Business Development Center
- Director of Student Support Services
- Tutoring Program Director, Title III

5/96

Dyersburg State Community College

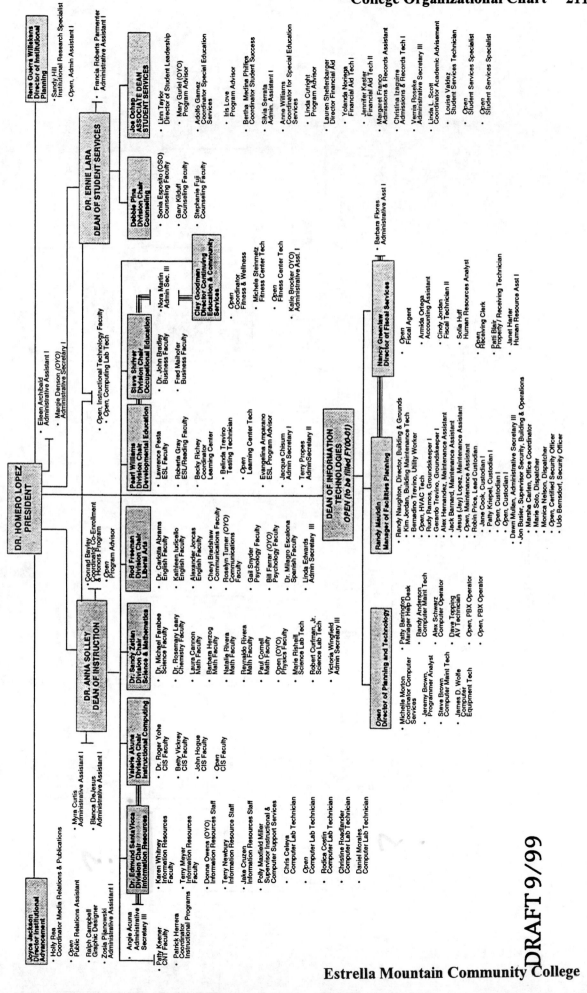

ESTRELLA ▴ MOUNTAIN ▴ COMMUNITY ▴ COLLEGE
ORGANIZATIONAL CHART 1999 - 2000

DRAFT 9/99

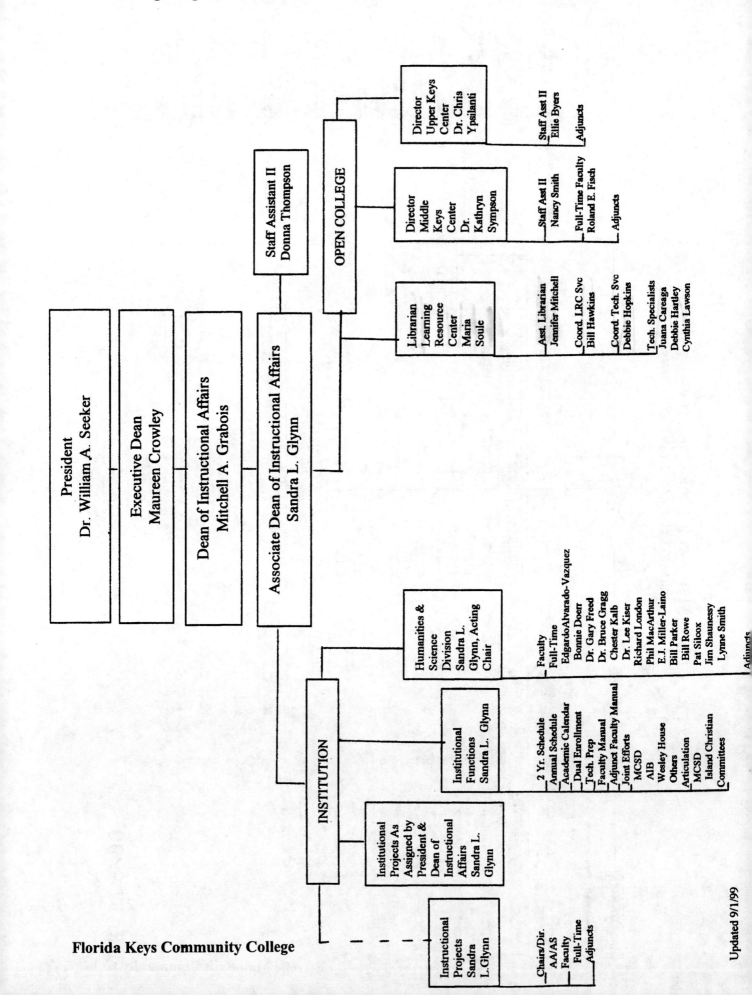

Florida Keys Community College

Updated 9/1/99

HARRISBURG AREA COMMUNITY COLLEGE

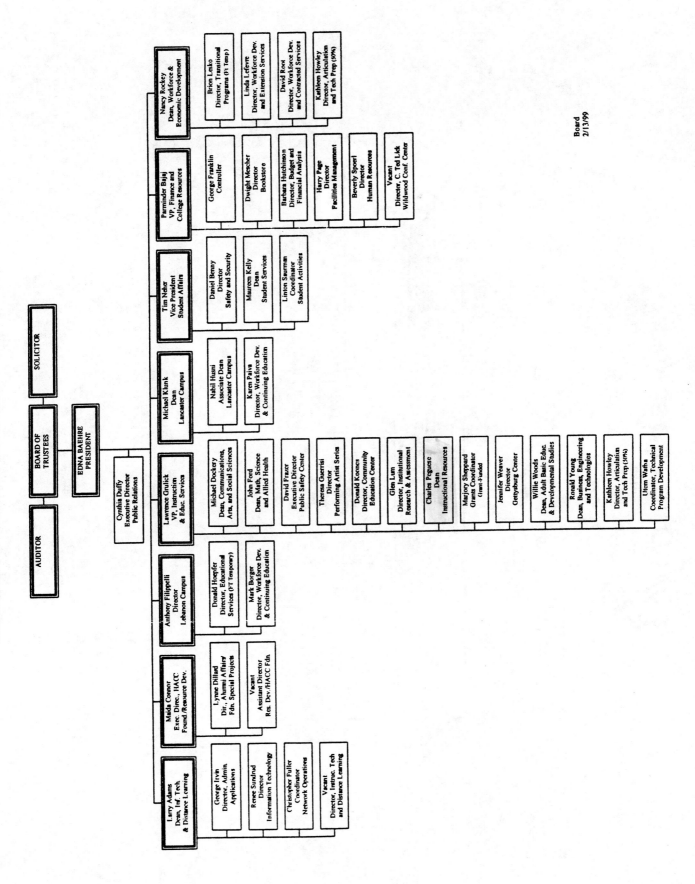

Board
2/13/99

Main Campus

ACADEMIC PROGRAMS

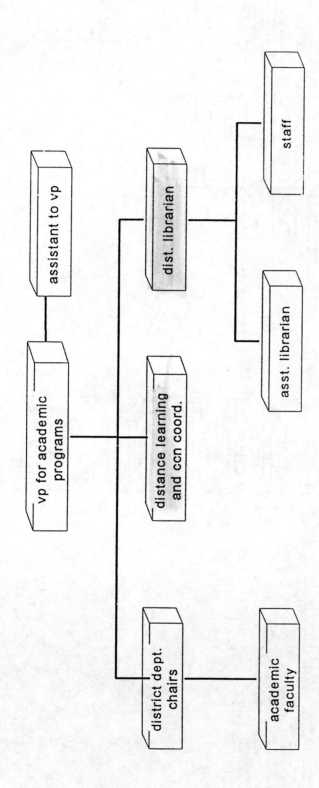

Branch #1

GRENADA CENTER

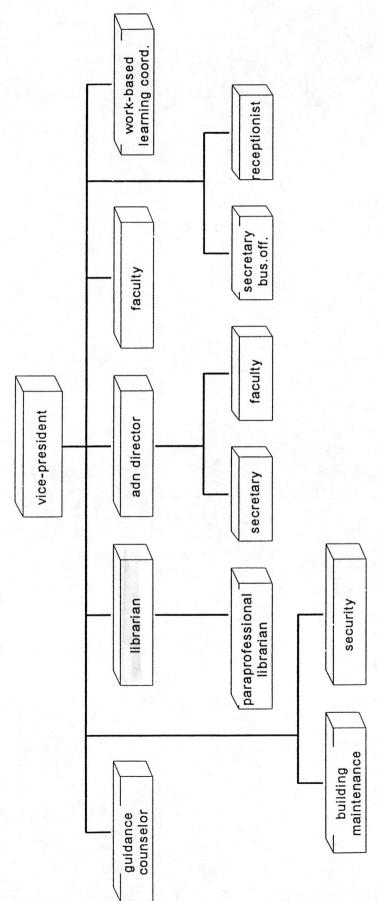

Branch #2

RIDGELAND CAMPUS

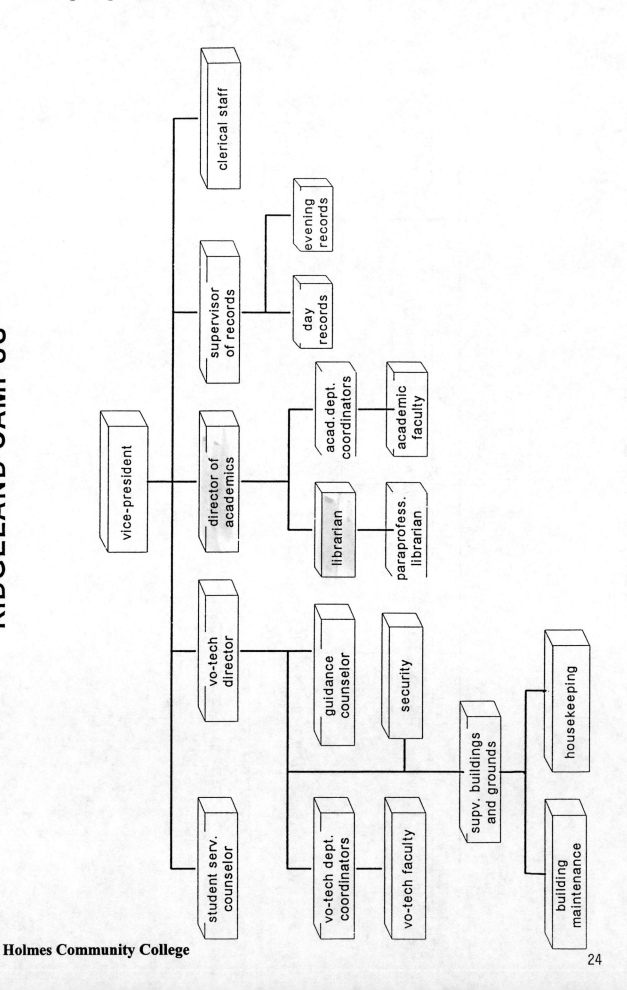

Hutchinson Community College and Area Vocational School

May 2000

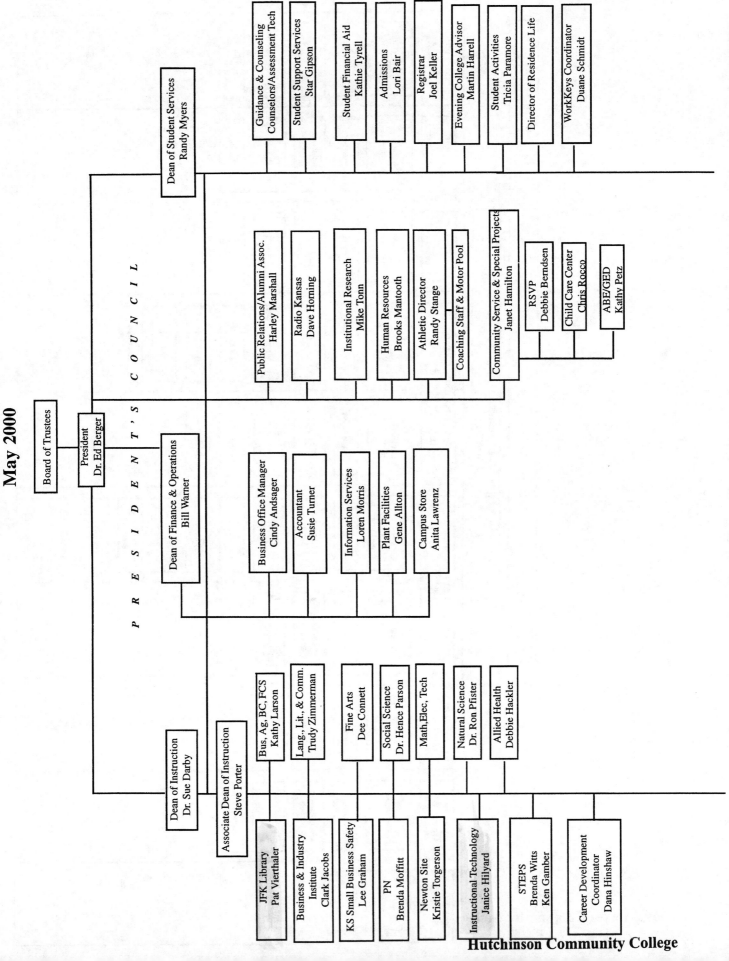

Board of Trustees

President
Dr. Ed Berger

PRESIDENT'S COUNCIL

Dean of Student Services
Randy Myers

- Guidance & Counseling
  Counselors/Assessment Tech
- Student Support Services
  Star Gipson
- Student Financial Aid
  Kathie Tyrell
- Admissions
  Lori Bair
- Registrar
  Joel Keller
- Evening College Advisor
  Martin Harrell
- Student Activities
  Tricia Paramore
- Director of Residence Life
- WorkKeys Coordinator
  Duane Schmidt

- Public Relations/Alumni Assoc.
  Harley Marshall
- Radio Kansas
  Dave Horning
- Institutional Research
  Mike Tonn
- Human Resources
  Brooks Mantooth
- Athletic Director
  Randy Stange
- Coaching Staff & Motor Pool
- Community Service & Special Projects
  Janet Hamilton
  - RSVP
    Debbie Berndsen
  - Child Care Center
    Chris Rocco
  - ABE/GED
    Kathy Petz

Dean of Finance & Operations
Bill Warner

- Business Office Manager
  Cindy Andsager
- Accountant
  Susie Turner
- Information Services
  Loren Morris
- Plant Facilities
  Gene Allton
- Campus Store
  Anita Lawrenz

Dean of Instruction
Dr. Sue Darby

Associate Dean of Instruction
Steve Porter

- Bus, Ag, BC, FCS
  Kathy Larson
- Lang., Lit., & Comm.
  Trudy Zimmerman
- Fine Arts
  Dee Connett
- Social Science
  Dr. Hence Parson
- Math, Elec, Tech
- Natural Science
  Dr. Ron Pfister
- Allied Health
  Debbie Hackler

- JFK Library
  Pat Vierthaler
- Business & Industry
  Institute
  Clark Jacobs
- KS Small Business Safety
  Lee Graham
- PN
  Brenda Moffitt
- Newton Site
  Kristie Torgerson
- Instructional Technology
  Janice Hilyard
- STEPS
  Brenda Witts
  Ken Gamber
- Career Development
  Coordinator
  Dana Hinshaw

Hutchinson Community College

Iowa Lakes Community College

BOARD OF TRUSTEES

BOARD SECRETARY
Clark Marshall

COLLEGE PRESIDENT
Jim Billings

EXEC. DIR. Plant Services Delaine Hiney	VICE PRES. Administration Tom Herbst	EXEC. DIR. Finance Bob L'Heureux	EXECUTIVE CAMPUS DEAN Estherville Ellengray Kennedy	EXECUTIVE CAMPUS DEAN Emmetsburg Dr. Dave Nixon	EXEC. DIR. Cont Ed Econ Dev Clark Marshall	EXEC. DIR. Plan-Dev Judy Cook	EXEC. DIR. Marketing Jane Campbell	EXEC. CHAIR Inst Advancement Tammy Biggs
New Facilities	Human Resources	Central Business Office	ASSOC. DEAN OF STUDENT SERVICES Julie Carlson	ASSOC. DEAN / E'BURG CAMPUS Val Newhouse	Economic Development	Resource Development	Admissions	Fund Raising
Plant Services	Staff Development	Computer Center	Instructional Programs	Instructional Programs	Continuing Ed	Planning	Marketing	Foundations
	Alternative High Schools		Campus Office	Campus Office	Small Business Development Center	Institutional Effectiveness	Public Relations	Alumni Association
	Algona, Spencer & Spirit Lake Centers		Technology Center	Special Needs	Industrial Training Programs	Title III Director	Printing Services	Student Scholarships
	Records & Enrollment		Libraries	Children's Center	Third Age College	Accreditation	Summer Student Orientation	
			Counseling / Placement	Nursing Programs	Retired & Senior Volunteer Pgm			
			Educational Equity	Secondary Programs				
			Developmental Education	T & I Resale				
			Student Records	Food Service				
			Athletics	College Farm				
			Financial Aid/ Veterans Affairs	Bookstore				
			Student Gov't Leadership	Wellness Center				
			Housing	Housing				
			TRIO Programs	Intramurals				
			Intramurals					

Iowa Lakes Community College

KELLOGG COMMUNITY COLLEGE

Institutional Reporting System
July 1, 1999

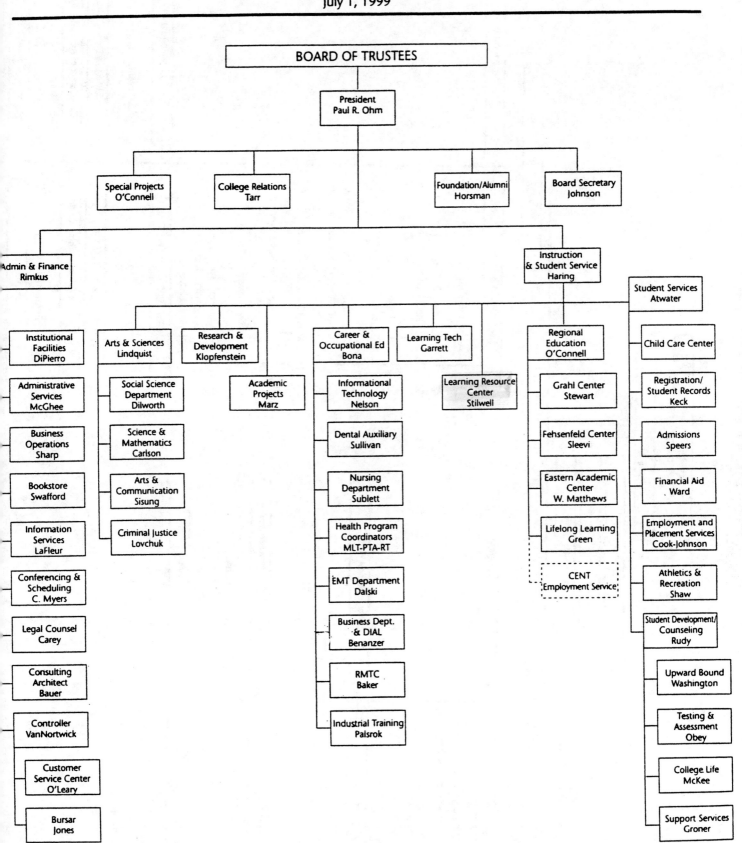

BOARD OF TRUSTEES

President
Paul R. Ohm

Special Projects
O'Connell

College Relations
Tarr

Foundation/Alumni
Horsman

Board Secretary
Johnson

Admin & Finance
Rimkus

Instruction
& Student Service
Haring

Student Services
Atwater

Institutional
Facilities
DiPierro

Arts & Sciences
Lindquist

Research &
Development
Klopfenstein

Career &
Occupational Ed
Bona

Learning Tech
Garrett

Regional
Education
O'Connell

Child Care Center

Administrative
Services
McGhee

Social Science
Department
Dilworth

Academic
Projects
Marz

Informational
Technology
Nelson

Learning Resource
Center
Stilwell

Grahl Center
Stewart

Registration/
Student Records
Keck

Business
Operations
Sharp

Science &
Mathematics
Carlson

Dental Auxiliary
Sullivan

Fehsenfeld Center
Sleevi

Admissions
Speers

Bookstore
Swafford

Arts &
Communication
Sisung

Nursing
Department
Sublett

Eastern Academic
Center
W. Matthews

Financial Aid
Ward

Information
Services
LaFleur

Criminal Justice
Lovchuk

Health Program
Coordinators
MLT-PTA-RT

Lifelong Learning
Green

Employment and
Placement Services
Cook-Johnson

Conferencing &
Scheduling
C. Myers

EMT Department
Dalski

CENT
Employment Service

Athletics &
Recreation
Shaw

Legal Counsel
Carey

Business Dept.
& DIAL
Benanzer

Student Development/
Counseling
Rudy

Consulting
Architect
Bauer

RMTC
Baker

Upward Bound
Washington

Controller
VanNortwick

Industrial Training
Palsrok

Testing &
Assessment
Obey

Customer
Service Center
O'Leary

College Life
McKee

Bursar
Jones

Support Services
Groner

Kellogg Community College

KIRTLAND COMMUNITY COLLEGE

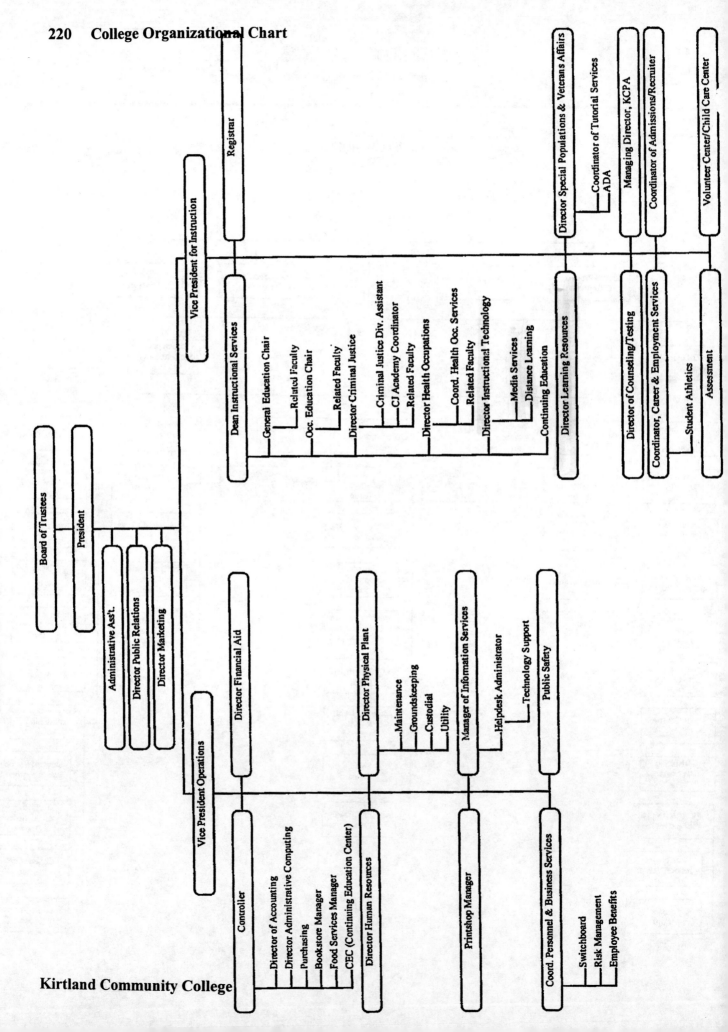

Kirtland Community College

Manatee Community College
Organizational Chart

Dr. Sarah Pappas
President

Dr. James Woods
CEO, Venice Campus

Dr. John Rosen
VP Academic Affairs

Dr. Tom Davenport
Director
Workforce Development

Phil McClung
Director Continuing
and Adult Education

Dr. Mike Mears
Associate Dean
of Instruction

Carol Singer
Associate Dean
of Instruction

Darlene Wedler-Johnson
Associate Dean
of Instruction

Cal Winger
Director Institute of
Alcohol and Drug Education

Alan Richardson
VP Business and
Administrative Services

Margaret Beck
Director of Human Resources

Tom Flowers
Director of Business Services
and Public Safety

Karen Kester
Director of Finance

TBA
Director of Facilities

Alvin Dugan
Supervisor of Maintenance

John Veselenak
Assistant Director
Facilities

Tom Cleary
VP of Planning and Effectiveness

Sue Clayton
Library Department Chair

Marge Dooley
Director of Resource
Development

Lou Macri
Director Computer Services

Su-hua Men
Director Institutional Research

Katherine Walker
Director Public Affairs

Dr. Don Bowman
VP Student Development
and Enrollment Planning

TBA
Registrar

Susan Goodpaster
Director of Recruitment

Anders Nilsen
Director Financial Aid

Dr. Paul Nolting
Student Development Services

Dee Dee Gatch
Coordinator Career
Resource Center

Greg Fierro
Coordinator Disabled
Student Services

George Sanders
Director of Athletics

TBA
Advisor Student Activities

Appendix A—Nicolet College Organization Chart

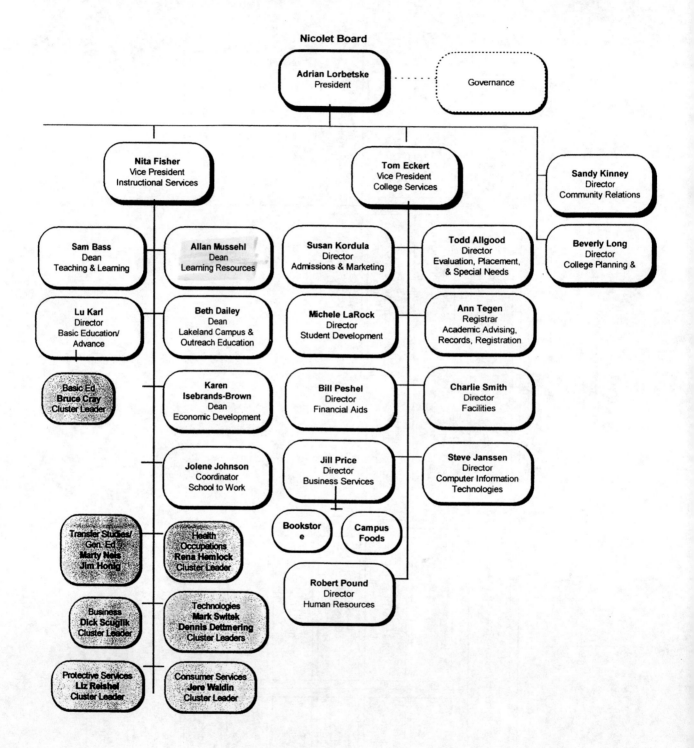

Nicolet Board

Adrian Lorbetske
President

Governance

Nita Fisher
Vice President
Instructional Services

Tom Eckert
Vice President
College Services

Sandy Kinney
Director
Community Relations

Sam Bass
Dean
Teaching & Learning

Allan Mussehl
Dean
Learning Resources

Susan Kordula
Director
Admissions & Marketing

Todd Allgood
Director
Evaluation, Placement,
& Special Needs

Beverly Long
Director
College Planning &

Lu Karl
Director
Basic Education/
Advance

Beth Dailey
Dean
Lakeland Campus &
Outreach Education

Michele LaRock
Director
Student Development

Ann Tegen
Registrar
Academic Advising,
Records, Registration

Basic Ed
Bruce Cray
Cluster Leader

**Karen
Isebrands-Brown**
Dean
Economic Development

Bill Peshel
Director
Financial Aids

Charlie Smith
Director
Facilities

Jolene Johnson
Coordinator
School to Work

Jill Price
Director
Business Services

Steve Janssen
Director
Computer Information
Technologies

Transfer Studies/
Gen. Ed
**Marty Neis
Jim Honig**

Health
Occupations
Rena Hemlock
Cluster Leader

Bookstore

**Campus
Foods**

Business
Dick Scuglik
Cluster Leader

Technologies
**Mark Switek
Dennis Dettmering**
Cluster Leaders

Robert Pound
Director
Human Resources

Protective Services
Liz Reishel
Cluster Leader

Consumer Services
Jere Waldin
Cluster Leader

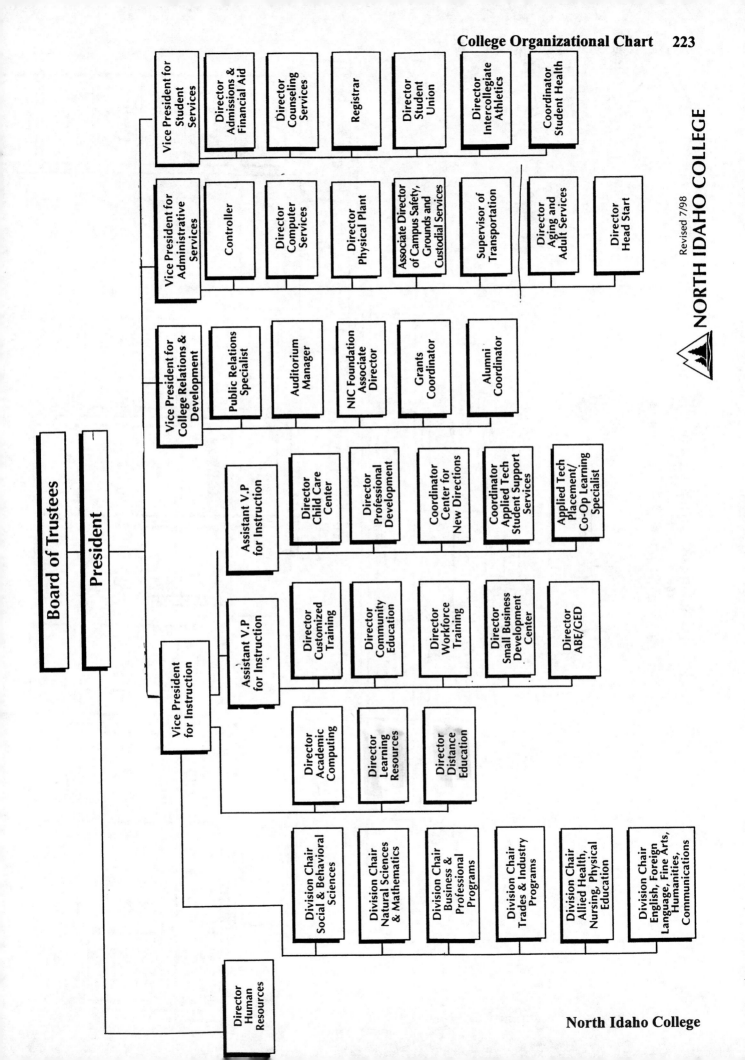

North Idaho College

SERIES NUMBER: 311

Northeast Iowa Community College
"The College for All the Possibilities"
1999-2000

Citizens of NICC District

Board of Trustees

President

Office of Institutional Research, Grants & Alumni Gifts, Private Giving

Assistant to the President-Resource Development [Barb]

Assistant to the President-Research Grants & Alumni [Catherine]

Vice-President for Economic Development Services [Ken]

Economic Development Consulting Services

Vice-President for Administrative Services* [Bob]

- Accounting & Financial Forecasting
- Human Resources
- Computer Information Services
- Business Services/ Purchasing
- Continuing Education Financial
- Switchboard

Executive Vice-President for Student & Academic Affairs [Darwin]

- Distance Learning [Kathy G.]
- Marketing, News & Publications [Kathy H.]
- Enrollment Services & Admissions [Lee & Martha]
- Centers [Oelwein, Manchester, Chickasaw County]

Provost for Student and Academic Affairs Calmar [Jim]

- Department Chairs
- Faculty
- Dairy Foundation
- Continuing Education Director [Alt. H.S.]
- Library Learning Center
- Day Care Center
- Office Manger Student Services
- Food Service*
- Print Shop
- Maintenance*
- Bookstore*
- Security

Provost for Student and Academic Affairs Peosta & Dubuque [Karla]

- Ag. Safety Center
- Department Chairs
- Faculty
- Day Care Center
- Continuing Education Director [Alt. H.S.]
- Library
- Bookstore*
- Switchboard
- Learning Center [PAVE]
- Food Service*
- Print Shop
- Security
- Vice-Provost & Dept. Chair
- Coordinator of Student Services
- Maintenance*

Northeast Iowa Community College

Our Structure

NAVAJO COUNTY COMMUNITY COLLEGE DISTRICT GOVERNING BOARD
(NORTHLAND PIONEER COLLEGE)

Office of the President

Assistant to the President

Director of Marketing & Public Relations

Vice President for Instructional Services	Vice President for Administrative Services	Vice President for Student Services	Dean of Information Services	Director of Institutional Research and Planning	Director of Native American Program Services
Apache County Programs /Centers	Bookstore	Academic Advising	Computer Services		
Developmental Services	Business Office	Admissions	Library Services		
Division of Liberal Arts	Campus Coordinators	Athletics	Networking & Telecommunication Systems		
Division of Business & Technologies	District Office	Career Services			
Division of Science & Mathematics	Facilities/Maintenance	Financial Aid			
Extended Learning Services	Purchasing	Personnel			
Instructional Support Services	Transportation	Registrar			
Satellite Programs/ Centers		Residence Halls			
		Special Needs			
		Student Activities			

Vice President for Instructional Services
Judith E. Doerr

DIVISION OF LIBERAL ARTS Pat Wolf, Dean	DIVISION OF BUSINESS & TECHNOLOGY Mark Workman, Dean	DIVISION OF SCIENCE & MATHEMATICS Brenda Manthei, Dean	EXTENDED LEARNING SERVICES Joel Eittreim, Director	INSTRUCTIONAL SUPPORT SERVICES Charles Kermes, Assoc. Dean	DEVELOPMENTAL SERVICES Heidi Fulcher, Director
Art	Administrative Information Services	Agriculture	Alternative Education	Academic Assessment	The Learning Cornerstone
Anthropology	Aviation	Astronomy	Community Outreach	Faculty Evaluation	Developmental Reading
Child Development	Business	Biology	Community Service Programs	Instructional Program Applications	Developmental Writing
Correctional Services	Computer Information Systems	Chemistry	Continuing Education	Instructional Report Development	Developmental Math
Criminal Justice	Computer Technology	Cosmetology	Contracted Instruction	Program Review	Study Skills
Education	Construction Technology	Emergency Medical Training	Enrichment Courses		ABE/GED (instruction)
English	Drafting Technology	Fire Science	Small Business Development		ESL/Citizenship
Geography	Electronics Technology	Forestry	Special Events		Learning Assistance
History	Industrial Arts Technology	Geology	Summer Sessions		TLC Tutoring
Honors Colloquia	Industrial Technology	Health Sciences			Placement
Human Development	Photography Technician	Home Economics			Student Writing Centers
Human Services	School-to-Work	Math			
Humanities	Small Business Management	Medical Assistant			
Language	Tech Prep	Nursing			
Legal Assistant	Welding Technology	Nursing Assistant			
Library Science		Occupational Therapy Assistant (*Proposed*)			
Music		Physics			
Philosophy		Turfgrass Management			
Political Science					
Psychology					
Speech/Theatre					
Sociology					

**SATELLITE PROGRAMS
Ron Troutman, Coordinator**

GED & Credit by Exam
Satellite Center Programming (Navajo County)
  Dept. of Corrections
  Heber
  Keams Canyon
  Whiteriver

**APACHE COUNTY PROGRAMS
Robert Parnell, Coordinator**

Satellite Center Programming (Apache County)
  Springerville/ Eagar
  St. Johns
  Sanders

Northland Pioneer College

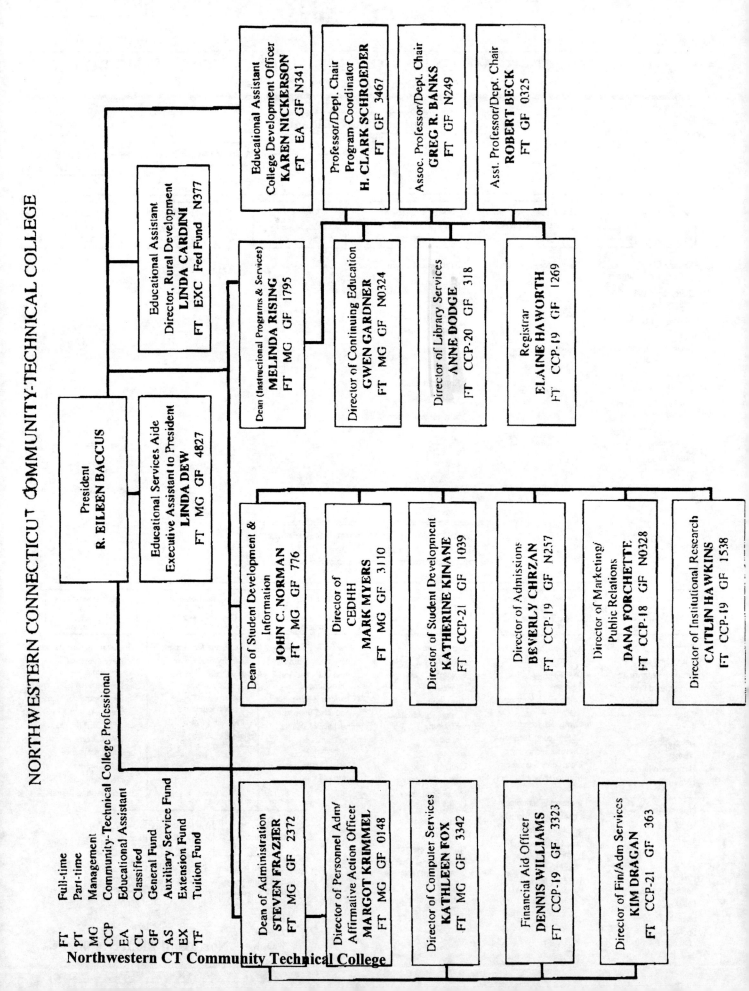

NORTHWESTERN CONNECTICUT COMMUNITY-TECHNICAL COLLEGE

FT   Full-time
PT   Part-time
MG   Management
CCP   Community-Technical College Professional
EA   Educational Assistant
CL   Classified
GF   General Fund
AS   Auxiliary Service Fund
EX   Extension Fund
TF   Tuition Fund

Northwestern CT Community Technical College

Educational Assistant
College Development Officer
KAREN NICKERSON
FT EA GF N341

Professor/Dept. Chair
Program Coordinator
H. CLARK SCHROEDER
FT GF 3467

Assoc. Professor/Dept. Chair
GREG R. BANKS
FT GF N249

Asst. Professor/Dept. Chair
ROBERT BECK
FT GF 0325

Educational Assistant
Director, Rural Development
LINDA CARDINI
FT EXC Fed Fund N377

Dean (Instructional Programs & Services)
MELINDA RISING
FT MG GF 1795

Director of Continuing Education
GWEN GARDNER
FT MG GF N0324

Director of Library Services
ANNE DODGE
FT CCP-20 GF 318

Registrar
ELAINE HAWORTH
FT CCP-19 GF 1269

President
R. EILEEN BACCUS

Educational Services Aide
Executive Assistant to President
LINDA DEW
FT MG GF 4827

Dean of Student Development &
Information
JOHN C. NORMAN
FT MG GF 776

Director of
CEDHH
MARK MYERS
FT MG GF 3110

Director of Student Development
KATHERINE KINANE
FT CCP-21 GF 1039

Director of Admissions
BEVERLY CHRZAN
FT CCP-19 GF N257

Director of Marketing/
Public Relations
DANA FORCHETTE
FT CCP-18 GF N0328

Director of Institutional Research
CAITLIN HAWKINS
FT CCP-19 GF 1538

Dean of Administration
STEVEN FRAZIER
FT MG GF 2372

Director of Personnel Adm/
Affirmative Action Officer
MARGOT KRIMMEL
FT MG GF 0148

Director of Computer Services
KATHLEEN FOX
FT MG GF 3342

Financial Aid Officer
DENNIS WILLIAMS
FT CCP-19 GF 3323

Director of Fin/Adm Services
KIM DRAGAN
FT CCP-21 GF 363

OKALOOSA-WALTON COMMUNITY COLLEGE
-- ORGANIZATIONAL CHART 1999-2000 --

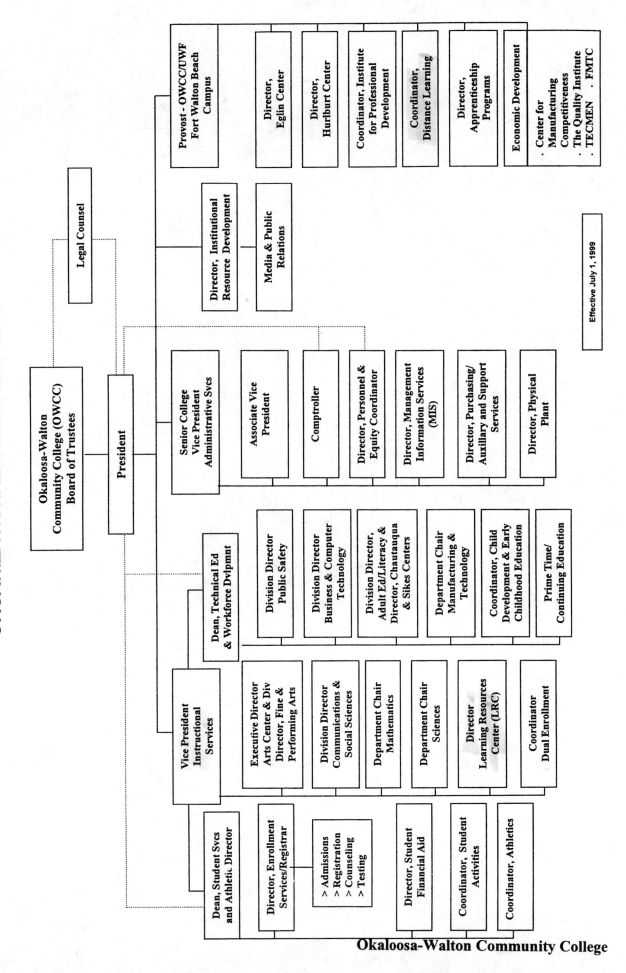

Okaloosa-Walton Community College (OWCC) Board of Trustees

Legal Counsel

President

Provost - OWCC/UWF Fort Walton Beach Campus

Director, Eglin Center

Director, Hurlburt Center

Coordinator, Institute for Professional Development

Coordinator, Distance Learning

Director, Apprenticeship Programs

Economic Development

. Center for Manufacturing Competitiveness
. The Quality Institute
. TECMEN   . FMTC

Director, Institutional Resource Development

Media & Public Relations

Senior College Vice President Administrative Svcs

Associate Vice President

Comptroller

Director, Personnel & Equity Coordinator

Director, Management Information Services (MIS)

Director, Purchasing/ Auxiliary and Support Services

Director, Physical Plant

Effective July 1, 1999

Dean, Technical Ed & Workforce Dvlpmnt

Division Director Public Safety

Division Director Business & Computer Technology

Division Director, Adult Ed/Literacy & Director, Chautauqua & Sikes Centers

Department Chair Manufacturing & Technology

Coordinator, Child Development & Early Childhood Education

Prime Time/ Continuing Education

Vice President Instructional Services

Executive Director Arts Center & Div Director, Fine & Performing Arts

Division Director Communications & Social Sciences

Department Chair Mathematics

Department Chair Sciences

Director Learning Resources Center (LRC)

Coordinator Dual Enrollment

Dean, Student Svcs and Athletic Director

Director, Enrollment Services/Registrar

> Admissions
> Registration
> Counseling
> Testing

Director, Student Financial Aid

Coordinator, Student Activities

Coordinator, Athletics

ACADEMIC/VOCATIONAL INSTRUCTION
Organizational Chart

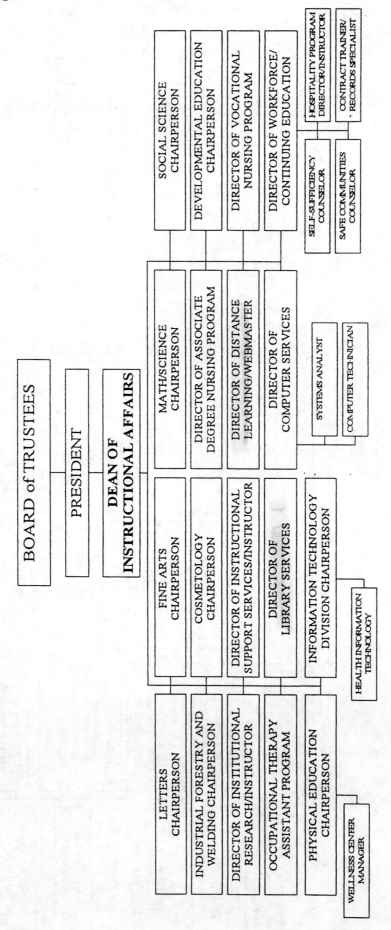

Panola College

Appendix 1.5.2.

Paul Smith's College
Academic Affairs
Fall 1999

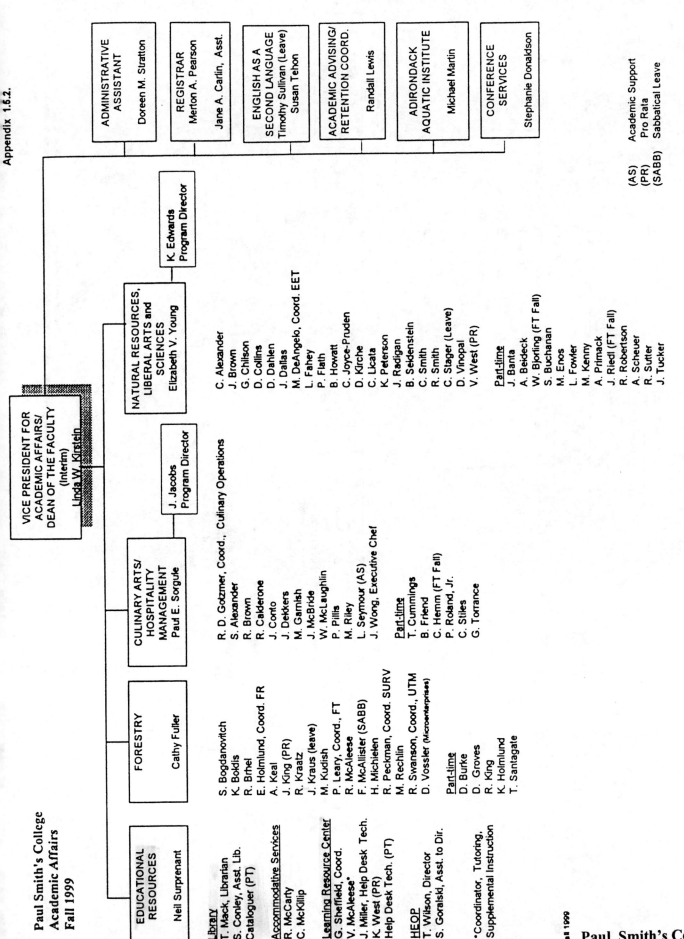

VICE PRESIDENT FOR ACADEMIC AFFAIRS/ DEAN OF THE FACULTY (Interim)
Linda W. Kirstein

ADMINISTRATIVE ASSISTANT
Doreen M. Stratton

REGISTRAR
Merton A. Pearson
Jane A. Carlin, Asst.

ENGLISH AS A SECOND LANGUAGE
Timothy Sullivan (Leave)
Susan Tehon

ACADEMIC ADVISING/ RETENTION COORD.
Randall Lewis

ADIRONDACK AQUATIC INSTITUTE
Michael Martin

CONFERENCE SERVICES
Stephanie Donaldson

(AS)   Academic Support
(PR)   Pro Rata
(SABB) Sabbatical Leave

EDUCATIONAL RESOURCES
Neil Surprenant

FORESTRY
Cathy Fuller

CULINARY ARTS/ HOSPITALITY MANAGEMENT
Paul E. Sorgule

NATURAL RESOURCES, LIBERAL ARTS and SCIENCES
Elizabeth V. Young

J. Jacobs
Program Director

K. Edwards
Program Director

Library
T. Mack, Librarian
S. Conley, Asst. Lib.
Cataloguer (PT)

Accommodative Services
R. McCarty
C. McKillip

Learning Resource Center
G. Sheffield, Coord.
V. McAleese*
J. Miller, Help Desk Tech.
K. West (PR)
Help Desk Tech. (PT)

HEOP
T. Wilson, Director
S. Goralski, Asst. to Dir.

*Coordinator, Tutoring, Supplemental Instruction

S. Bogdanovitch
K. Boldis
R. Brhel
E. Holmlund, Coord. FR
A. Keal
J. King (PR)
R. Kraatz
J. Kraus (leave)
M. Kudish
P. Leary, Coord., FT
R. McAleese
F. McAllister (SABB)
H. Michielen
R. Peckman, Coord. SURV
M. Rechlin
R. Swanson, Coord., UTM
D. Vossler (Microenterprises)

Part-time
D. Burke
D. Groves
R. King
K. Holmlund
T. Santagate

R. D. Gotzmer, Coord., Culinary Operations
S. Alexander
R. Brown
R. Calderone
J. Conto
J. Dekkers
M. Garnish
J. McBride
W. McLaughlin
P. Pillis
M. Riley
L. Seymour (AS)
J. Wong, Executive Chef

Part-time
T. Cummings
B. Friend
C. Hemm (FT Fall)
P. Roland, Jr.
C. Stiles
G. Torrance

C. Alexander
J. Brown
G. Chilson
D. Collins
D. Dahlen
J. Dallas
M. DeAngelo, Coord. EET
L. Fahey
P. Flath
B. Howatt
C. Joyce-Pruden
D. Kirche
C. Licata
K. Peterson
J. Radigan
B. Seidenstein
C. Smith
R. Smith
C. Stager (Leave)
D. Vinopal
V. West (PR)

Part-time
J. Banta
A. Beideck
W. Bjorling (FT Fall)
S. Buchanan
M. Enos
L. Fowler
M. Kenny
A. Primack
J. Riedl (FT Fall)
R. Robertson
A. Scheuer
R. Sutter
J. Tucker

Fall 1999

Paul Smith's College

Pierce College
Organization Chart
August 1999

Board of Trustees

District President
Steve Wall

Affirmative Action Officer
Kelly Brooks
Director of College Relations
Dale Stowell
Director of Development
Cherry Tinker
Director of Human Resources
Jan Bucholz
Director of Institutional Research
Lynne Stamoulis

Institutional Technology
Dean
Dan Russ

Vice President
Administrative Services
Alan Spence

Executive Vice President
Extended Learning
Ed Brewster

Pierce College
at Puyallup
President
District Executive for
Student Services
Steve Wall

Campus
Vice President
Learning and
Student Success
Mary Chikwinya

Pierce College
at Fort Steilacoom
President
District Executive for
Instruction
Michele Johnson

Campus
Vice President
Learning and
Student Success
Sara L. @Sunny# Burns

Director
Library/Media Services
Debra Gilchrist

Pierce College

PRINCE GEORGE'S COMMUNITY COLLEGE
Continuing Education and Evening Programs
Administrative Organization Functions 1998-1999

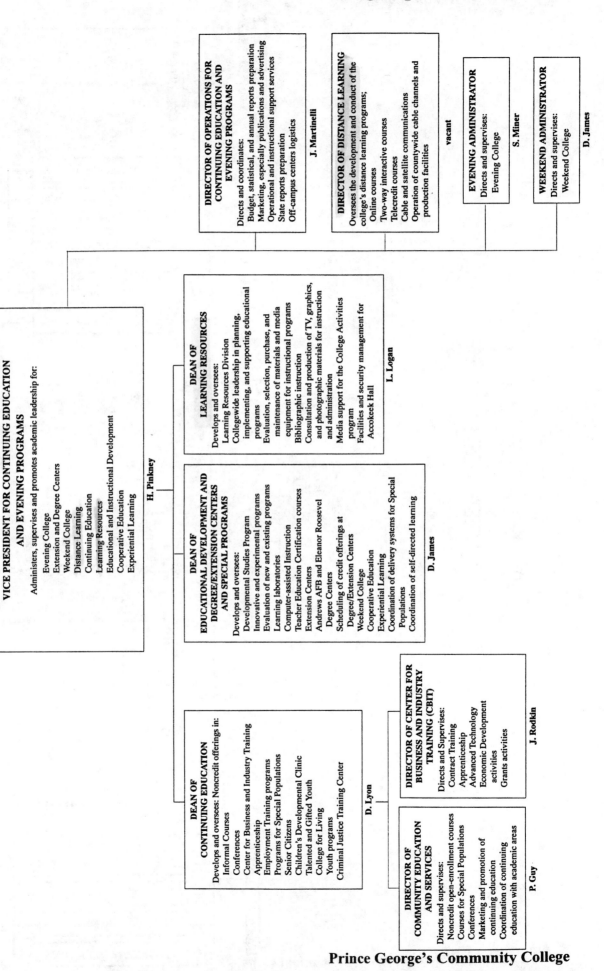

VICE PRESIDENT FOR CONTINUING EDUCATION AND EVENING PROGRAMS

Administers, supervises and promotes academic leadership for:

Evening College
Extension and Degree Centers
Weekend College
Distance Learning
Continuing Education
Learning Resources
Educational and Instructional Development
Cooperative Education
Experiential Learning

H. Pinkney

DIRECTOR OF OPERATIONS FOR CONTINUING EDUCATION AND EVENING PROGRAMS

Directs and coordinates:

Budget, statistical, and annual reports preparation
Marketing, especially publications and advertising
Operational and instructional support services
State reports preparation
Off-campus centers logistics

J. Martinelli

DIRECTOR OF DISTANCE LEARNING

Oversees the development and conduct of the college's distance learning programs;
Online courses
Two-way interactive courses
Telecredit courses
Cable and satellite communications
Operation of countywide cable channels and production facilities

vacant

EVENING ADMINISTRATOR

Directs and supervises:
Evening College

S. Miner

WEEKEND ADMINISTRATOR

Directs and supervises:
Weekend College

D. James

DEAN OF LEARNING RESOURCES

Develops and oversees:
Learning Resources Division
Collegewide leadership in planning, implementing, and supporting educational programs
Evaluation, selection, purchase, and maintenance of materials and media equipment for instructional programs
Bibliographic instruction
Consultation and production of TV, graphics, and photographic materials for instruction and administration
Media support for the College Activities program
Facilities and security management for Accokeek Hall

L. Logan

DEAN OF EDUCATIONAL DEVELOPMENT AND DEGREE/EXTENSION CENTERS AND SPECIAL PROGRAMS

Develops and oversees:
Developmental Studies Program
Innovative and experimental programs
Evaluation of new and existing programs
Learning laboratories
Computer-assisted Instruction
Teacher Education Certification courses
Extension Centers
Andrews AFB and Eleanor Roosevel
Degree Centers
Scheduling of credit offerings at Degree/Extension Centers
Weekend College
Cooperative Education
Experiential Learning
Coordination of delivery systems for Special Populations
Coordination of self-directed learning

D. James

DEAN OF CONTINUING EDUCATION

Develops and oversees: Noncredit offerings in:
Informal Courses
Conferences
Center for Business and Industry Training
Apprenticeship
Employment Training programs
Programs for Special Populations
Senior Citizens
Children's Developmental Clinic
Talented and Gifted Youth
College for Living
Youth programs
Criminal Justice Training Center

D. Lyon

DIRECTOR OF CENTER FOR BUSINESS AND INDUSTRY TRAINING (CBIT)

Directs and Supervises:
Contract Training
Apprenticeship
Advanced Technology
Economic Development activities
Grants activities

J. Rodkin

DIRECTOR OF COMMUNITY EDUCATION AND SERVICES

Directs and supervises:
Noncredit open-enrollment courses
Courses for Special Populations
Conferences
Marketing and promotion of continuing education
Coordination of continuing education with academic areas

P. Guy

FIGURE 2
ORGANIZATION CHART

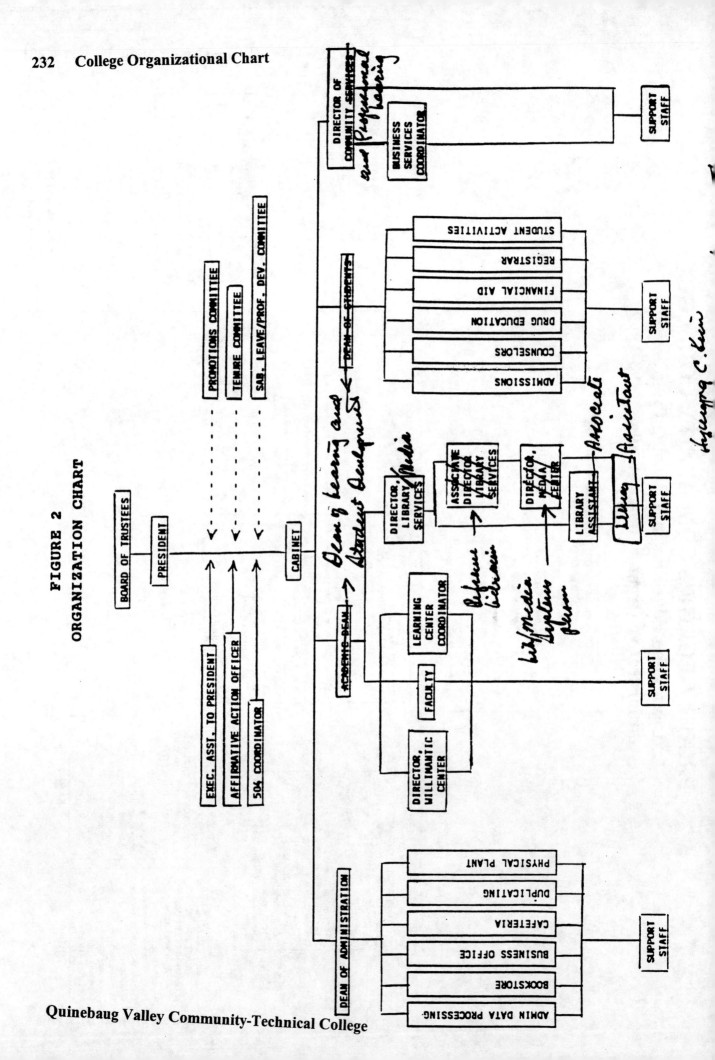

Quinebaug Valley Community-Technical College

Educational Programs

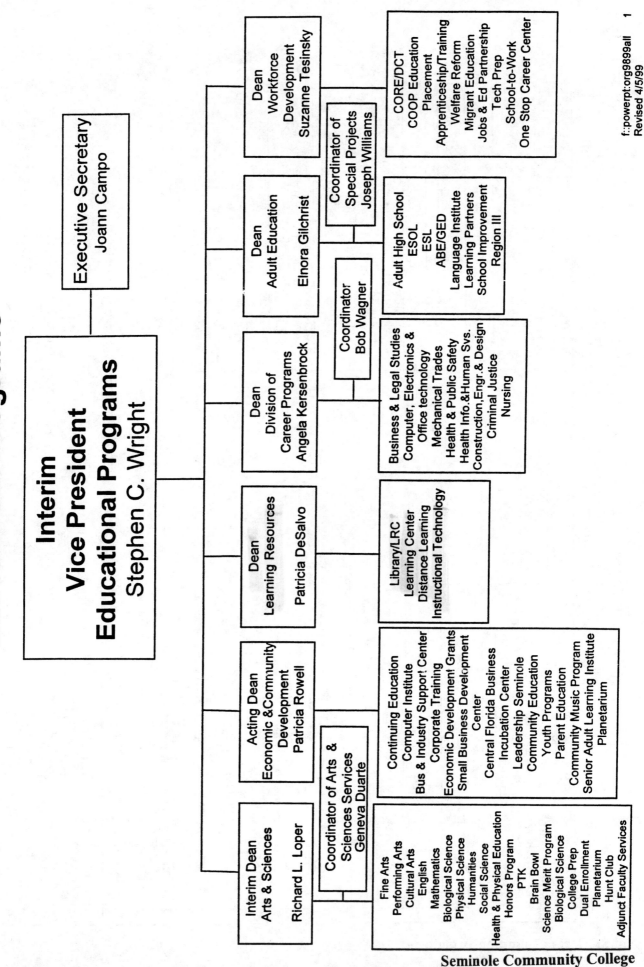

**Interim
Vice President
Educational Programs**
Stephen C. Wright

Executive Secretary
Joann Campo

Dean
Workforce
Development
Suzanne Tesinsky

Coordinator of
Special Projects
Joseph Williams

CORE/DCT
COOP Education
Placement
Apprenticeship/Training
Welfare Reform
Migrant Education
Jobs & Ed Partnership
Tech Prep
School-to-Work
One Stop Career Center

Dean
Adult Education
Elnora Gilchrist

Adult High School
ESOL
ESL
ABE/GED
Language Institute
Learning Partners
School Improvement
Region III

Coordinator
Bob Wagner

Dean
Division of
Career Programs
Angela Kersenbrock

Business & Legal Studies
Computer, Electronics &
Office technology
Mechanical Trades
Health & Public Safety
Health Info.&Human Svs.
Construction,Engr.& Design
Criminal Justice
Nursing

Dean
Learning Resources
Patricia DeSalvo

Library/LRC
Learning Center
Distance Learning
Instructional Technology

Acting Dean
Economic &Community
Development
Patricia Rowell

Continuing Education
Computer Institute
Bus & Industry Support Center
Corporate Training
Economic Development Grants
Small Business Development
Center
Central Florida Business
Incubation Center
Leadership Seminole
Community Education
Youth Programs
Parent Education
Community Music Program
Senior Adult Learning Institute
Planetarium

Interim Dean
Arts & Sciences
Richard L. Loper

Coordinator of Arts &
Sciences Services
Geneva Duarte

Fine Arts
Performing Arts
Cultural Arts
English
Mathematics
Biological Science
Physical Science
Humanities
Social Science
Health & Physical Education
Honors Program
PTK
Brain Bowl
Science Merit Program
Biological Science
College Prep
Dual Enrollment
Planetarium
Hunt Club
Adjunct Faculty Services

Seminole Community College

f::powerpt:org9899all   1
Revised 4/5/99

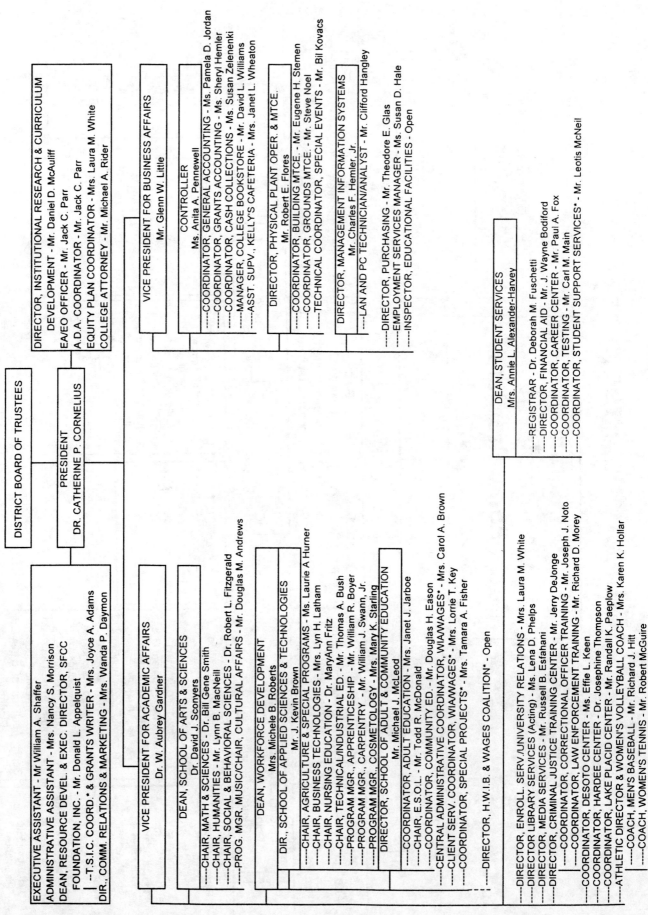

2000-2001 SOUTH FLORIDA COMMUNITY COLLEGE ORGANIZATIONAL CHART

7/24/00

DISTRICT BOARD OF TRUSTEES

PRESIDENT
DR. CATHERINE P. CORNELIUS

EXECUTIVE ASSISTANT - Mr William A. Shaffer
ADMINISTRATIVE ASSISTANT - Mrs. Nancy S. Morrison
DEAN, RESOURCE DEVEL. & EXEC. DIRECTOR, SFCC
FOUNDATION, INC. - Mr. Donald L. Appelquist
-T.S.I.C. COORD.* & GRANTS WRITER - Mrs. Joyce A. Adams
DIR., COMM. RELATIONS & MARKETING - Mrs. Wanda P. Daymon

DIRECTOR, INSTITUTIONAL RESEARCH & CURRICULUM
DEVELOPMENT - Mr. Daniel D. McAuliff
EA/EO OFFICER - Mr. Jack C. Parr
A.D.A. COORDINATOR - Mr. Jack C. Parr
EQUITY PLAN COORDINATOR - Mrs. Laura M. White
COLLEGE ATTORNEY - Mr. Michael A. Rider

VICE PRESIDENT FOR BUSINESS AFFAIRS
Mr. Glenn W. Little

CONTROLLER
Ms. Anita A. Pennewell
----COORDINATOR, GENERAL ACCOUNTING - Ms. Pamela D. Jordan
----COORDINATOR, GRANTS ACCOUNTING - Ms. Sheryl Hemler
----COORDINATOR, CASH COLLECTIONS - Ms. Susan Zelenenki
----MANAGER, COLLEGE BOOKSTORE - Mr. David L. Williams
----ASST. SUPV., KELLY'S CAFETERIA - Mrs. Janet L. Wheaton

DIRECTOR, PHYSICAL PLANT OPER. & MTCE.
Mr. Robert E. Flores
----COORDINATOR, BUILDING MTCE. - Mr. Eugene H. Stemen
----COORDINATOR, GROUNDS MTCE. - Mr. Steve Noel
----TECHNICAL COORDINATOR, SPECIAL EVENTS - Mr. Bil Kovacs

DIRECTOR, MANAGEMENT INFORMATION SYSTEMS
Mr. Charles F. Hemler, Jr.
----LAN AND PC TECHNICIAN/ANALYST - Mr. Clifford Hangley

----DIRECTOR, PURCHASING - Mr. Theodore E. Glas
----EMPLOYMENT SERVICES MANAGER - Ms. Susan D. Hale
----INSPECTOR, EDUCATIONAL FACILITIES - Open

DEAN, STUDENT SERVICES
Mrs. Annie L. Alexander-Harvey
----REGISTRAR - Dr. Deborah M. Fuschetti
----DIRECTOR, FINANCIAL AID - Mr. J. Wayne Bodiford
----COORDINATOR, CAREER CENTER - Mr. Paul A. Fox
----COORDINATOR, TESTING - Mr. Carl M. Main
----COORDINATOR, STUDENT SUPPORT SERVICES* - Mr. Leotis McNeil

VICE PRESIDENT FOR ACADEMIC AFFAIRS
Dr. W. Aubrey Gardner

DEAN, SCHOOL OF ARTS & SCIENCES
Dr. David J. Sconyers
----CHAIR, MATH & SCIENCES - Dr. Bill Gene Smith
----CHAIR, HUMANITIES - Mr. Lynn B. MacNeill
----CHAIR, SOCIAL & BEHAVIORAL SCIENCES - Dr. Robert L. Fitzgerald
----PROG. MGR. MUSIC/CHAIR, CULTURAL AFFAIRS - Mr. Douglas M. Andrews

DEAN, WORKFORCE DEVELOPMENT
Mrs. Michele B. Roberts
----DIR., SCHOOL OF APPLIED SCIENCES & TECHNOLOGIES
Mr. J. Kevin Brown
----CHAIR, AGRICULTURE & SPECIAL PROGRAMS - Ms. Laurie A Hurner
----CHAIR, BUSINESS TECHNOLOGIES - Mrs. Lyn H. Latham
----CHAIR, NURSING EDUCATION - Dr. MaryAnn Fritz
----CHAIR, TECHNICAL/INDUSTRIAL ED. - Mr. Thomas A. Bush
----PROGRAM MGR., APPRENTICESHIP - Mr. William R. Boyer
----PROGRAM MGR., CARPENTRY - Mr. William J. Swann, Jr.
----PROGRAM MGR., COSMETOLOGY - Mrs. Mary K. Starling
----DIRECTOR, SCHOOL OF ADULT & COMMUNITY EDUCATION
Mr. Michael J. McLeod
----COORDINATOR, ADULT EDUCATION - Mrs. Janet J. Jarboe
----CHAIR, E.S.O.L. - Mr. Todd R. McDonald
----COORDINATOR, COMMUNITY ED. - Mr. Douglas H. Eason
----CENTRAL ADMINISTRATIVE COORDINATOR, WIA/WAGES* - Mrs. Carol A. Brown
----CLIENT SERV. COORDINATOR, WIA/WAGES* - Mrs. Lorrie T. Key
----COORDINATOR, SPECIAL PROJECTS* - Mrs. Tamara A. Fisher

----DIRECTOR, H.W.I.B. & WAGES COALITION* - Open

----DIRECTOR, ENROLL. SERV./UNIVERSITY RELATIONS - Mrs. Laura M. White
----DIRECTOR, LIBRARY SERVICES (Acting) - Ms. Lena D. Phelps
----DIRECTOR, MEDIA SERVICES - Mr. Russell B. Esfahani
----DIRECTOR, CRIMINAL JUSTICE TRAINING CENTER - Mr. Jerry DeJonge
----COORDINATOR, CORRECTIONAL OFFICER TRAINING - Mr. Joseph J. Noto
----COORDINATOR, LAW ENFORCEMENT TRAINING - Mr. Richard D. Morey
----COORDINATOR, DESOTO CENTER - Ms. Effie L. Keen
----COORDINATOR, HARDEE CENTER - Dr. Josephine Thompson
----COORDINATOR, LAKE PLACID CENTER - Mr. Randall K. Paeplow
----ATHLETIC DIRECTOR & WOMEN'S VOLLEYBALL COACH - Mrs. Karen K. Hollar
----COACH, MEN'S BASEBALL - Mr. Richard J. Hitt
----COACH, WOMEN'S TENNIS - Mr. Robert McGuire

South Florida Community College

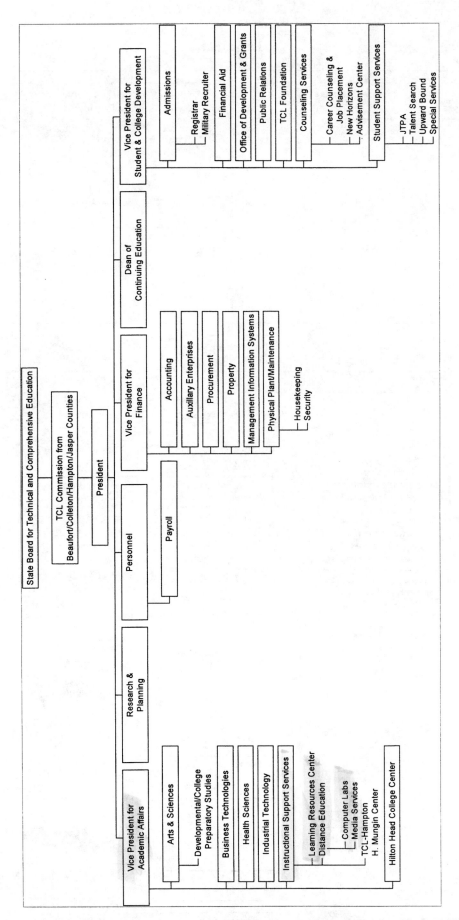

Technical College of the Low Country

TRIDENT TECHNICAL COLLEGE ORGANIZATION CHART

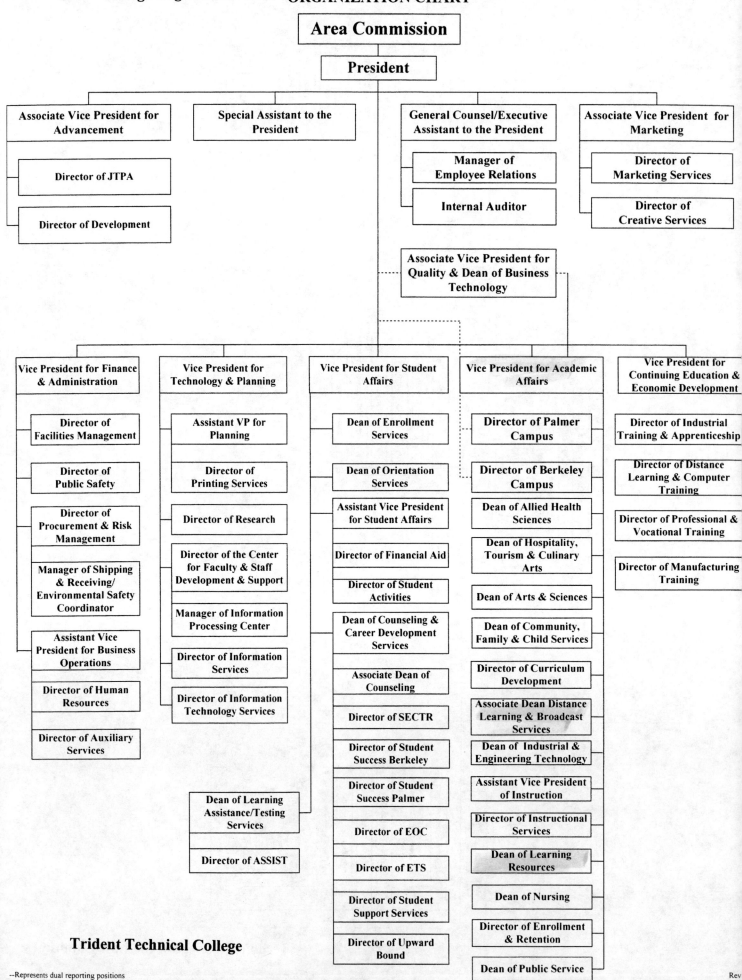

Area Commission

President

Associate Vice President for Advancement
- Director of JTPA
- Director of Development

Special Assistant to the President

General Counsel/Executive Assistant to the President
- Manager of Employee Relations
- Internal Auditor

Associate Vice President for Marketing
- Director of Marketing Services
- Director of Creative Services

Associate Vice President for Quality & Dean of Business Technology

Vice President for Finance & Administration
- Director of Facilities Management
- Director of Public Safety
- Director of Procurement & Risk Management
- Manager of Shipping & Receiving/ Environmental Safety Coordinator
- Assistant Vice President for Business Operations
- Director of Human Resources
- Director of Auxiliary Services

Vice President for Technology & Planning
- Assistant VP for Planning
- Director of Printing Services
- Director of Research
- Director of the Center for Faculty & Staff Development & Support
- Manager of Information Processing Center
- Director of Information Services
- Director of Information Technology Services
- Dean of Learning Assistance/Testing Services
- Director of ASSIST

Vice President for Student Affairs
- Dean of Enrollment Services
- Dean of Orientation Services
- Assistant Vice President for Student Affairs
- Director of Financial Aid
- Director of Student Activities
- Dean of Counseling & Career Development Services
- Associate Dean of Counseling
- Director of SECTR
- Director of Student Success Berkeley
- Director of Student Success Palmer
- Director of EOC
- Director of ETS
- Director of Student Support Services
- Director of Upward Bound

Vice President for Academic Affairs
- Director of Palmer Campus
- Director of Berkeley Campus
- Dean of Allied Health Sciences
- Dean of Hospitality, Tourism & Culinary Arts
- Dean of Arts & Sciences
- Dean of Community, Family & Child Services
- Director of Curriculum Development
- Associate Dean Distance Learning & Broadcast Services
- Dean of Industrial & Engineering Technology
- Assistant Vice President of Instruction
- Director of Instructional Services
- Dean of Learning Resources
- Dean of Nursing
- Director of Enrollment & Retention
- Dean of Public Service

Vice President for Continuing Education & Economic Development
- Director of Industrial Training & Apprenticeship
- Director of Distance Learning & Computer Training
- Director of Professional & Vocational Training
- Director of Manufacturing Training

Trident Technical College

--Represents dual reporting positions

Rev

UMPQUA COMMUNITY COLLEGE
BOARD OF DIRECTORS

PRESIDENT
(DR. JAMES M. KRABY)

Director of UCC Foundation
(TERRY SWAGERTY)

Vice President for Administrative Serv.
- Human Resources
(JOHN BLANCHARD)

- Director of Acct. Services (KIM GANDY)
- Director of Purch./Bookstore Mgr. (DAVE CLIFFORD)
- Director of Plant Op./Maint. (STEVE CHANEY)
- Security Officer (BEE ROBERSON)

Director of Community Relations, AA/EEO
(SONIA WRIGHT)

Vice President for Student Services
- Student Activities
(DR. JACKY HAGAN)

- Director of Admiss. & Records (DR. LARRY SHIPLEY)
- Director of Counseling Serv.
  - Assessment/testing
  - Academic Advising
  - Personal Counseling
  - Career Services
  (DR. LEON YOUNG)
- Director of Financial Aid
  - Federal F.A.
  - Scholarships
  - Student work-study
  - Veterans Affairs
  (CLAUDIA JUSTICE)
- Director of Facilities/Events
  - Facility Scheduling
  - Event Planning/Arrange
  - Jacoby Auditorium
  (MIKE HOFFMAN)
- Manager of Food Serv. (SARAH NEWELL)
- Director of JOBS Program (KAY TANO)

Asst. to President/Athletic Director
(DR. BILL BACHMAN)

Dean of Liberal Arts & Sciences
- Social Science Chr.
(DR. ROGER HAUGEN)

- Director for Health Occup. (SANDY HENDY)
- Business Dept. Chr. (JAN SHIPLEY)
- Humanities Dept. Chr. (DR. JIM O'NEILL)
- Science Dept. Chr. (DR. DALE RITTER)
- Fine/Performing Arts Chr. (MARIE RASMUSSEN)
- Health & PE Chr. (DR. BILL BACHMAN)

Vice President for Instruct. Services
(DR. BERTA DARGEN)

Dean of Career & Technical Train.
- Apprenticeship
- Fire Science
- Industry Training
- Cosmetology
(SHERRIL WELLS)

- Technical Dept. Chr. (DR. DALE BRYSON)
- Dir. Dev. Ed. - Disability Services (DORIS JOHNSON)
- Director of Adult Basic Skills Dev (RICK BOWMAN)
- Faculty Coord. for CWE/SFE (KAREN FAGER)

Director of Computer Serv.
(GEORGE ROTH)

- Dir. of Comm. Ed., Special Programs (SANDI SMICK)
- Director of Library Services (DAVID HUTCHISON)
- Director of Media Services (CHRIS BINGHAM)
- Director of Small Bus. Dev. Ctr. (TERRY SWAGERTY)

Umpqua Community College

Western Oklahoma State College
Organizational Chart 1999-2000

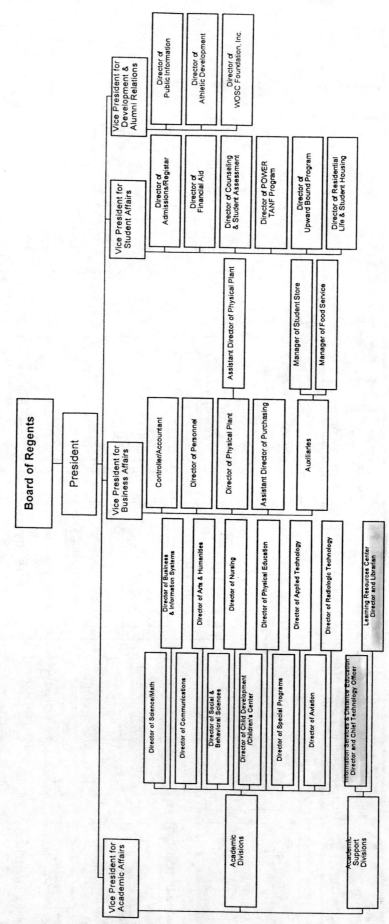

Board of Regents

President

Vice President for Business Affairs

Controller/Accountant

Director of Personnel

Director of Physical Plant

Assistant Director of Purchasing

Assistant Director of Physical Plant

Auxiliaries

Manager of Student Store

Manager of Food Service

Vice President for Student Affairs

Director of Admissions/Registrar

Director of Financial Aid

Director of Counseling & Student Assessment

Director of POWER TANF Program

Director of Upward Bound Program

Director of Residential Life & Student Housing

Vice President for Development & Alumni Relations

Director of Public Information

Director of Athletic Development

Director of WOSC Foundation, Inc.

Vice President for Academic Affairs

Academic Divisions

Director of Science/Math

Director of Business & Information Systems

Director of Communications

Director of Arts & Humanities

Director of Social & Behavioral Sciences

Director of Nursing

Director of Child Development /Children's Center

Director of Physical Education

Director of Special Programs

Director of Applied Technology

Director of Aviation

Director of Radiologic Technology

Academic Support Divisions

Information Services & Distance Education Director and Chief Technology Officer

Learning Resources Center Director and Librarian

D:\MyFiles\1999-2000 Organizational Chart.shw - krb

September 1999

YORK TECHNICAL COLLEGE

Executive Vice President
For Academic and Student Affairs

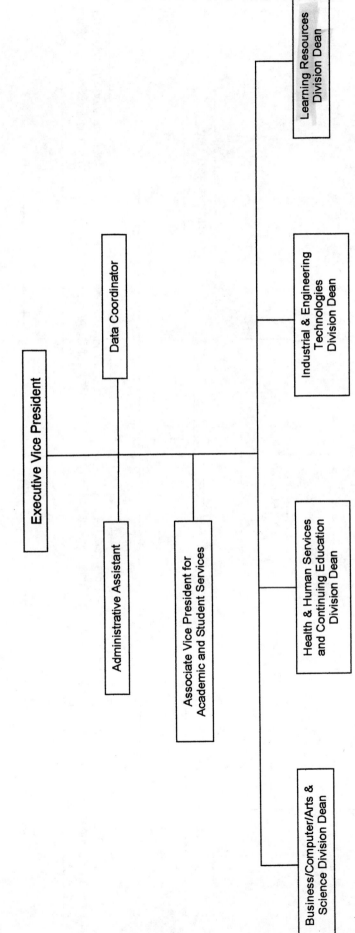

York Technical College

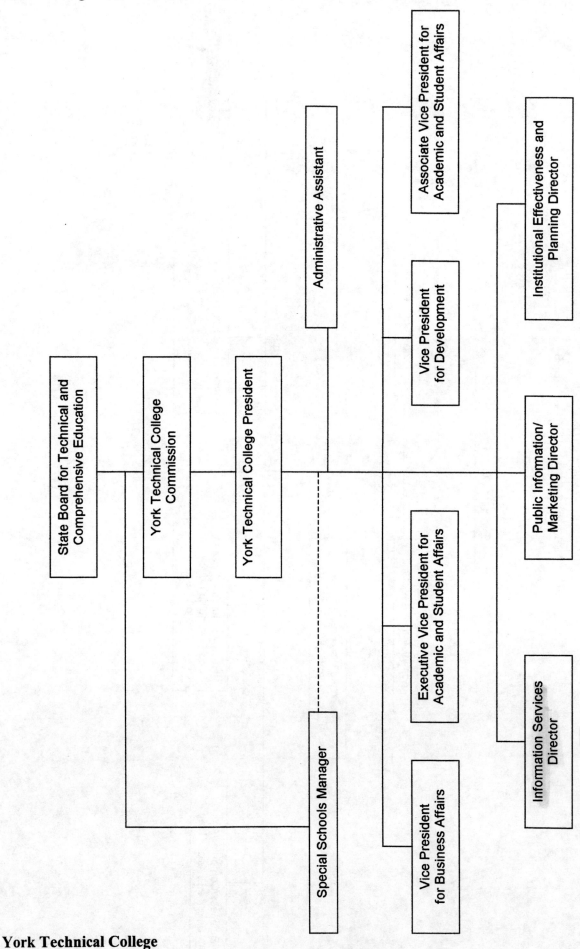

York Technical College

Library Organizational Charts

Blue Mountain Community College
Bossier Parish Community College
Carl Sandburg College
Central Florida Community College
College of DuPage
Columbus State Community College
Eastern Idaho Tech College
Edison Community College
Everett Community College
Gulf Coast Community College
Harrisburg Area Community College
Horry Georgetown Tech College
Hutchinson Community College
Manatee Community College
Miami Dade Community College - Kendall Campus
Monroe Community College
Northland Pioneer College
Norwalk Community Technical College
North Idaho College
Nunez Community College
Okaloosa-Walton Community College
Panola College
Pasadena City College
Pierce College
Portland Community College
St.Petersburg Junior College
Seminole Community College
Trident Tech College
Western Oklahoma
York Tech College

Blue Mountain Community College 1999-2000
Functional Unit: Information Technologies & Resources

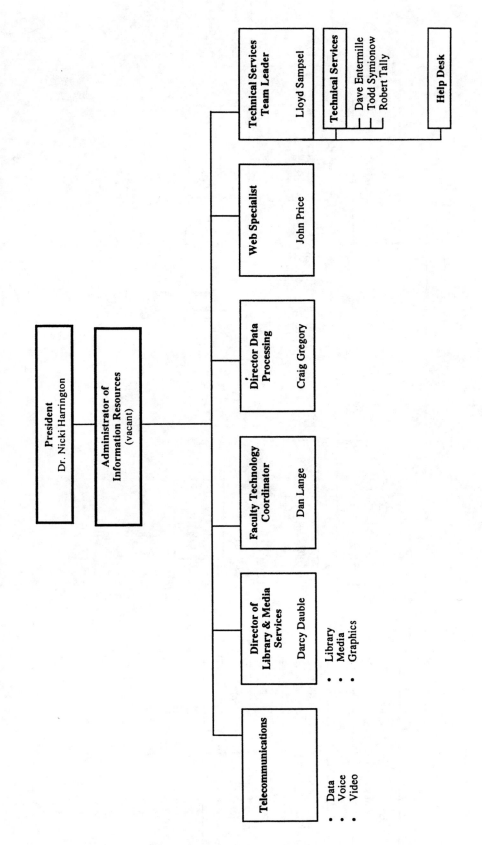

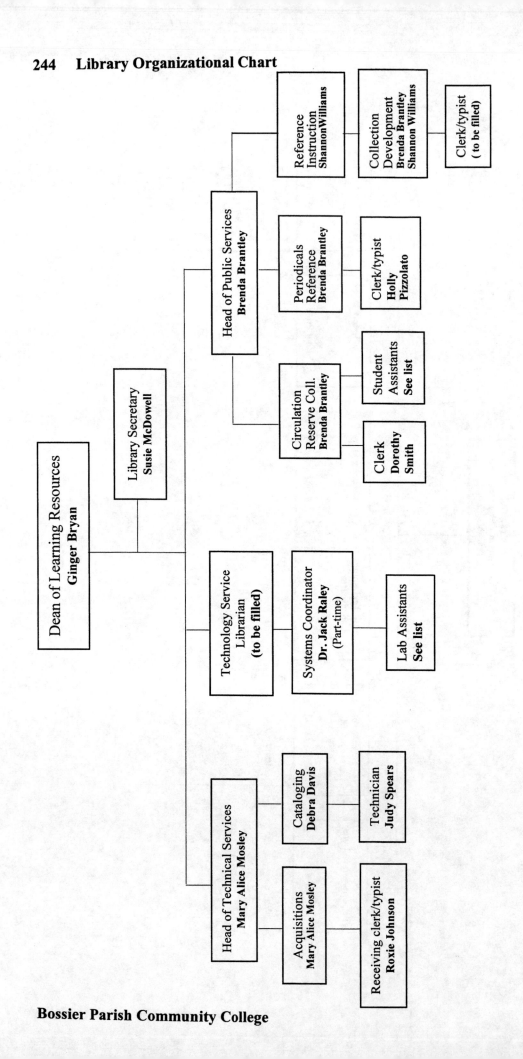

LRC CHART OF FUNCTIONS

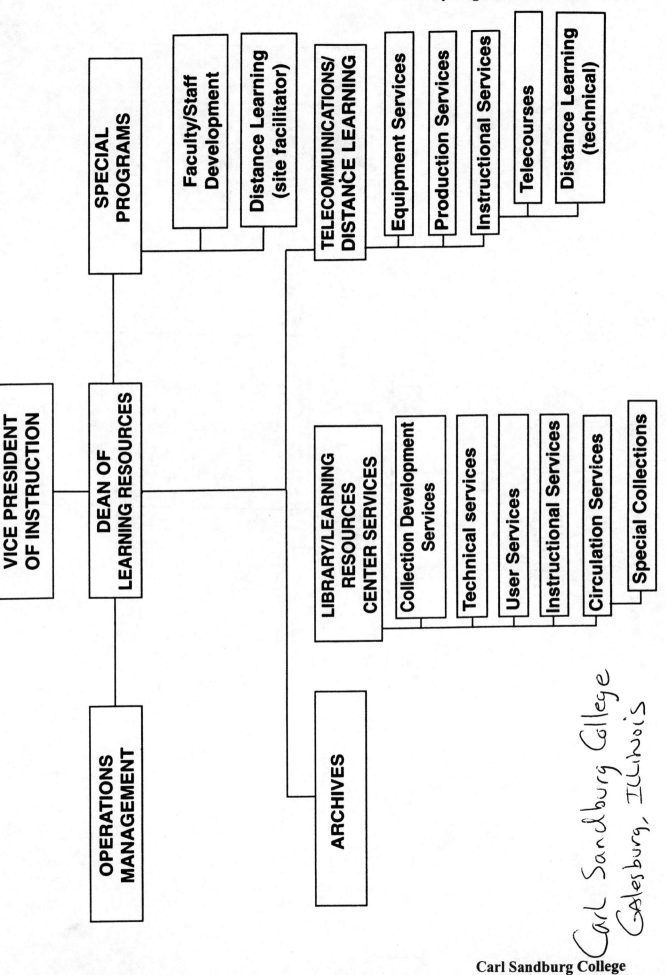

VICE PRESIDENT OF INSTRUCTION

DEAN OF LEARNING RESOURCES

OPERATIONS MANAGEMENT

SPECIAL PROGRAMS

Faculty/Staff Development

Distance Learning (site facilitator)

TELECOMMUNICATIONS/ DISTANCE LEARNING

Equipment Services

Production Services

Instructional Services

Telecourses

Distance Learning (technical)

ARCHIVES

LIBRARY/LEARNING RESOURCES CENTER SERVICES

Collection Development Services

Technical services

User Services

Instructional Services

Circulation Services

Special Collections

Carl Sandburg College
Galesburg, Illinois

Carl Sandburg College

CENTRAL FLORIDA COMMUNITY COLLEGE
Learning Resources Department
Organization Chart

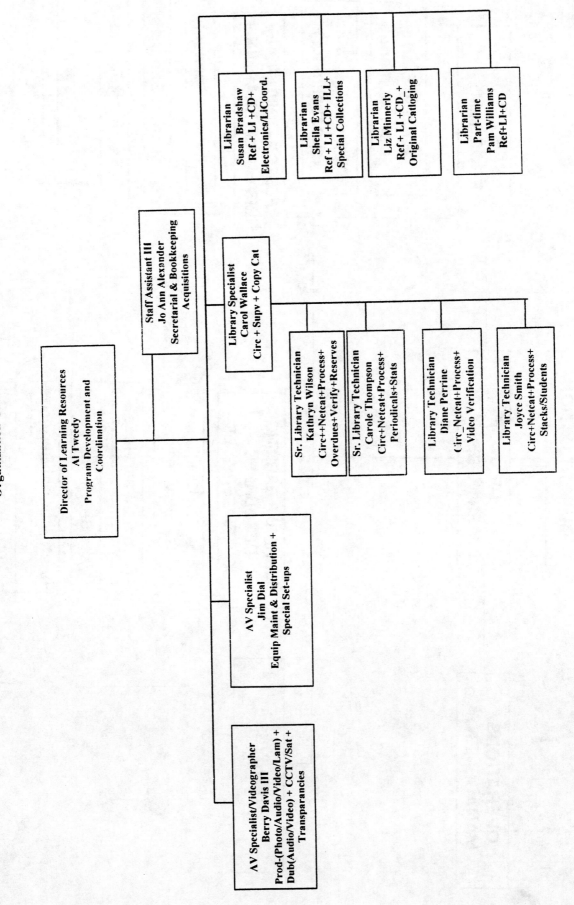

Director of Learning Resources
Al Tweedy
Program Development and
Coordination

Staff Assistant III
Jo Ann Alexander
Secretarial & Bookkeeping
Acquisitions

Librarian
Susan Bradshaw
Ref + LI +CD+
Electronics/LiCoord.

Librarian
Sheila Evans
Ref + LI +CD+ ILL+
Special Collections

Librarian
Liz Minnerly
Ref + LI +CD _+
Original Cattoging

Librarian
Part-time
Pam Williams
Ref+LI+CD

Library Specialist
Carol Wallace
Circ + Supv + Copy Cat

Sr. Library Technician
Kathryn Wilson
Circ++Netcat+Process+
Overdues+Verify+Reserves

Sr. Library Technician
Carole Thompson
Circ+Netcat+Process+
Periodicals+Stats

Library Technician
Diane Perrine
Circ_Netcat+Process+
Video Verification

Library Technician
Joyce Smith
Circ+Netcat+Process+
Stacks/Students

AV Specialist
Jim Dial
Equip Maint & Distribution +
Special Set-ups

AV Specialist/Videographer
Berry Davis III
Prod-(Photo/Audio/Video/Lam) +
Dub(Audio/Video) + CCTV/Sat +
Transparancies

9/30/1999

Central Florida Community College

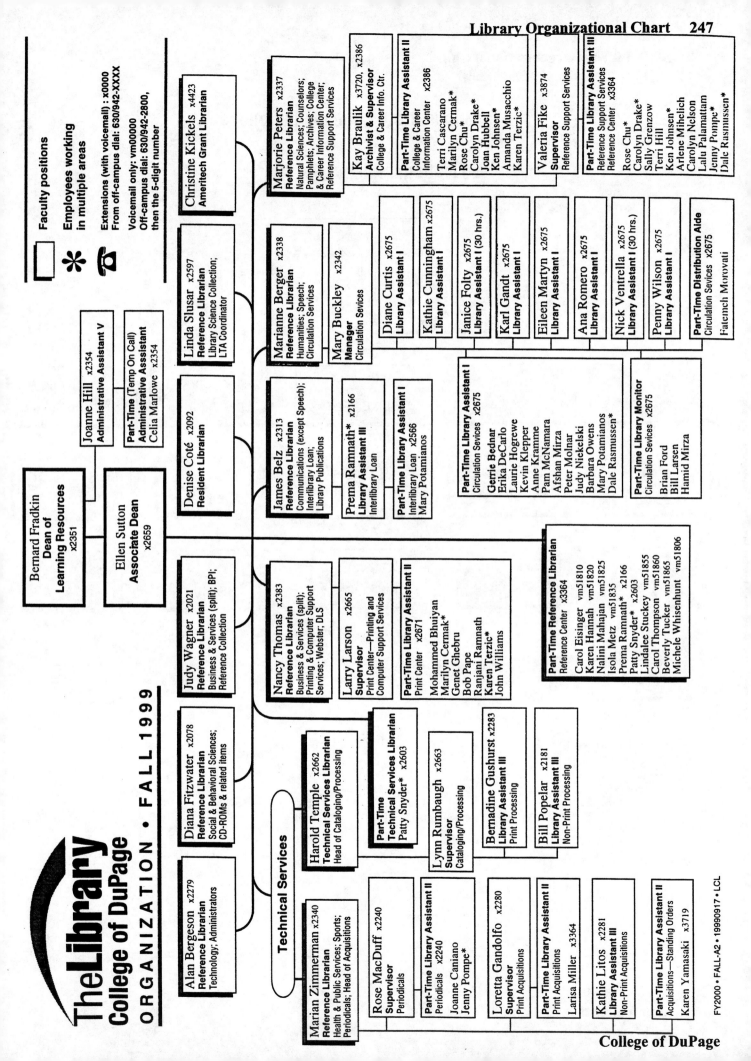

Columbus State Community College

Educational Resources Center

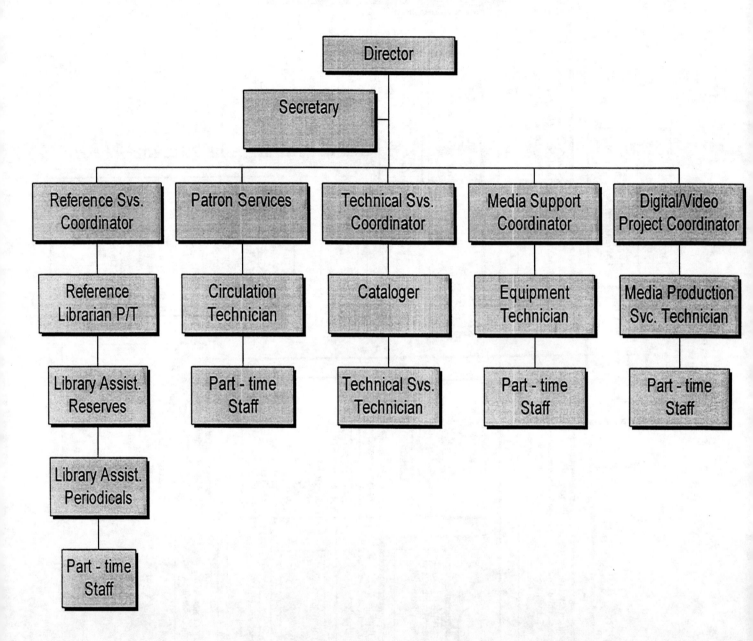

Information Technology Division

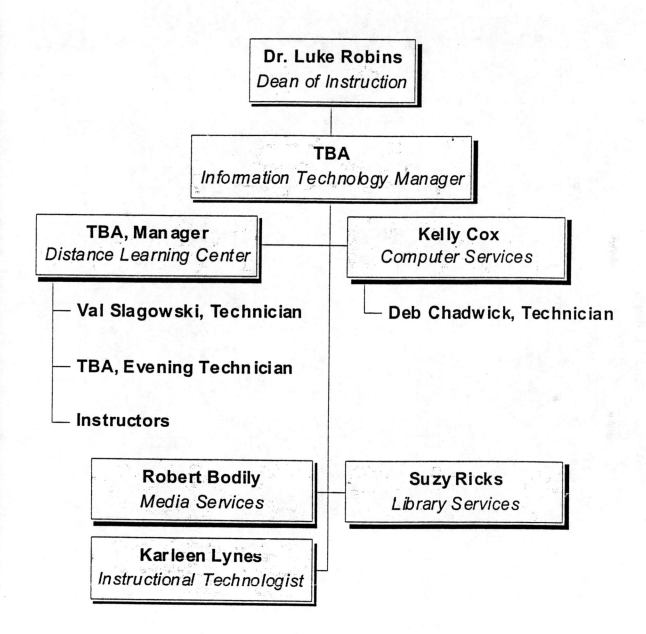

Dr. Luke Robins
Dean of Instruction

TBA
Information Technology Manager

TBA, Manager
Distance Learning Center

Kelly Cox
Computer Services

— **Val Slagowski, Technician**

— **Deb Chadwick, Technician**

— **TBA, Evening Technician**

— **Instructors**

Robert Bodily
Media Services

Suzy Ricks
Library Services

Karleen Lynes
Instructional Technologist

Organizational Charts

Rev. 7-99

Eastern Idaho Technical College

LEARNING RESOURCES ORGANIZATIONAL CHART
Edison Community College
Fort Myers, Florida

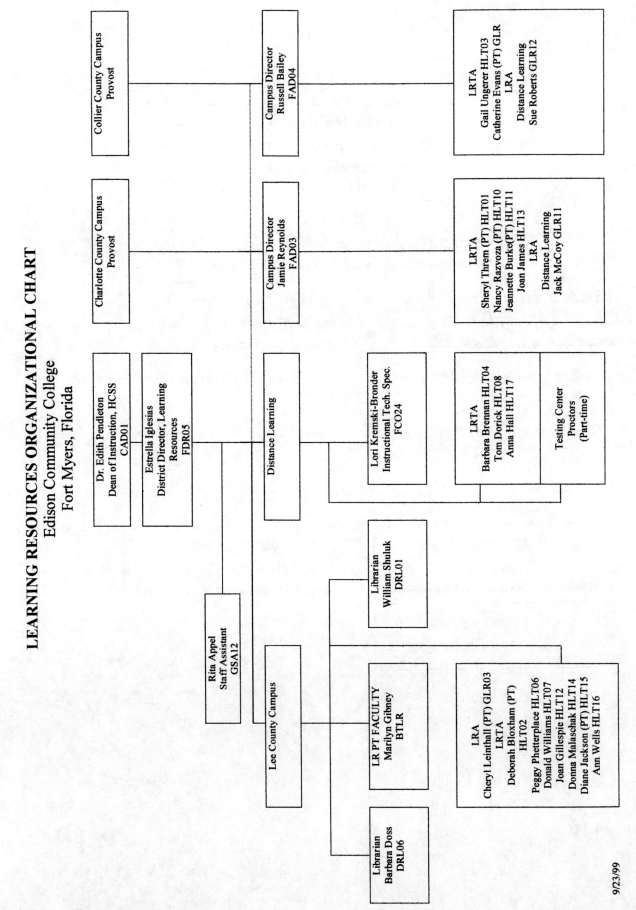

Collier County Campus Provost	
Charlotte County Campus Provost	
Dr. Edith Pendleton Dean of Instruction, HCSS CAD01	
Estrella Iglesias District Director, Learning Resources FDR05	
Campus Director Russell Bailey FAD04	
Campus Director Jamie Reynolds FAD03	
Distance Learning	
Rita Appel Staff Assistant GSA12	
Lee County Campus	
Lori Kremski-Bronder Instructional Tech. Spec. FCO24	
Librarian William Shuluk DRL01	
LR PT FACULTY Marilyn Gibney BTLR	
Librarian Barbara Doss DRL06	

LRTA
Gail Ungerer HLT03
Catherine Evans (PT) GLR
LRA
Distance Learning
Sue Roberts GLR12

LRTA
Sheryl Threm (PT) HLT01
Nancy Razvoza (PT) HLT10
Jeannette Burke(PT) HLT11
Joan James HLT13
LRA
Distance Learning
Jack McCoy GLR11

LRTA
Barbara Brennan HLT04
Tom Dorick HLT08
Anna Hall HLT17

Testing Center
Proctors
(Part-time)

LRA
Cheryl Leinthall (PT) GLR03
LRTA
Deborah Bloxham (PT) HLT02
Peggy Phetterplace HLT06
Donald Williams HLT07
Joan Gillespie HLT12
Donna Malaschak HLT14
Diane Jackson (PT) HLT15
Ann Wells HLT16

9/23/99

Edison Community College

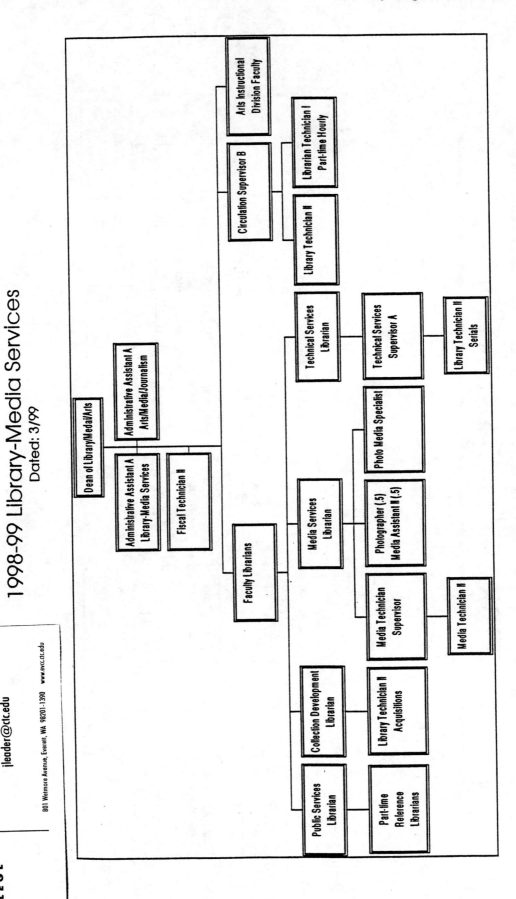

1998-99 Library-Media Services
Dated: 3/99

Jeanne P. Leader
Dean
*Library/Media/Arts and
Distance Learning*

425.388.9502
fax: 425.388.9144
jleader@ctt.edu

801 Wetmore Avenue, Everett, WA. 98201-1390   www.evcc.ctc.edu

Everett Community College

LIBRARY ORGANIZATION

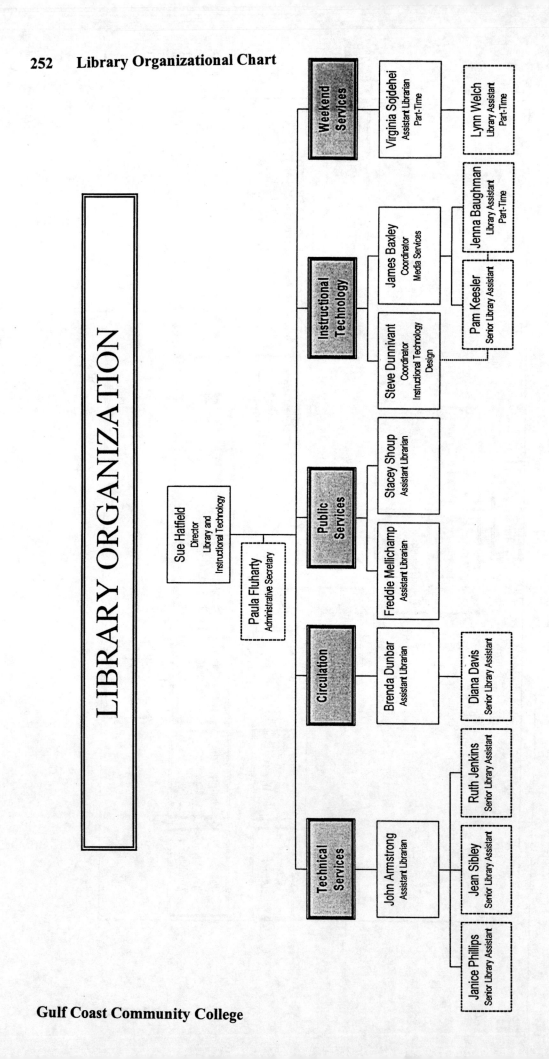

Sue Hatfield
Director
Library and
Instructional Technology

Paula Fluharty
Administrative Secretary

Technical Services

John Armstrong
Assistant Librarian

Janice Phillips
Senior Library Assistant

Jean Sibley
Senior Library Assistant

Ruth Jenkins
Senior Library Assistant

Circulation

Brenda Dunbar
Assistant Librarian

Diana Davis
Senior Library Assistant

Public Services

Freddie Mellichamp
Assistant Librarian

Stacey Shoup
Assistant Librarian

Instructional Technology

Steve Dunnivant
Coordinator
Instructional Technology
Design

James Baxley
Coordinator
Media Services

Pam Keesler
Senior Library Assistant

Jenna Baughman
Library Assistant
Part-Time

Weekend Services

Virginia Sojdehei
Assistant Librarian
Part-Time

Lynn Welch
Library Assistant
Part-Time

Gulf Coast Community College

INSTRUCTIONAL RESOURCES

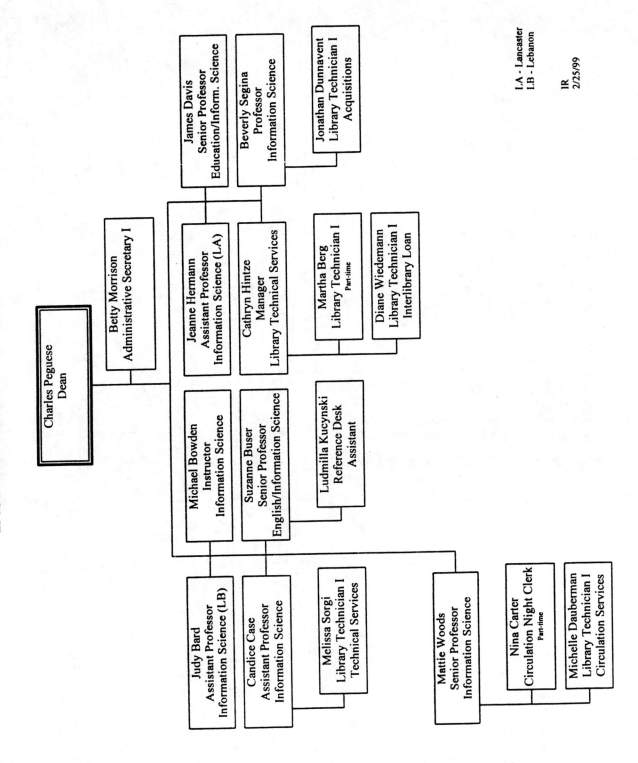

LA - Lancaster
LB - Lebanon

IR
2/25/99

Charles Peguese
Dean

Betty Morrison
Administrative Secretary I

James Davis
Senior Professor
Education/Inform. Science

Beverly Segina
Professor
Information Science

Jonathan Dunnavent
Library Technician I
Acquisitions

Jeanne Hermann
Assistant Professor
Information Science (LA)

Cathryn Hintze
Manager
Library Technical Services

Martha Berg
Library Technician I
Part-time

Diane Wiedemann
Library Technician I
Interlibrary Loan

Michael Bowden
Instructor
Information Science

Suzanne Buser
Senior Professor
English/Information Science

Ludmilla Kucynski
Reference Desk
Assistant

Judy Bard
Assistant Professor
Information Science (LB)

Candice Case
Assistant Professor
Information Science

Melissa Sorgi
Library Technician I
Technical Services

Mattie Woods
Senior Professor
Information Science

Nina Carter
Circulation Night Clerk
Part-time

Michelle Dauberman
Library Technician I
Circulation Services

Harrisburg Area Community College

Library/LRC Employee Hierarchy

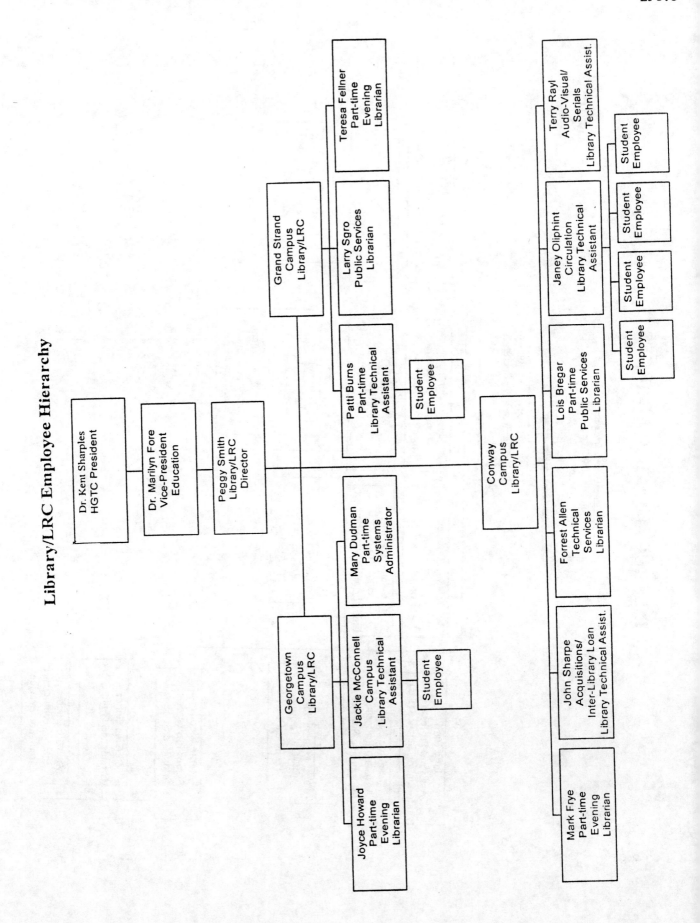

Internal Organizational Chart for John F. Kennedy Library
Hutchinson Community College

Director

```
                ┌──────────┬──────────┬──────────┐
                │          │          │          │
         ┌───────────┐ ┌──────────┐ ┌────────────┐ ┌──────────────┐
         │ Reference │ │Circulation│ │ Technical  │ │ Acquisitions │
         │           │ │           │ │  Services  │ │              │
         └───────────┘ └──────────┘ └────────────┘ └──────────────┘
```

Hutchinson Community College

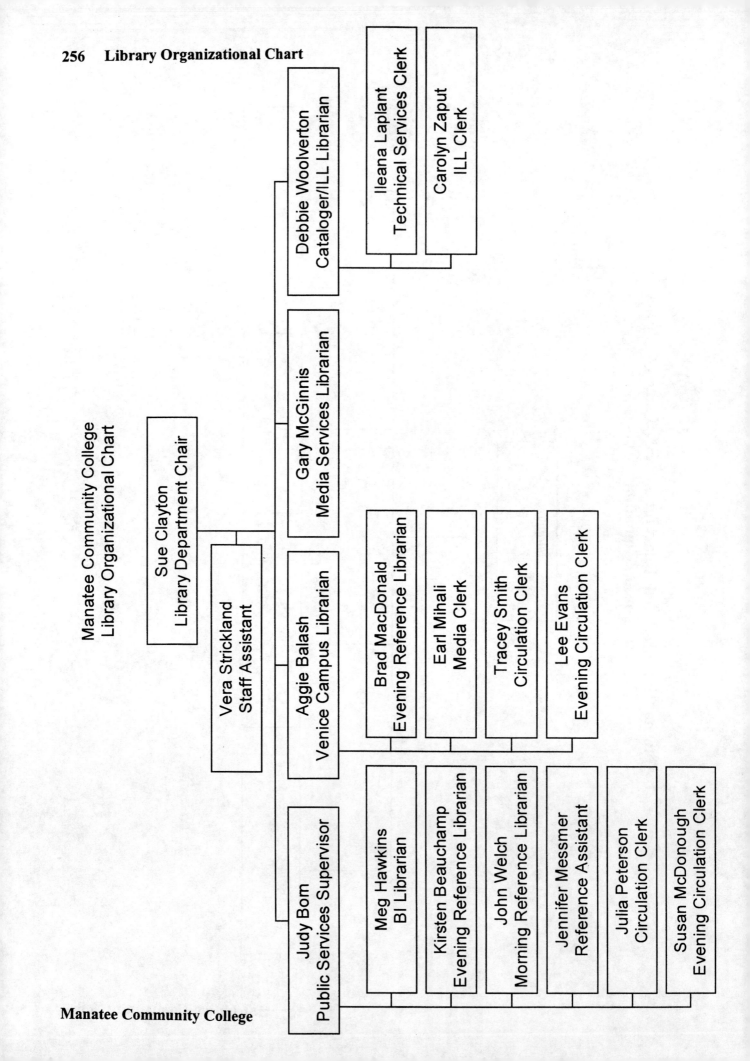

Manatee Community College
Library Organizational Chart

Sue Clayton
Library Department Chair

Vera Strickland
Staff Assistant

Debbie Woolverton
Cataloger/ILL Librarian

Ileana Laplant
Technical Services Clerk

Carolyn Zaput
ILL Clerk

Gary McGinnis
Media Services Librarian

Aggie Balash
Venice Campus Librarian

Brad MacDonald
Evening Reference Librarian

Earl Mihali
Media Clerk

Tracey Smith
Circulation Clerk

Lee Evans
Evening Circulation Clerk

Judy Bom
Public Services Supervisor

Meg Hawkins
BI Librarian

Kirsten Beauchamp
Evening Reference Librarian

John Welch
Morning Reference Librarian

Jennifer Messmer
Reference Assistant

Julia Peterson
Circulation Clerk

Susan McDonough
Evening Circulation Clerk

Manatee Community College

KENDALL CAMPUS LIBRARY

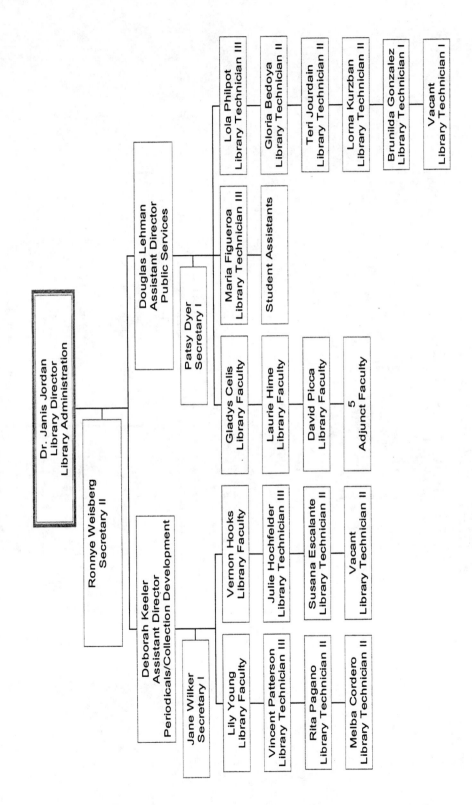

KENDALL CAMPUS LIBRARY
PUBLIC SERVICES

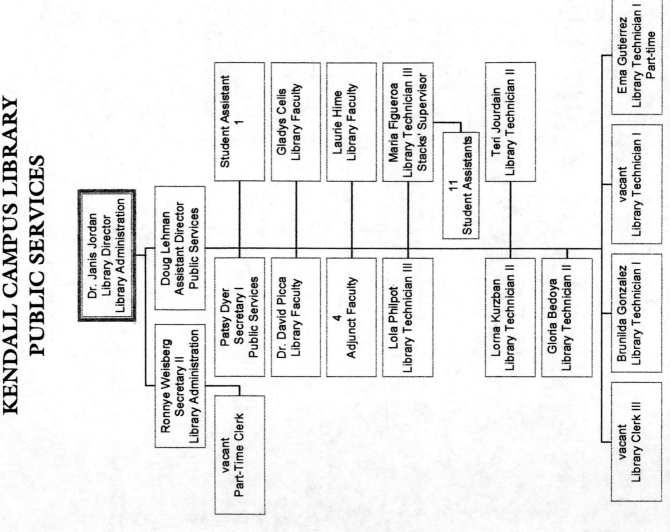

Dr. Janis Jordan
Library Director
Library Administration

Doug Lehman
Assistant Director
Public Services

Ronnye Weisberg
Secretary II
Library Administration

vacant
Part-Time Clerk

Patsy Dyer
Secretary I
Public Services

Student Assistant
1

Dr. David Picca
Library Faculty

Gladys Cells
Library Faculty

4
Adjunct Faculty

Laurie Hime
Library Faculty

Lola Philpot
Library Technician III

Maria Figueroa
Library Technician III
Stacks' Supervisor

11
Student Assistants

Lorna Kurzban
Library Technician II

Teri Jourdain
Library Technician II

Gloria Bedoya
Library Technician II

vacant
Library Clerk III

Brunilda Gonzalez
Library Technician I

vacant
Library Technician I

Ema Gutierrez
Library Technician I
Part-time

Miami-Dade Community College

KENDALL CAMPUS LIBRARY
COLLECTION DEVELOPMENT/PERIODICALS

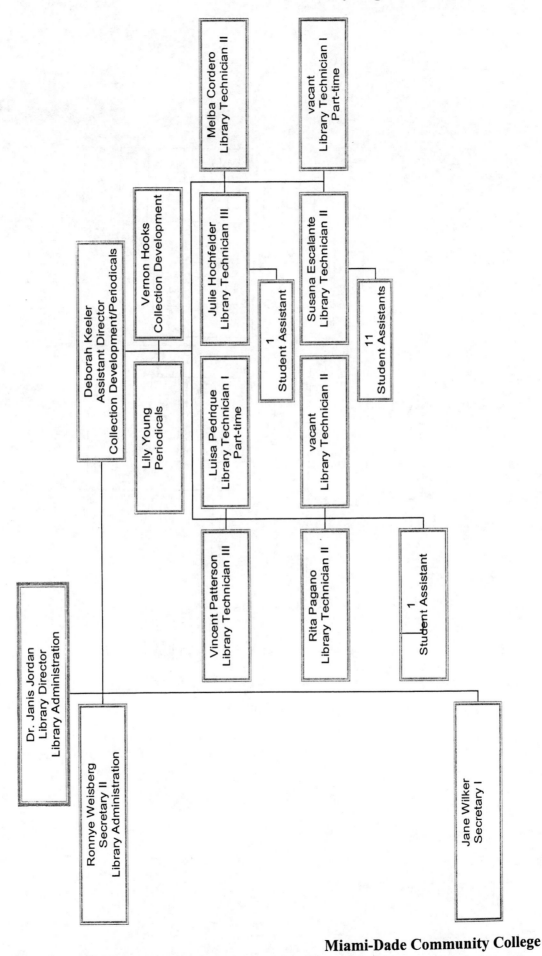

Miami-Dade Community College

c:\msoffice\powerpnt\libchart.ppt

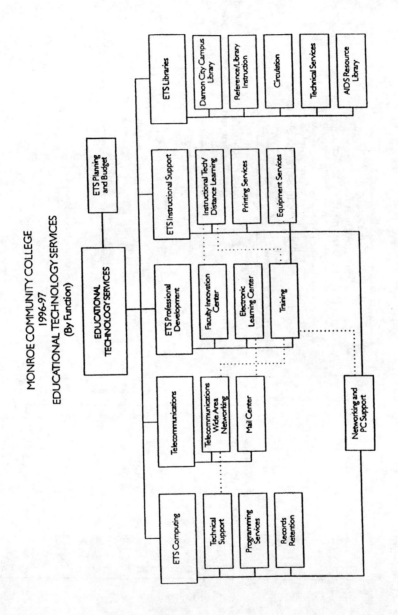

MONROE COMMUNITY COLLEGE
1996-97
EDUCATIONAL TECHNOLOGY SERVICES
(By Function)

EDUCATIONAL TECHNOLOGY SERVICES

ETS Planning and Budget

ETS Computing
- Technical Support
- Programming Services
- Records Retention

Telecommunications
- Telecommunications Wide Area Networking
- Mail Center

ETS Professional Development
- Faculty Innovation Center
- Electronic Learning Center
- Training

ETS Instructional Support
- Instructional Tech/ Distance Learning
- Printing Services
- Equipment Services

ETS Libraries
- Damon City Campus Library
- Reference/Library Instruction
- Circulation
- Technical Services
- AIDS Resource Library

Networking and PC Support

August 1, 1996
Page 5 of 5

Monroe Community College

Divison of Information Services - Organizational Chart

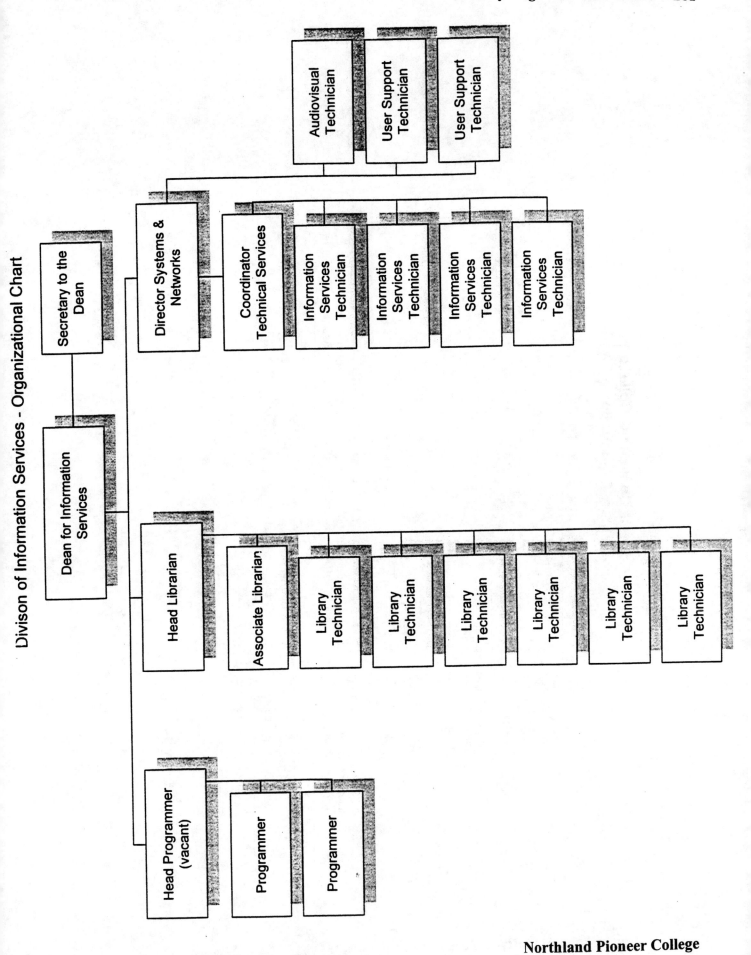

Northland Pioneer College

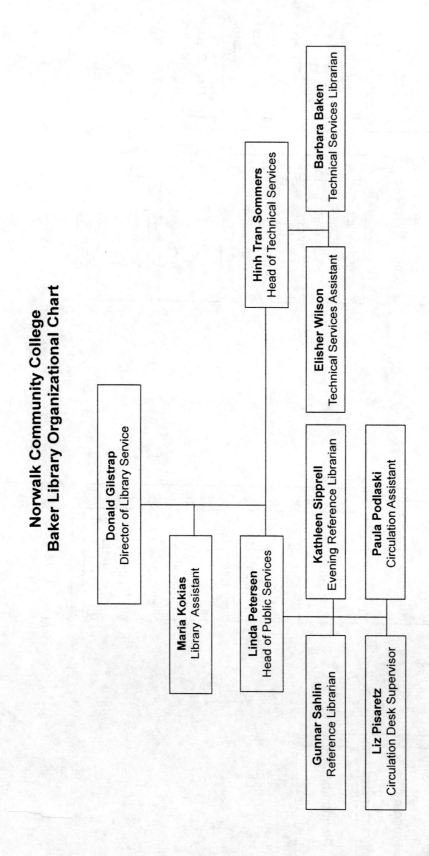

Norwalk Community College
Baker Library Organizational Chart

Donald Gilstrap
Director of Library Service

Maria Kokias
Library Assistant

Linda Petersen
Head of Public Services

Hinh Tran Sommers
Head of Technical Services

Barbara Baken
Technical Services Librarian

Elisher Wilson
Technical Services Assistant

Kathleen Sipprell
Evening Reference Librarian

Paula Podlaski
Circulation Assistant

Gunnar Sahlin
Reference Librarian

Liz Pisaretz
Circulation Desk Supervisor

Learning Resources Organizational Chart

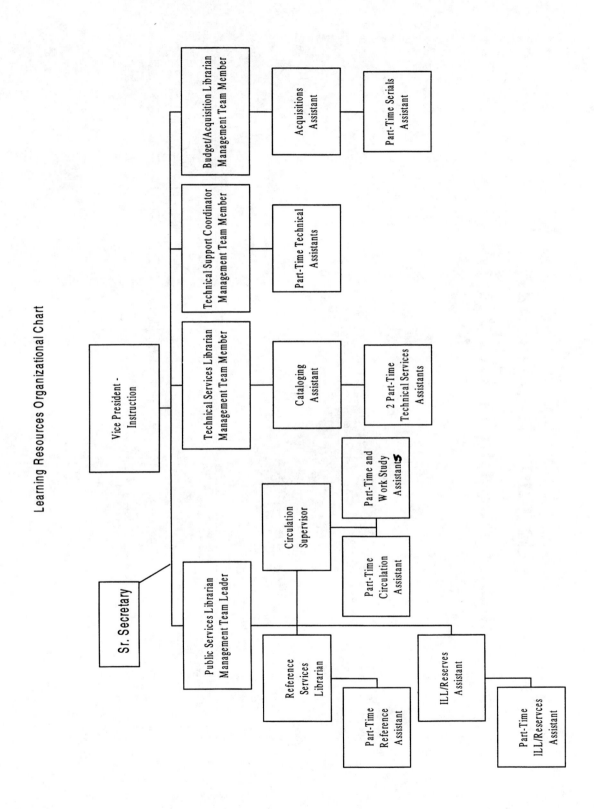

Organizational Chart
Nunez Community College Library

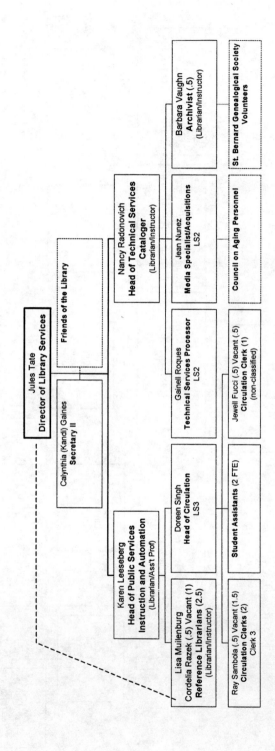

Jules Tate
Director of Library Services

Calynthia (Kandi) Gaines
Secretary II

Friends of the Library

Karen Leeseberg
Head of Public Services
Instruction and Automation
(Librarian/Ass't Prof)

Nancy Radonovich
Head of Technical Services
Cataloger
(Librarian/Instructor)

Lisa Mullenburg
Cordelia Razek (.5) Vacant (1)
Reference Librarians (2.5)
(Librarian/Instructor)

Doreen Singh
Head of Circulation
LS3

Gainell Roques
Technical Services Processor
LS2

Jean Nunez
Media Specialist/Acquisitions
LS2

Barbara Vaughn
Archivist (.5)
(Librarian/Instructor)

Ray Sambola (.5) Vacant (1.5)
Circulation Clerks (2)
Clerk 3

Student Assistants (2 FTE)

Jewell Fucci (.5) Vacant (.5)
Circulation Clerk (1)
(non-classified)

Council on Aging Personnel

St. Bernard Genealogical Society
Volunteers

LS=Library Specialist

June 6, 2000

Okaloosa-Walton Community College
Learning Resources Center
June 30, 1998

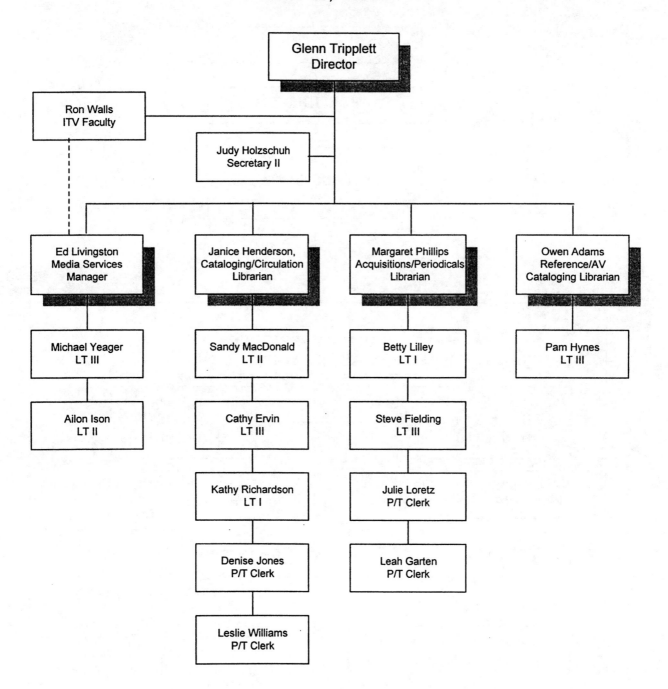

Panola College
Organizational Chart

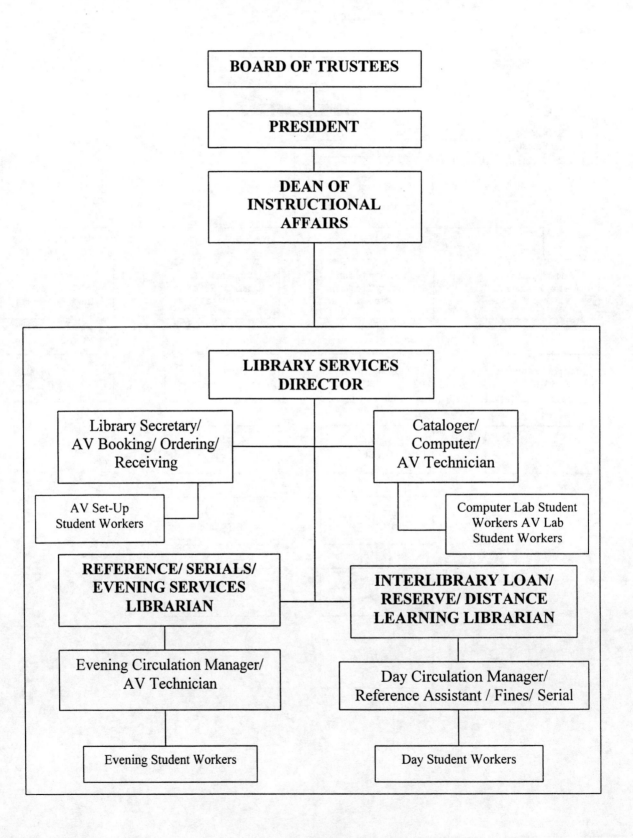

Shatford Library

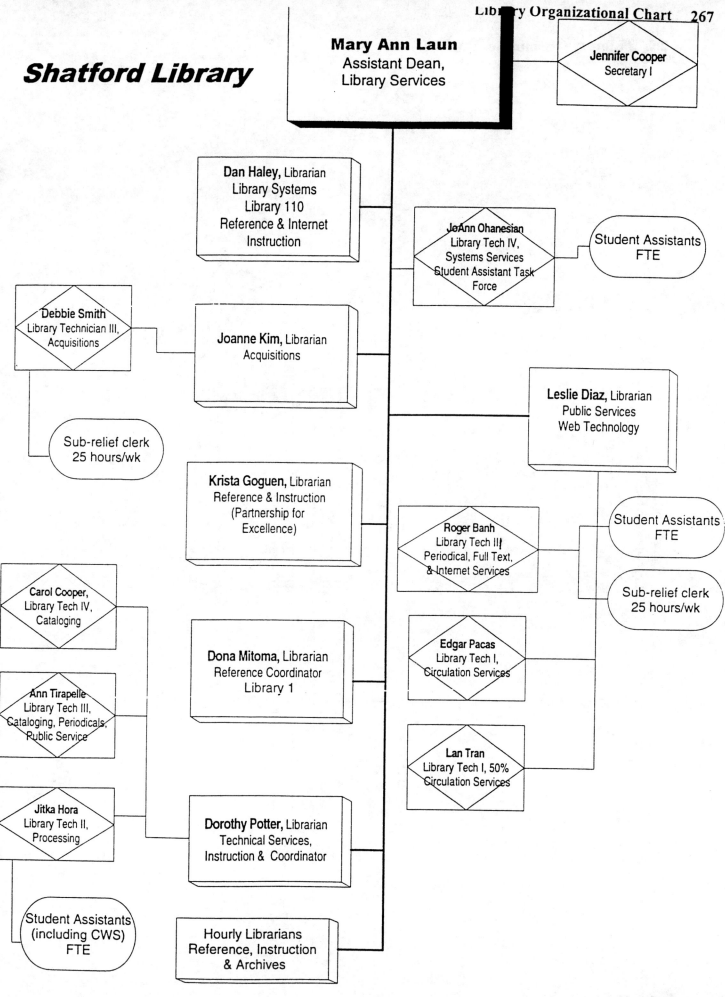

Mary Ann Laun
Assistant Dean,
Library Services

Jennifer Cooper
Secretary I

Dan Haley, Librarian
Library Systems
Library 110
Reference & Internet
Instruction

JoAnn Ohanesian
Library Tech IV,
Systems Services
Student Assistant Task
Force

Student Assistants
FTE

Debbie Smith
Library Technician III,
Acquisitions

Joanne Kim, Librarian
Acquisitions

Leslie Diaz, Librarian
Public Services
Web Technology

Sub-relief clerk
25 hours/wk

Krista Goguen, Librarian
Reference & Instruction
(Partnership for
Excellence)

Roger Banh
Library Tech III
Periodical, Full Text,
& Internet Services

Student Assistants
FTE

Sub-relief clerk
25 hours/wk

Carol Cooper,
Library Tech IV,
Cataloging

Dona Mitoma, Librarian
Reference Coordinator
Library 1

Edgar Pacas
Library Tech I,
Circulation Services

Ann Tirapelle
Library Tech III,
Cataloging, Periodicals,
Public Service

Lan Tran
Library Tech I, 50%
Circulation Services

Jitka Hora
Library Tech II,
Processing

Dorothy Potter, Librarian
Technical Services,
Instruction & Coordinator

Student Assistants
(including CWS)
FTE

Hourly Librarians
Reference, Instruction
& Archives

Pasadena City College

Pierce College
Library/Media Services

Organization

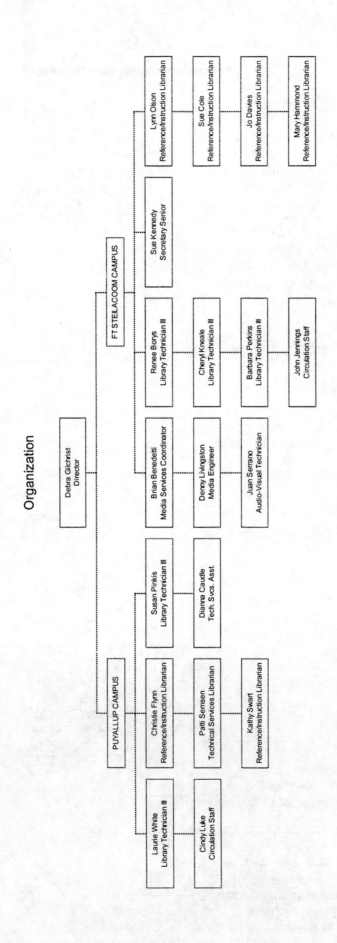

Pierce College

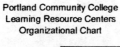

Portland Community College
Learning Resource Centers
Organizational Chart

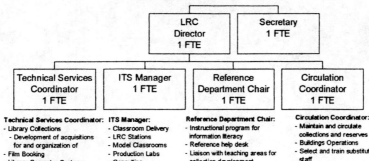

| LRC Director 1 FTE | Secretary 1 FTE |

| Technical Services Coordinator 1 FTE | ITS Manager 1 FTE | Reference Department Chair 1 FTE | Circulation Coordinator 1 FTE |

Technical Services Coordinator:
- Library Collections
  - Development of acquisitions for and organization of
- Film Booking
- Library Computer Systems

Supervise: 5 FTE

Role of a Coordinator/Chair:
- Assist in selecting staff
- Schedule and assign work
- Monitor/evaluate performance
- Provide training, staff development & well-being of the team
- Prioritize work and expenditures
- Help monitor portions of the budget
- Coordinate work with other LRC units
- Help plan for and manage LRC

ITS Manager:
- Classroom Delivery
- LRC Stations
- Model Classrooms
- Production Labs
- Consulting
- Events/Campus Special
- Instructional Tech
- WebCT

Supervise: 12 FTE

Role of Instructional Computing Facilitator:
- Coordinate student access to micro labs
- Coordinate faculty support for instructional computing

Reference Department Chair:
- Instructional program for information literacy
- Reference help desk
- Liaison with teaching areas for collection development

Monitor: 5.83 FTE

Circulation Coordinator:
- Maintain and circulate collections and reserves
- Buildings Operations
- Select and train substitute staff

Supervise: 14 FTE

Library Organizational Chart

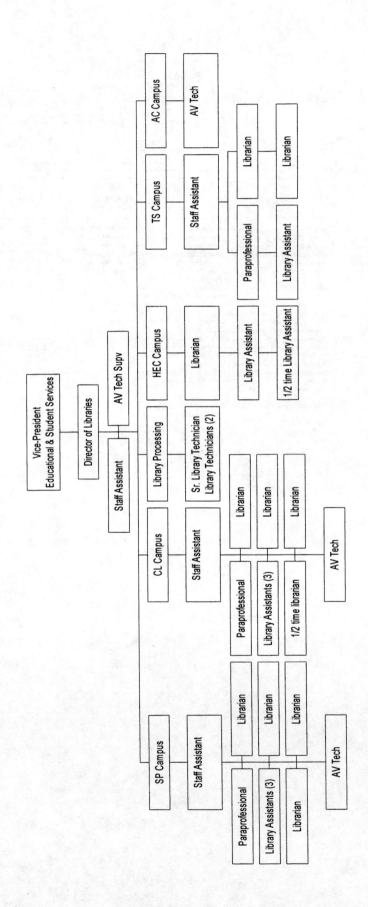

St. Petersburg Junior College

f::powerpt:org9899all   12
Revised 4/5/99

Learning Resources

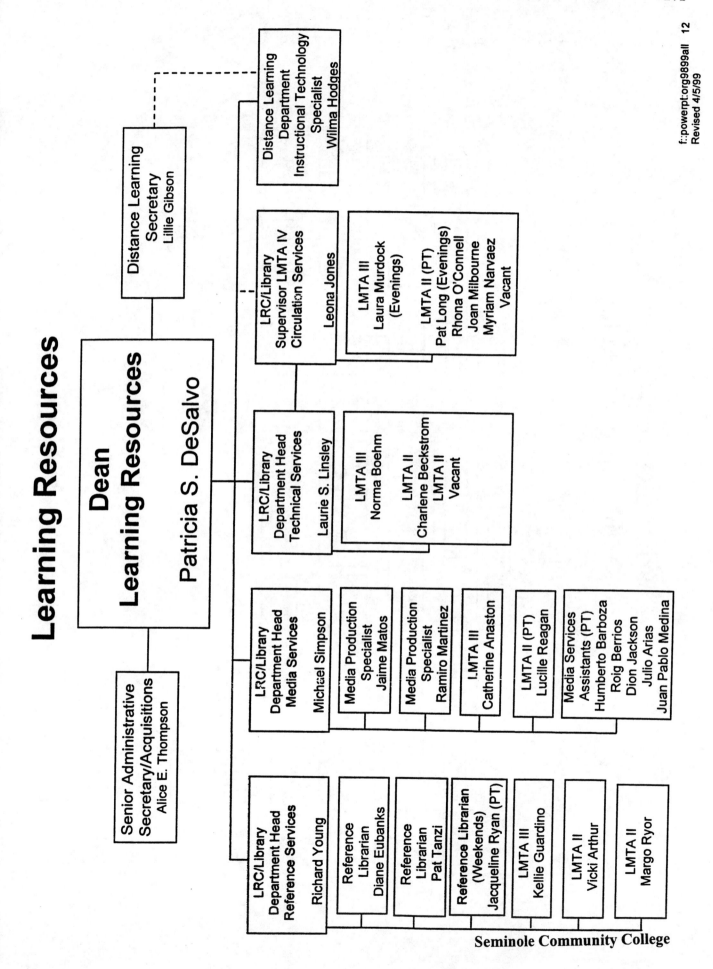

**Dean
Learning Resources**

Patricia S. DeSalvo

Distance Learning
Secretary
Lillie Gibson

Distance Learning
Department
Instructional Technology
Specialist
Wilma Hodges

Senior Administrative
Secretary/Acquisitions
Alice E. Thompson

LRC/Library
Supervisor LMTA IV
Circulation Services

Leona Jones

LMTA III
Laura Murdock
(Evenings)

LMTA II (PT)
Pat Long (Evenings)
Rhona O'Connell
Joan Milbourne
Myriam Narvaez
Vacant

LRC/Library
Department Head
Technical Services

Laurie S. Linsley

LMTA III
Norma Boehm

LMTA II
Charlene Beckstrom
LMTA II
Vacant

LRC/Library
Department Head
Media Services

Michael Simpson

Media Production
Specialist
Jaime Matos

Media Production
Specialist
Ramiro Martinez

LMTA III
Catherine Anaston

LMTA II (PT)
Lucille Reagan

Media Services
Assistants (PT)
Humberto Barboza
Roig Berrios
Dion Jackson
Julio Arias
Juan Pablo Medina

LRC/Library
Department Head
Reference Services

Richard Young

Reference
Librarian
Diane Eubanks

Reference
Librarian
Pat Tanzi

Reference Librarian
(Weekends)
Jacqueline Ryan (PT)

LMTA III
Kellie Guardino

LMTA II
Vicki Arthur

LMTA II
Margo Ryor

Seminole Community College

Learning Resources Centers
Main/Palmer/Berkeley

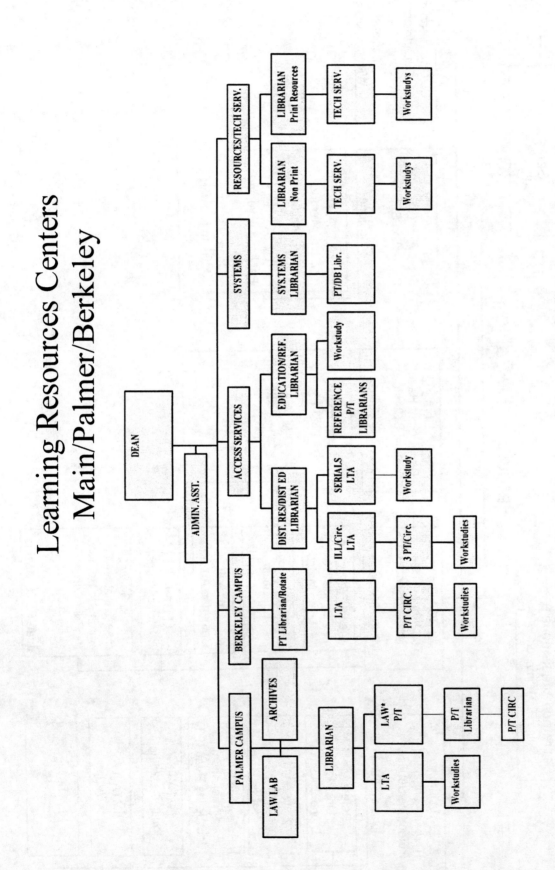

Trident Technical College

5/22/00

LRC Hierarchy
The following diagram shows the hierarchy for the LRC.

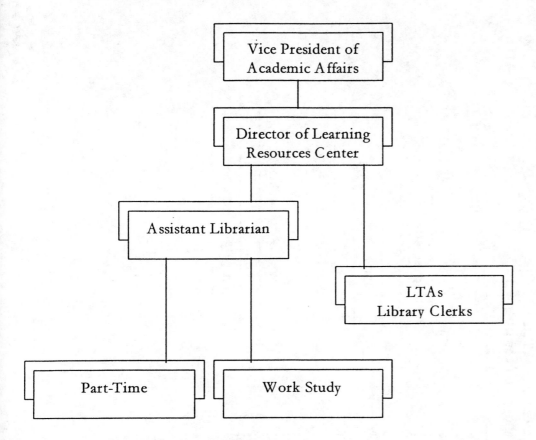

Revised September 1999

YORK TECHNICAL COLLEGE

Learning Resources Division

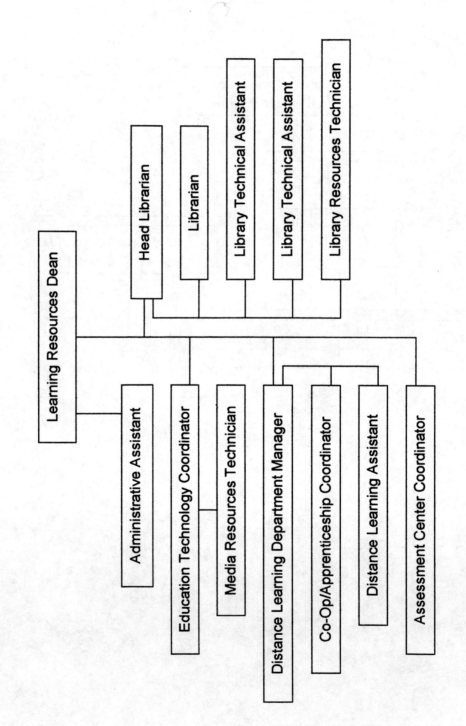

York Technical College

Selected Readings

Cervenka, Patricia A., <u>Survey on Job Descriptions</u>. Littleton, Colo.;
    Fred B. Rothman, 1997.

This publication was sponsored by the American Association of Law Libraries. Findings for this report were compiled from 56 law libraries that responded to a survey conducted by the author. The sample job descriptions presented cover a wide range of positions in academic, county/court and law firm/corporate law libraries, with a variety of duties and tasks. The book emphasizes the importance of constant updating of job descriptions and the usefulness of those updates in performance evaluations.

DeLon, Barbara, "Job Descriptions: What They Are, Are Not, and Can Be,"
    <u>College & Research Libraries News</u>. 55 (June 1994): 339-40

The author gives us the most multifaceted picture and myriad of uses of job descriptions. She stresses the importance of accuracy and flexibility to fit the changing needs of the organization. Her advice is to make job descriptions work for you.

Eustis, Joanne D. and Donald J. Kenney, Comp., ed. Laura A. Rounds,
    <u>Library Reorganization and Restructuring: A SPEC Kit.</u> (215)
    Washington, D.C.: Association of Research Libraries, Office of Management
    Services, 1996.

This survey tries to explain how librarians are meeting the challenge of both information technology developments and declining resources by redesigning their organizations. 53 ARL libraries responded to this survey. 17 of the libraries have already either completed or were in the process of completing a library-wide reorganization.

Out of the 35 libraries that answered positively to reorganization, the libraries not included before had a formal planning process in place. The outcomes that were mentioned the most as a result of reorganization were the joining of units within the libraries, new partnerships with other units within the college, shift of emphasis from print to electronic resources, elimination of some services and less emphasis on catalog maintenance.

Foote, Elizabeth, "Sources and Information on Organizational Change In
    The Community College," <u>New Directions For Community Colleges</u>.
    No. 102 (Summer 1998): 99 - 106.

This article is part of a special issue on organizational change in community colleges. It offers an annotated bibliography of the current ERIC literature on organizational change. Some of the citations are actual case studies of community colleges that have worked through change. The author also gives information on practical models for managing organizational change.

Knapp, Scott Edward, "Formal Organizational Structure in Two-Year
        Colleges," Dissertation Abstracts International 49-07A (1988):
        1677 - 1788.

This dissertation studied the formal organization structure of two-year colleges as
demonstrated by their organizational charts. The study set out to determine the prevailing
models (if any) of formal organization structures at the colleges, as well as determining
the relationship between certain institutional variables and the prevailing models. A total
of 756 schools responded to this survey. The results of this study will help those who
have responsibilities for organizational design by showing them alternative models for
future decision-making and planning.

Levin, John S. "Making Sense of Organizational Change, "New Directions
        For Community Colleges. No. 102 (Summer 1998): 43 - 54.

This article is also part of a special issue on organizational change in the community
college. Results of surveys done on community colleges demonstrate that organizational
change encompasses the interplay between external and internal forces. Community
colleges do not remain motionless. They change their approaches, programs and their
relationships with their environment in order to survive and still maintain their purpose.

Library Support Staff Resource Center, "Library Paraprofessional Job
        Classifications and Descriptions." 1999.
        <http://www.lib.rochester.edu/ssp/overview/jobdescr.htm>
        (13 June 2000).

This Web site lists library paraprofessional job classifications and descriptions within the
United States, Canada and Australia. While most of the information in this site comes
from the United States, there are good hyperlinks to job descriptions, job outlooks,
earnings and education/experience in both Canada and Australia. Under the United States
category there are separate listings for Academic, Federal, School and Public Libraries,
as well as the American Library Association Policy Statement.

Ray, Tom H. and Pat Hawthorne, Comp., ed. C. Brigid Welch.
        Librarian Job Descriptions in ARL Libraries a SPEC Kit (194).
        Washington, D.C.: Association of Research Libraries, Office of
        Management Services, 1993

This SPEC Kit was developed to give examples of job descriptions in
Academic libraries. The 73 respondent libraries reported accurate and current reviews of
traditional public and technical service responsibilities. When position vacancies occur,
redefining positions becomes necessary to accommodate new service offerings, shortage
of economic resources and compliance with the Americans with Disabilities Act.

Job/position descriptions are also used in the performance rating system. Samples of
job/position descriptions, annual reviews and evaluations are also provided in this report.

Ryan, Joe, "Jobs for Information Professionals." <u>Writing Job Descriptions.</u> 1999.
<http://web.syr.edu/~jryan/infopro/jobs.html> (13 June 2000).

This web site includes "Information Resources for Information Professionals." The
hyperlink to Writing Job Descriptions leads the viewer to a page that gives examples of
resume writing, cover letters and interview resources. The viewer is also guided to two
books to aid in the job search. Syracuse University also has additional hyperlinks on this
page that lead to other interview resource areas. In addition, Internet job listings are also
provided from many different countries.

Stambaugh, Laine: "Are Your Library Support Staff Classifications Ready for the
    Twenty-First Century?" <u>Library Administration & Management</u>. 14 (Summer
    2000): 167-171.

Library personnel at the University of Oregon have developed an experimental job
classification system that has been useful in creating and classifying new library support
staff positions. A designated "library spec team," working together with campus human
resource managers and library personnel, identified patterns of typical tasks and
benchmarks to be used in delineating the differences between levels of library
technicians. The spec team combined a Position Analysis Survey with face-to-face staff
interviewing to identify essential functions and responsibilities of each position
classification. Included in the article is a "Summary of Tips for a Successful Job
Classification Study."

Stambaugh, Laine and Joni Gomez, Comp.: <u>Library Support Staff</u>
    <u>Position Classification Studies</u> (SPEC Kit 252.) Washington, D.C.: Association of
    Research Libraries, 1999.

This study looks at support staff in 59 ARL libraries, examines the process for classifying
these positions, and makes salary and title comparisons with positions outside of the
library. Other questions it deals with are: When was a previous classification study done?
Why is a current study being done? Are the library or human resources doing the study?
If the library is doing the study; what is the person's position who is doing the study?
Also, what were the results of the classification study in both human and economic
terms?

The outcome of this study showed the growing importance of support staff positions.
Survey respondents with experience in classification studies felt the library should be in
charge of revamping its classification system to ensure more accuracy and fit within
appropriate salary schedules.

Woodsworth, Anne, <u>Patterns and Options for Managing Information
Technology on Campus.</u> Chicago: American Library Association, 1991.

Although published in 1991 and based on interviews between 1986 and 1989, this book
remains a good starting point for exploring models and options for managing information
systems both collegewide as well as within your library. One model is Librarian as CIO
in which the library director has the vision and leadership to assume responsibility for
academic computing or telecommunications networking.

Zenelis, John and Jean Dorrian, Comp. <u>Non-Librarian Professionals:</u> a
SPEC Kit. (212) Washington, D.C.: Association of Research
Libraries, Office of Management Services, 1995. SPEC Kit 212

This flyer concentrates on findings at 95 ARL (Association of Research Libraries)
institutions to reveal the results of hiring applicants without the M.L.S. degree for
professional positions. The authors place the emphasis on how these positions are defined
as well as how the candidates are recruited. How the appointee is oriented to the nature of
his/her responsibilities after being hired, is also addressed. This document provides
departmental position descriptions or specializations for the non-M.L.S. professionals
who were hired.

About the Editors and Section

Aggie Balash (M.L.S., University of South Florida) is a librarian at Manatee Community College, Venice. Aggie has been with MCC as a faculty librarian for 10 years, serving in public service position on both campuses. She has been active in many campus activities. Previously Aggie spent 11 years at the University of South Florida's Sarasota campus as serials librarian, managing a collection of 1200-1300 titles and devoting a quarter of her time to the reference desk. Aggie served on a College Center for Library Automation (CCLA) standing committee on Bibliographic Quality Control for two years, and has been a member of the Florida Library Association and ACRL. Aggie provided the Review of Literature and Index for this publication.

Judy Born (A.M.L.S., University of Michigan) is public services supervisor for Manatee Community College, Bradenton. She has over 20 years experience in academic and public libraries. Judy as been on the faculty at MCC for the past 10 years and is active on many campus committees. She has served on the CJCLS Bibliographic Instruction Committee and is currently serving on the Publications Committee. She developed a series of college guides, which were awarded Best of Show from the LAMA. She has published a series of articles on Floridiana for the Florida Library Association Journal. Judy currently services on the College Center for Library Automation (CCLA) Circulation Committee and on the committees for Electronic Resources, Continuing Education and Reciprocal Borrowing at the Tampa Bay Library Consortium (TBLC).

Sue Clayton (M.L.S., East Carolina University) is library department chair at Manatee Community College (MCC) Bradenton and has been with the MCC library for 10 years. Her interest in becoming a librarian began when she was an assistant children's librarian in North Carolina in 1977. After acquiring an M.L.S. degree, Sue moved to Bradenton, Fl., in 1989 as a supervisor of technical services at Manatee County Public Library. In 1990, Sue became technical services supervisor at MCC, where she has also supervised acquisitions and collection development. As department chair, Sue is a working librarian who continues to handle acquisitions,, the library computer network and administrative task. She administered the survey and compiled results for this book.

The Community and Junior College Libraries Section of ACRL

The purpose of the Community and Junior College Libraries Sections (CJCLS) is to contribute to library services and librarianship through those activities which related to libraries and learning resource centers and which support the educational programs in community and junior colleges and equivalent institutions.

CJCLS Home Page: http://www.glendale.cc.ca.us/cjcls

INDEX

Reporting Structure Cont.
Vice President for College 210
Vice President for Continuing Education & Evening Programs 231
Vice President Educational Programs 233
Vice President of Planning and Effectiveness 22-24, 221
Vice President of Instruction 209, 220, 223
Vice President of Instructional Services 13-16, 19, 222, 227
Vice President of Learning Systems & Technology 207

State
Arizona 68-69, 211, 225, 261
California 267
Connecticut 226, 232
Florida 13-14, 15-16, 17-18, 19-20, 21, 22-23, 24-25, 26-27, 35-36, 37-38, 39-40, 54-55, 56-57, 58-60, 73-74, 75, 83, 84, 89-90, 91, 92, 93-94, 95-96, 121-122, 123-124, 125-126, 145-148, 158-159, 160-161, 162-163, 168-169, 170, 181, 182, 183, 184, 185, 186-188, 189-192, 209, 227, 233, 234, 245, 246, 250, 252, 256, 257-259, 265, 270, 271
Idaho 63-67, 101-106, 223, 249, 263
Illinois 71-72, 113-114, 247
Indiana 151-152
Iowa 41-43, 139-140, 218, 224
Kansas 45-46, 153-154, 155-156, 217, 255
Louisiana 70, 157, 180, 208, 244, 264
Maryland 207, 231
Michigan 171-173, 174, 219, 220
Mississippi 214-216
Missouri 136-137
Montana 49-53
Nebraska 30-33
New York 61-62, 77-78. 97-98, 229, 260
Ohio 47-48, 81-82, 127-128, 129-130, 131, 132-133, 134-135, 164-165, 248
Oklahoma 85-87, 196-198, 238
Oregon 76, 107-108, 109-110, 111-112, 193, 194, 195, 237, 243, 269
Pennsylvania 213, 253, 274
South Carolina 235, 236, 239, 254, 272-273
Tennessee 138, 166-167, 210
Texas 202-204, 228, 266
Utah 28-29, 115-116, 117-119, 143-144
Washington 230, 251, 268
Wisconsin 99-100, 141-142, 175-177, 178-179, 199-201, 222